THE WIDOW SPY

MY CIA JOURNEY FROM THE
JUNGLES OF LAOS TO PRISON IN MOSCOW

MARTHA D. PETERSON

Copyright c 2012 by Martha D Peterson

Red Canary Press
Wilmington, North Carolina
www.widowspy.com

Photos courtesy of H. Keith Melton and from personal collections

Cover photo by Nikolai Orlov, 1997, Moscow, Russia

Publisher's Cataloging-in-Publication data

Peterson, Martha Denny.
 The Widow spy : my CIA journey from the jungles of Laos to prison in Moscow /
Martha Denny Peterson.
 p. cm.
 Includes index.
 ISBN 978-0-9838781-2-4
 ISBN 978-0-9838781-5-5 (e-book)

1. Peterson, Martha Denny. 2. United States. Central Intelligence Agency --Biography.
3. Intelligence officers --United States --Biography. 4. Spies --United States --
Biography. 5. United States --Foreign relations --Soviet Union. 6. Vietnam War, 1961-
1975 --Campaigns --Laos. 7. United States. Central Intelligence Agency --History --
20th century. I. Title.

JK468.I6 P459 2012
327.12730092/2 --dc22   2011962072

Dedicated

to

John Peterson

Acknowledgements

I wish to acknowledge with gratitude all those who have contributed to this book. I include those who offered me the experiences of my lifetime: my parents, Dorothy and Riley Denny, my sister Mary-Alice, my late husband, John, my husband, Steve, and my two children, Tyler and Lora.

This book first came into its early form in a memoir writing course under the wonderful guidance of Agnes Macdonald. Along with my two classmates, Eleanor Price and Risa Kell, I developed new styles to express my journey and ideas, a safe place to try out different approaches. With their generous comments as well as weekly requirements to produce pages, I found inspiration to write and value in their audience.

I wish to thank my literary agent Dan Mandel of Sanford Greenberger and Associates, who coached me through many long months of shaping the story and then searched tirelessly for an opening in the publishing world. I also want to thank Robert Wallace, whose constant confidence in my efforts kept me motivated and dedicated to telling my story.

My two editors, Roberta Igler and Mary-Alice Denny, brought a fresh view to the story and offered me critical suggestions which transformed a personal story into a professional non-fiction account of one woman's amazing experiences during notable periods in history. Ann McCray provided me technical guidance as well as spiritual enthusiasm as a coach and mentor.

Without the assistance of my friend, T. Dewi Rowlands, who encouraged a strict schedule, pushing me to complete the endless details, keeping my spirits high and my efforts focused, this book may not have seen publication.

And to you the reader, I appreciate that you have expressed a continuing interest in the Cold War and its significant legacy to today's world.

Finally, to those who continue the work of the CIA in dangerous and unpredictable places: Celebrate our victories, no matter how silently.

Contents

Prologue

Before I left for work that balmy spring morning in McLean, Virginia, I placed my casually worded note on the kitchen counter where my kids couldn't miss it. It was April 1997. Tyler was seventeen and Lora was fifteen. They had the day off from school with no plans, so I didn't have to compete with more interesting options. Who knew what made me decide to tell them on this particular day, wondering how they would react to my secret. Maybe this wouldn't be a big deal to them, but I was apprehensive.

Friends at work warned me, if I waited too long for this true confession, my children would be angry that I had not trusted them. I always stressed to my children that their only choice was to tell the truth. Now I had to admit that I had lied to them.

Lora called me around 10:00 a.m., having been awakened by her voracious hunger pangs. Sleepily, she asked me what was up and why we had to meet for lunch. I knew her immediate focus was on the meal at hand, breakfast. As a toddler, she had climbed out of her crib with a thump, then padded her pajama'd feet down the hall, shimmied up on her chair, expecting me to instantly produce her cereal. Then the only noise was the clink of her spoon as she shoveled fuel into her little empty tank. When she finished, her happy countenance awakened as she climbed into my lap for cuddles. Her morning craving for food had not changed, except now she had to fix her own cereal.

I replied that I wanted to meet them for lunch because they had a day off for Good Friday. I sensed this aroused her curiosity because I never met them for lunch. She agreed to get Tyler up in time to arrive in McLean by noon. I assured her that Tyler knew where the Roy Rogers was.

I had been parked for fifteen minutes when Tyler wheeled his Chevy Blazer into the spot next to mine. Tumbling into my car, Lora in front and Tyler in back, they asked, "So what's up?" Funny, after all the roles I had played in my life, I had not devised a suitable preamble for what I was about to tell them. So, I just blurted out: "I work for CIA." Lora looked puzzled. Tyler replied quickly, which amazed me. Yet again, how knowledgeable he was: "She's a spy." We all laughed together at how absurd this sounded: Mom a spy.

I filled the unsettled silence by explaining why lying had been my only option. I worried about telling them this secret when they were younger because children don't fully understand why being exposed as a CIA officer could pose a real danger to a family living abroad. When we went overseas in 1992 right after the Gulf War, I had to be certain that, if their school bus were hijacked and they were confronted by terrorists, they didn't have in their brain the fact that I worked for CIA. They could tell "the truth" as they knew it. But now, in their teens, I told them I trusted them with my secret. And besides, we were in the States with no enemy lurking at the corner to ambush their school bus.

They sensed I was uneasy admitting my lie. I looked at both of them wondering whether I had waited too long to tell them. My daughter's next question, tinged with a hint of resentment, confirmed that I probably had. "What *else* aren't you telling us, Mammi?" But then, I saw a faint smile bloom on her lips, almost enjoying the fact that she had caught me in a lie. Tyler smiled too. Relieved that they weren't offended, I knew they were curious about who I really was. I decided to tell them the whole story, even though I have always found it difficult to tell, not wanting to sound like I was bragging.

We drove to CIA Headquarters (HQS) about a mile down the road where I suggested we have lunch in the cafeteria. I included the fact that we could visit the gift shop, which snagged their immediate interest in addition to the food. As we turned into the main CIA entrance drive, seeing it through their eyes, I realized the guard house ahead appeared disappointingly unimpressive. I had registered them as official guests earlier that day. When I came to a stop at the security gate, the guard asked for their photo IDs. Their eyes revealed their shock at this guard addressing them directly. He seriously scrutinized their IDs, leaning close to my window to compare their faces to the photos. He handed back their IDs along with a red government "V" badge indicating they were visitors labeled "Escort Required." They were impressed by the formality of entering CIA. To this day, they recall how awed they were at this official attention.

Heading to the large three-story covered parking garage at the rear of the compound, we passed the front of the main building. This view is often featured on the news although neither of them said they recalled it. I had probably changed channels or at least didn't point it out to them when it came on TV as the backdrop for some spy story. As I pulled into my reserved parking place on the lowest level of the parking garage, Lora remarked snidely that I sure didn't have a very good parking place. My colleagues would have screamed in laughter at her comment. How could she know that having a reserved space in the garage was a coveted and distinct privilege earned through years of hard work? The alternative to a reserved spot lay in the far reaches of what was known as "West Lot," the parking lot for all but those lucky or warranted to be assigned parking spaces in the closer lots and the parking garage. I didn't correct her impression, but told her how a covered parking place kept me sheltered from icy winter elements and torrid Washington, D.C. summer heat.

My story was going to shocked them, but I planned to be selective as I unrolled my past. Walking the long sidewalk to the new HQS building, I slowly started my story by telling them about meeting their father, Steve, in Moscow in 1975 when we were both working there in the midst of the Cold War. Past the badge machines, we rode the escalator down to the ground floor while I pointed to the replica of the U-2 spy plane suspended in the four-story atrium. I told them about Gary Powers being shot down in the Soviet Union in 1960 when I was about their age. They listened intently while they looked around at the people and the building, still amazed at where they were.

In the first floor atrium, we entered the historical collection where an actual World War II Enigma code machine, uniforms, and other espionage articles of that era are displayed. Only mildly interested in this museum, Lora and Tyler were more eager to learn what I had done. As we moved down the hall past the portraits of the former Directors on the way to the front lobby of the main HQS building, I wondered how this part of my story would affect them.

General Donovan's impressive larger-than-life-size statue posed near the right front wall under the saying, "Ye shall know the truth, and the truth shall set you free." I described his significance as the Chief of the OSS and revealed that I had recently received the Donovan Award for my accomplishments throughout my career. I knew I was planting seeds of curiosity with this comment. We moved to the center of the lobby where we stood in the center of the over-sized CIA medallion emblazoned in the various shades of gray marble. This place and my apparent intimacy with it amazed them.

I walked them to the other side of the lobby where granite stars are carved deeply into the wall. Standing there with my children, I read aloud the inscription above the stars: "In Honor of Those Members of the Central Intelligence Agency Who Gave Their Lives in the Service of Their Country." We sat down together on the bench facing this imposing, yet silent, wall of stars.

How do you reveal to your children that you had a life long before them, before their father, and before our quiet family home in Annandale, Virginia? Tears came to my eyes as I looked at my children who saw my welling emotion.

"I was married once before your father. His name was John Peterson. We met in college." I looked into their eyes as they stared at me, unbelieving and silent. "He was a Green Beret in Vietnam and then he joined CIA. He was a brave, wonderful man." Quietly I continued. "He was killed in 1972."

They blinked. Tears rolled down my cheeks. I turned to the stars and whispered, "John's star is here." I moved to the wall and gently touched the star I knew was his. They followed me, Lora's small hand lovingly and gently taking mine. Tyler slipped his arm protectively around me, both sharing my newly revealed sadness.

Moments passed in silence. I pointed to John's star in the glass-framed book beneath the stars containing a mix of names and anonymous spaces for each star on the wall. After we stood together unspeaking and looking at the wall of stars, they each touched John's star, tenderly, as I had. They understood. But I knew they would have more questions after they reflected on this new reality.

Without words, we walked back up the stairs and headed to the more current exhibit of Cold War spy paraphernalia on loan from Keith Melton, the spy gear authority and collector. I knew this would interest them, especially my connection to the articles on display. The glass cases and wall exhibits, I explained with new animation, contained actual spy paraphernalia that Melton had collected after the fall of the Soviet Union. Among the items were miniature cameras, concealed daggers and guns, gas masks, Berlin Wall barbed wire, miniature listening devices and all kinds of concealment devices - all the cool spy gear that made spy thrillers exciting.

Tyler and Lora were eager to know whether I had used any of this and what I had done. I told them to wait until we had lunch in the cafeteria when I would tell them the rest of my story. I thought to myself that maybe this was too much for them to absorb all in one day. Mom a CIA spy. Mom married before. And now the Moscow story.

CHAPTER 1

PAKSE, Laos - July 1971

John and I left Vientiane and headed south for Pakse, the third largest city in Laos (population 35,000). Our transport was an old C-47 twin-engine prop plane of "Terry and the Pirates" vintage. It was affectionately nicknamed "50 Kip" since its tail numbers were 50K and *kip* was the name of the local Lao currency. Inside, entering from the tail, the aisle sloped steeply up to the cockpit, making it much easier to exit down to the rear door than to board uphill. The seats, two on one side, one on the other, accommodated 40 passengers. John and I found seats together, which somewhat eased my growing anxiety over our new adventure.

I had forgotten how noisy prop planes are and how jolting the take-off. The Air America pilot in a no-name khaki uniform and proper captain's hat with the same no-name insignia, lined the plane up at the end of the runway for take-off, set the brake, and started revving the engines until they both screamed and shook. When the engines reached their highest pitch, the pilot released the brake, and we roared down the runway. After an alarmingly long taxi, we finally lifted off the bumpy concrete runway. Banking over the city, I saw Vientiane's maze of dirt roads branching from very few paved boulevards, lots of small houses on stilts with thatched roofs, and the wide, forceful muddy brown Mekong River that runs nearly the entire length of the border between Laos and Thailand. The plane's engines wound down some, the plane leveled off, and I relaxed for the final leg of our trip to our new home in the most southern city in Laos.

We had spent two days in Vientiane, checking into the office and meeting people who would be our lifeline for anything we needed once we arrived "up country" in Pakse. The people I met were cordial, but it became apparent that I was a spouse, one of many and not unique. They asked whether I wanted to work, and I always said yes although I was uncertain what work they were referring to. I filled out a personal history statement (PHS), a multi-page form, which included information on my education, work history, parents, sister, marriage, residences and relatives working overseas or foreign relatives. The form was long yet straightforward. A security officer gave me a briefing, but overall they were uniformly indifferent to me.

While in Vientiane, John and I dined on remarkably fine French cuisine at Madeleine's, a restaurant leftover from the French occupation, where we ate delicious cream of mushroom soup, probably the best I have ever eaten. The mushrooms were fresh, almost crispy in the heavy rich cream with a heavenly hint of fine sherry. We also enjoyed a local hangout for Americans, The Spot, in the Lan Xang Hotel, complete with a live band playing Yellow River and Country Roads. John ran into a few men he knew from Washington, D.C. I was introduced as "my wife," but I always added "Marti" with my handshake. I was beginning to understand what it meant to be a CIA spouse. Just something John was issued, like a car, a house, a desk, a wife.

Our plane landed once in a small town enroute to Pakse where CIA officers and their families were living. We had originally been assigned there, but plans had changed when the American women and children had been evacuated from Pakse after a serious North Vietnamese Army mortar attack in April 1971. This made John and I, a couple without children, better suited to go to Pakse. It was all the same to me, and I think John was happier because he knew there was more action in Pakse.

As we approached the airport in Pakse, I saw rugged mountains to the east. I knew from my study of Laos that this was the Bolovens Plateau, approximately 3500 feet above sea level. South Vietnam lay to the east just beyond these mountains. We circled the very small airport with an equally short runway. Our landing was bumpy, testifying to the crude concrete and deteriorating effects of annual rainy seasons. We taxied to the front of a shed-sized corrugated building. I laughed as I thought to myself that there was no "Welcome to Pakse" sign. Airport workers rolled the stairs to the rear of the plane and we proceeded downhill to the door. Hot sticky humid air blasted us immediately.

John identified our fellow passengers as primarily Lao and some Thai. I never could tell the difference. No other American women were on the plane and only a couple of American men. I noted that the farther east we traveled, the taller we became in contrast to the local population. This made it easier for us to see over crowds, but also more difficult to remain inconspicuous.

Once on the ground we waited at the tail of the plane where they unloaded a wide variety of luggage - duffle bags, over-filled canvas bags, old fashioned suitcases with the clicking flop down latches, nondescript lumpy bundles, and finally our two pieces of luggage. Imagine, we traveled to the opposite side of the earth with one suitcase each, having shipped the rest of our belongings in one large trunk. Our life was to be very simple.

The Lao and Thai passengers dispersed, getting rides into town by local taxi, small cars with open windows to circulate air heavy, a mixture of dust and humidity. Others were picked up by friends to ride to town by truck or motorcycle. Some just started walking down the dirt airport exit road in the direction of the city.

Carl, the chief of our small office in Pakse, met us planeside. We shook hands. He said he was glad to see us, especially John, since he helped fill the manpower shortage in Pakse. Carl, middle aged in his forties with a silver crew-cut, very tan, compact and strong looking, friendly and polite, had a clipped military manner. He drove a tan Jeep Wagoneer, although it might have been cream or white originally, given its thick coating of dust over dirt. John loaded our bags in the rear as I slid into the back seat across an inch of gritty dirt. The Jeep was fresh air cooled, windows wide-open blowing in dust from the airport road. Carl turned onto the two-lane main road, the only paved road to run the length of Pakse. No sidewalks or curbs, just packed dirt in front of small hut shops and houses that lined the main road. I mentally recorded all I was seeing, wondering how I would become accustomed to my new life in this remote primitive town.

"How was your trip?" Carl asked, looking at me through the dust in his rear-view mirror. "Are you interested in working?" he added, all in one breath. I wondered, *What work? Doing what?* But I answered out loud with a smile, "Great. Sure." He nodded.

Carl made a left onto a dirt road into what he called the American compound, distinguished by a tall metal radio antenna in the corner of the yard of a large yellow two-story stucco European style house. I learned later that this was the home of Elsie and her husband, Jim, Chief of Air Operations, nicknamed Gray Fox, because he had bright silver hair and lots of experience. Carl gestured to various points of interest, like the school on the right, abandoned when families with American kids were evacuated after the mortar attack earlier in the spring. Next to the school was the US Army detachment office where the American medic lived and worked. I made a mental note of this for possible future reference.

He pointed left to a parking lot shaded under a bright green plastic corrugated roof. It resembled a 1950s drive-in, but there were no girls on roller-skates in sight. Carl identified the building situated behind the awning as the Annex. We didn't stop there but continued down the dirt lane, a series of huge potholes, which we fell into and out of and into again. The Jeep had oversized tires and a good driver who knew how to navigate through the series of holes. I later learned that another spouse had been told by the medic that jolting too fast into these potholes caused her abdominal pain, likely bruised ovaries. Interesting diagnosis and believable from what I was experiencing.

A right turn took us past the tennis courts, but no adjoining pool or club house, and past another lane off to the left with four more houses. A short distance ahead, Carl stopped in front of a wooden house identical to the all others, saying, "This is your house." *Could this be it?* I climbed out of the Jeep, scooting dirt out with me. "This is a Lao-style house," Carl offered intuitively to my silent question of where the glass windows and front door were.

He led the way into the screened-in first floor through a screened door that banged closed behind us. A mildew stained tan hemp rug covered the concrete floor. Four old, beaten rattan chairs circled a coffee table in the far corner. I ventured to picture us drinking coffee there in the morning before work or sipping cold beers in the evening. Circular water stains on the coffee table evidenced similar habits of previous residents. I took comfort knowing we were among a long line of those who came before us and probably would follow us.

Turning around to follow John's voice, I saw a huge pile of dusty olive drab sandbags extending out in a square from the back wall. I asked John quietly, "What's that?" He said simply, "Our bunker." My mind flashed back at that moment, taking in what he just said. Bunker. Incoming rounds, deafening explosions. I had watched often-repeated broadcasts from Vietnam. *Bunker* meant bad things happening. I pictured soldiers diving into bunkers. Slowing my thoughts, I caught John's eye. He gestured for me to follow.

Behind ceiling-to-floor stacked sand bags was a small storage room with empty shelves on one wall and a single bare cot along the opposite wall. Carl explained it was our pantry for food although I noted there was none. A large but silent air conditioner filled the small window at the far end of the pantry. I tried to put together what I was seeing, but decided that I'd think about details tomorrow.

The kitchen was to the left out of the bunker. Kitchen. A 1950's Formica table with four chairs, all bright cheery yellow. Sink. Stove. Refrigerator. Full-size upright freezer. In the corner stood a three-foot-tall ceramic jug on a stand with a spigot at the bottom. "What's that?" I asked anyone, and Carl filled in the blank. "That's your water filter. You put boiled water in the top and it filters out all the minerals." Very simple.

The single window on the back wall had a screen. I could see closed shutters on the outside. A single bare light bulb hung over the table. I discovered this light bulb attracted all kinds of flying insects. It also was the mess hall for small lizards called *chinchuk*s, who hung around the light bulb to easily pick off their airborne dinner. One night not long after our arrival, I cooked up vegetable stir-fry on rice, served our plates and sat down across from John. That's when I had my first personal encounter with a *chinchuk*, who proceeded to relieve himself in my plate. Without a word, John removed my plate to the sink and served me a clean plate, but not before I made him run off the *chinchuk*. Eventually I became used to sharing my home with the resident *chinchuk* population, which worked on keeping the insect population in check. The kitchen had the basics, four of each—plates, bowls, glasses, cups and stainless flatware, as well as two oversized pots, just enough to prepare uncomplicated meals.

Next to the bunker was a simple toilet in a closet with no sink. Beside that was the laundry room with a washer with an old-fashioned wringer attached, no dryer. I quickly decided to relegate laundry exclusively to our maid who we had hired by the second day.

John and I could survive and probably even enjoy this simple existence. As people do when they look at a prospective house they might want to rent, I judged this one as livable, if primitive. John told me later that he watched me and was proud that I reacted reasonably to the bunker and the basic nature of the house. I told him it didn't surprise me although deep down I truly was. I assured him, though, I wouldn't have embarrassed us by running shrieking from the house. In a moment of self-discovery, I realized I mentally made a note of questions to ask John later. This became my habit as I encountered all kinds of new experiences.

Carl led us upstairs to the second floor with its empty screened porch running along the front of the house. I suppose we could have had porch chairs out there to catch a sunset or sunrise, but we never thought of it. Inside

I took in the ordinary combination living room and dining room. A two-stool bamboo bar occupied the front corner, typical of a beach Tiki bar in Hawaii. I thought this might be useful when entertaining. With only two stools, however, it limited us to small parties. (I came to realize that the best parties were just the two of us.)

The three-seater sofa, a love seat and two chairs were framed with bruised banana-colored bamboo. The cushions were covered in soiled beige muslin. The matching five-foot diameter round rattan coffee table provided a focal point, functional for hors d'oeuvres and drinks. At first, I thought the furniture was ugly, but I soon grew to like the well-used look and comfort. Plus, it fit the style of the house and how we were to live.

The large Danish modern teakwood dining room table and six matching chairs set up a unique counterpoint to early bruised banana rattan and Tiki bar. But my home wasn't entered in a design contest. It dawned on me as I looked at the dining room table that I would have to carry dinner up the stairs when we had guests. Our parties would be small or at least a limited number of courses. An air conditioner labored in the window in the corner of room, struggling to barely cool, and ineffective in eliminating the humidity. No pictures and only basic Woolworth lamps rounded out the decor. Throughout the house, the windows had wooden shutters that closed on the outside. Upstairs, the screens were covered on the inside with a sheet of thick, dirty yellowed translucent plastic, leaving the screens without function. I presumed the plastic kept the dirt and humidity at bay, but I'd ask John.

I saw the bathroom behind the dining room. The doorway had a one-tile high threshold, which I knew I would find tricky to remember in the middle of the night. A deep porcelain tub on feet stood next to the pedestal sink. A large tank hung on the wall over the toilet. A circular loop at the end of a chain dangling from the tank started the flushing reservoir mechanism. The whole bathroom sparkled with white tile, a clean nearly sterile look. A shoulder-high window over the tub looked out on the back lot, our view when showering. This window provided live entertainment, as the *chinchuks* hunted down and munched up the mosquitoes and spiders, the insects' legs hanging out in all directions as they were slowly chewed by their predators.

John explained the windows, screens, and shutters later that night. No glass in the windows prevented shards of glass from flying in all directions in the event of a mortar attack. I gave myself a point or two when he added that the plastic was an attempt to keep out the dust and humidity. I never figured out why there were screens, if they were covered with plastic. Probably the screens came first, plastic later. During the rainy season, the shutters were kept closed to keep out torrential rain. The reality was that we left them closed year round to help insulate the house from the tropical heat. John also added that, in the event of an attack, the shutters would cut down on concussive damage, the impact of an explosion, which could turn a body to jello inside, even if not hit directly. More than this I did not want to know on the first night.

The remaining rooms were predictable. Three bedrooms, the master bedroom to the left with an air conditioner, which distinguished it as the master bedroom, the two other bedrooms sparsely furnished and muggy hot without air conditioners. Our double platform bed had a mattress on top of wooden slats. Actually, it was comfortable and easy to make. The furniture included a dresser and a freestanding wardrobe, the closet. The house smelled of hot wood, like a cabin at summer camp, or a Finnish sauna.

No TV or radio broadcasts, no newspapers. No connection to the outside world. Pakse was our home for the next two years. We often laughed and figured when starting at the bottom, the only way to go is up. We assumed we had a long career and lifetime together.

After the tour of the house, Carl suggested we go to the Annex and meet our Pakse colleagues. As we left the house, we didn't lock the doors since there were no locks. We bumped back through the potholes and parked in the number one space under the green shade. As we entered a small outer office, Carl greeted a smiling Lao civilian in Lao, "Sah bye dee," as the young man jumped up from his desk. Typical Lao with brown eyes, dark brown hair and a friendly smile, he wore a white shirt and dark slacks, not a military uniform as I expected.

Through another door and a lounge with sofas, down a narrow hallway to the first door on the right, Carl stopped and punched some buttons on a small box beside the doorknob. The door clicked, releasing the latch and allowing him to open it. This was my first experience with a cipher lock. Cipher locks contain four or five numbered buttons in a row, which, when pressed in the correct secret sequence, release the inner bolt.

Inside was the Support Office. I met the man who was to be my first and great friend as well as my first boss in Pakse, Mac. He was the finance officer and taught me a lot about the Agency and the realities of life in the field. Next I met Dick, the chief of support, pleasant but businesslike. When he asked if I liked the house, of course I said yes. I knew that was the right answer, especially in front of Carl. Joe AKA Somsak, the logistics officer, worked in this office. He just smiled and shook my hand. Somsak was his Lao code name. All the American men had to use their code names when identifying themselves over the radio: John became Tamak, Leon became Khamsing, Bill was Noy, Dick was Rattana, Tom was Chanh. The men in everyday conversation referred to each other by their Lao names, too.

Passing back through the lounge, Carl led us upstairs to the left and through another cipher lock. Different numbers, I was to learn. They all had different numbers. We entered the inner sanctum of the Agency's operations in this small city in southern Laos. In reality, it was a jumbled assortment of desks in cheap wood paneled office spaces. The people I met seemed very friendly and welcoming.

The office at the top of the stairs to the left was the communications office, or commo. The Dutch door top half stood open where commo officers posted our daily news as well as sports scores on the bulletin board. This is where the most sensitive communications equipment was located and the commo officers sent encoded messages electronically from Pakse to the offices in Vientiane, the office that oversaw all operations in Laos, as well as to HQS. Entering behind the Dutch door required a much higher security clearance than I ever possessed while in Pakse. Actually, I never had a need to enter this office.

As we met a parade of people, I learned that all new people were quickly adopted and invited over since they were fresh meat for learning what was new at home, meaning HQS. New arrivals could also be used as allies in local office disputes. We discovered it was best to be good listeners and not get too enmeshed in partisan issues. Better to be neutral and friendly with everyone in this all too small community.

As I met these people in the office I wondered how I could ever remember their names or associate who went with which husband or wife. But of course this was foolish. I came to know them all way too well. As I said, our parties for two were always the best.

Another room straight ahead with a giant thick door was the vault, not unlike any bank vault at home. I saw safes lined up along the back wall. This vault became my haunt, my personal domain. A large roll of brown paper on a spool perched on the table to the right as we proceeded along the hallway. My dad wrapped Christmas boxes with an identical roll of brown paper. Strange how this simple detail, even out of context, made the place feel more familiar.

I met Jerol, Tom's wife and an Agency spouse, who was a local hire on a contract called WAE, short for "when-actually-employed." They hired me under the same arrangement, WAE, notable because WAEs accrue no benefits, work for minimal GS-4 pay, and have no career future. Like Jerol, I worked part-time, which meant we had all afternoons free, working Monday through Saturday. Not that I found excitement outside the office other than reading, eating, drinking, sewing my clothes, and shopping in primitive local markets.

My office tour complete, Jerol invited me to her house that afternoon. She and her husband, Tom, also invited John and me for dinner that first night. So, now we had plans and potential friends. As John was immediately sucked into the work vortex that first morning, I hitched a ride back to our house to unpack, no big challenge with just our two suitcases. I began to feel lost and alone, sitting in my Lao house, John clearly off and running at work. I wondered whether I could find anything meaningful for me in this place.

The office did not attract me, as the secretarial work they offered was not something that I had done particularly well in the past. I smiled recalling my previous secretarial experience at the University Of North Carolina (UNC) in Chapel Hill, while I was working on my Master's degree in 1969 before John and I were married and while he served in Vietnam.

To be hired as a secretary in the UNC School of Nursing, I had to talk my way into the job when the interviewer commented that the typing test I took as part of my application did not meet their minimum standard. She was obviously desperate to fill the job of a part-time secretary, so she obligingly suggested that I probably typed exclusively on an electric typewriter, as I had taken the test on a manual. I nodded. I was relieved she didn't see me on my first day of work trying to figure out how to turn on the IBM Selectric, which hid the on/off lever under the front right corner of the keyboard frame.

My job was to type all the lecture notes for the nursing school lecturers, a subject I found fascinating. Those typewriters had no delete or replace capability, just miles of white out tape and gallons of liquid correction fluid. I worked sixteen hours a week at $2.00 an hour, and this is what I lived on. So, although the pay was going to be better this time, I wasn't anxious to regress to facing the tedium of secretarial work again. But that's what they offered.

Around 3:00 p.m. that first afternoon, Jerol came walking down the lane to pick me up. In her friendly, caring way, she sensed my feelings of abandonment. We went to her house, identical to ours, just around the corner. A white picket fence stood in front of her Lao house, which seemed incongruous. I guess the fence was an attempt to make the housing compound look like a typical all-American neighborhood for the benefit of the children, who were now gone.

Later that summer, they put those white pickets to good use. One Sunday afternoon, we had gathered on the tennis court to watch friends Pru and Dick defeat another couple in a spirited tennis match. In her exuberance over winning, Pru tried to jump over the net. Not clearing it, she landed on her knee. Clearly, she had injured herself, as she could not stand. Two pickets strapped around her leg stabilized her knee while they flew her to a nearby military clinic upcountry for X-rays. She had broken her kneecap. Interestingly, Pru's accident was a godsend to me, as I visited her every afternoon to do small favors for her, getting to know her and to find out what life was really like there in Pakse. We became close friends, and she taught me much about being an Agency spouse.

Jerol and Tom's house was nicely decorated with local Lao and Thai artifacts she had collected in the year they had been there. They turned their porch area on the first floor into a living room, and we settled there for an afternoon of frosty daiquiris. These improved my mood. She shared behind the scenes details of who-was-who in the office. As we finished off a blender or two, she fixed dinner. It was probably pushing 9:00 p.m. when the men arrived. I couldn't believe it was so late.

During dinner, Jerol and Tom talked about the current controversy regarding where we should live. Evidently, they didn't want to move across the river away from the airport as Tom thought the airport was the best evacuation point in the event of a North Vietnamese Army (NVA) attack directly on Pakse. Carl saw the airport as the main target for an enemy attack, given the example of the previous spring's mortar shelling of the airport with both long and short shots landing all around the target. Tom said Carl was on the verge of giving everyone an ultimatum. Move or leave. Carl was in charge, no matter others' opinions. Eventually, all the married couples moved, including John and me, Jerol and Tom, Lora and Roger and Elsie and Jim, while the single men remained in the housing compound near the airport. The rationale was that they could defend themselves with no dependents to protect.

18

From John's journal:

30 July 1971-

Dinner conversations focused on the last evacuation, the rocket attack on Pakse in May [1971] and the possibility of another. All homes in the compound had bunkers, and everyone slept with their emergency radio by the bedsides. The decision had been made that the north side of the Sedong River, across the one-way bridge, would be safer for families. Houses had been identified, and work had commenced to Americanize them. There was much argument from some of the couples that the compound was safer and closer to the airstrip in case of evacuation by air. The counter argument was that the airstrip was always susceptible to attack and, therefore, anyone living near the airstrip was in danger, especially in the event of short or misguided rounds. In the last rocket attack, the rockets had been so inaccurate that they landed scattered throughout Pakse on both sides of the Sedong River. Those moving to the north side claimed they were in the line of enemy marching into the city. The bachelors didn't speak. They stayed in the compound. Eventually, all the families moved; the arguments were never resolved, as the enemy never shelled the city again.

After we ate, we drank more and, finally, John and I walked back to our house. It was past midnight, a long first day. I remember telling John how abandoned I felt on his leaving me alone. He said I'd get used to it. He explained that was what work in the field was. Long days, seven-day weeks. He was right.

After a week, the office had completed a low-level security clearance so that I could begin part-time work. I was assigned to the support office to work with Mac. He had me type long lists of numbers in finance ledgers, requiring absolute accuracy. Mac also taught me how to find inevitable mistakes in the columns of typed numbers.

Monthly, we counted the *kip* he stored in his vault, literally millions of *kip*, to satisfy the monthly audit requirement. The official exchange rate was 500 *kip* to the US dollar when I first arrived, but later it was down to 1000 kip to the dollar. When we went shopping on the local economy, we literally had to carry a shopping bag full of *kip*. When Mac paid the local Lao troops in *kip*, he placed bundled packets of *kip* into cartons and trucked out to where the troops where stationed. This was clearly not his favorite day because he had to wear a sidearm. Mac often told me he strongly disliked being around any kind of weapons, and I shared his feelings. Although acknowledging we were in a war zone, Mac and I preferred to remain far to the rear of the action.

Mac taught me a lot about our mission in Laos. He helped me understand that even though what we were doing seemed small in scale, Laos was important to the US war effort in Vietnam. He pointed out that a couple dozen CIA officers in southern Laos were managing to prevent vital supplies and manpower from reaching the enemy in South Vietnam. They actually provided essential force protection to the huge US military presence in South Vietnam. I began to understand how CIA functioned in these types of areas. It wasn't the amount of manpower applied, but rather the smart use of limited resources, which had an enormous effect on the ongoing course of the war. John told me he was proud to have this mission in Laos, that if the US Army had been given this role in Laos, they would have thrown thousands of men into the effort. The CIA did it with relatively few highly skilled, dedicated officers. John's and Mac's explanation made sense to me.

22 July 1971

My second day on the job, or semi on the job. Trailing around like a puppy dog. Looking interested, asking questions, removed from the scene, but at least we are here. No more orientations. Got an early start with Noy to a site, his site. Small unit operations, same as I did in Vietnam, only now I watched Lao troopers scampering off choppers much as I did a few years ago. Mixed feelings. Would like to be out there and not here, but other times I am content not being out there. Returned to Pakse. Not much happening. Got the use of a Jeep for three days. Marti and I took a ride through Pakse. She's taking this well, the M-16 in the bedroom, the 9mm pistol, the bug-out kit. We spent tonight by ourselves. Beautiful to be together.

I came to learn that there was a status difference between being a paramilitary (PM) AKA knuckle dragger officer versus a foreign intelligence (FI) officer. The FI case officers did the classic operations job, recruiting local spies who could tell the case officers information about the activities of the North Vietnamese Army. Also, good spy recruits successfully infiltrated and reported on the local government and the Lao communist organization, the Pathet Lao, so that CIA kept on top of power influences in the region. The case officers met with their agents covertly and paid them for information. I didn't know the relative value of the sources, nor was I included in processing any of their reporting. But some of them used a lot of smoke and mirrors.

John had high opinions of two FI officers, Roger and Jack. John said they knew their business, so I assumed they produced good intelligence from their agents. Notorious among the less respected FI officers was Slippery Jerry, hence the nickname. Once, he gave me a photo to put in a file, presumably a picture of a meeting site where he met an important secret agent. In reality, it was a picture of a crude dugout canoe pulled up on the beach of an unidentified river. Arrows on the picture pointed to the right of the boat, but off the picture. These arrows, Jerry told me, indicated where the meeting site was located. But I could see it wasn't even in the picture. This was all fictional, I knew. It made as much sense as putting an X on the side of a boat to mark the spot where the fishing had been good.

I sensed tension between the PM and FI officers; the former feeling that their role in the office was the essence of why we were in Pakse, the latter knowing that the intelligence they collected was not only critical to the PM mission in Pakse, but also to the larger picture of what was happening in Laos and the entire region.

The PM officers, including John, Dick, Leon, Bill, Bob, and Tom, ran the Lao irregular troops. These Lao troops deployed into the jungle battlefield to interdict the NVA troops' march to South Vietnam. The PM officers also sent out smaller teams, called "roadwatch teams," who reported on the movements of the NVA troops and war materiel moving down the Ho Chi Minh trail to South Vietnam. PM officers also trained the Lao irregulars and roadwatch teams. Overall, the Lao troops were not considered consistently disciplined or dependable.

31 July 1971

A huge operation was launched against Saravane. Khamsing's intel teams "secured" the HLZ, eight men strong, with one HT-2 radio, one 45-caliber pistol and one cross bow. When the first chopper landed 500 m south of Saravane's airstrip, the intel team leader asked Khamsing how many troops were landing. When Khamsing replied 1200, the team leader thought a moment and said, "I hope that will be enough." The intel team leader knew that Lao troops often took off their uniforms and weapons and disappeared into the jungle rather than fight.

The roadwatch teams dispersed along the Ho Chi Minh trail and reported by radio any sightings of enemy troops or materiel moving south. From this information, plans were devised to deploy the irregular Lao troops in battalions. Occasionally, these small teams returned to Pakse to be fully debriefed and re-supplied.

After working for Mac for four months, the office moved me upstairs to work for the FI officers. As a spouse, regardless of my Master's degree or previous work experience, my job was to type whatever they asked and to work for anyone who needed my skills. Twice a week, I became the pouch queen, responsible for double wrapping envelopes from that familiar roll of brown paper, making sure every corner had tape over and around it to make it tamper proof. Couriers hand-carried these packages in locked, sealed courier bags to Vientiane.

I also became the filing clerk. Talk about lowest on the totem pole. On Saturday mornings, Joyce gave me a foot-high stack of cables, every cable that had come in that week. My mission was to decide to file or shred them. Human nature as it was as well as my limited understanding of the subtle importance of many of the cables, I shredded more than I filed. Dick came into my office one day. "Can you find this cable for me?" he asked. Of course I could. But I was thinking, *I wonder if I shredded this one?* So, I looked in all the right files but never found it. Somehow, I convinced him that I probably hadn't filed it yet. He shrugged and thanked me.

I could logically defend my exuberance in my shredding practices. We were to keep the files in the office down to a certain linear footage, so if we had to destroy the paper files before evacuating, we would have time to complete the shred as prescribed by burn guidelines. Therefore, my shredding was clearly warranted. When the office closed eventually, they shredded it all. Interestingly, when the US Embassy in Tehran was overrun in 1978, the CIA officers shredded all the cables. But the Iranians reconstituted the shredded material into whole legible pages. It was then that CIA upgraded the shredders from producing straight strips to crosscut shred to prevent this from happening again. Our shredder in Pakse in 1971-1972 was like the original one in Tehran.

Over time, I became familiar with the personalities in the office, avoiding some, enjoying others. I identified our reports officer, Billy, as one of the latter. On a wall in his oversized office extending up to skylights hung a 20-foot map of the Pakse area, called Military Region Four (MR IV). On the map he stuck colored pins, which denoted all enemy and friendly troop presence and movements. He had scrounged a tall library-type rolling stepladder. Occasionally Billy asked me to update the map, sticking pins into designated locations, each denoted by the six-number map coordinate. For some reason, this made me feel like a part of the ongoing war effort, knowing that where I put some of the pins, an NVA group or troop movement of enemy trucks had been sighted. I could also see where our Lao troops were located and understand John's daily activities better.

As his main role, Billy accumulated reporting from FI officers and wrote comprehensive reports on the status of the war. He sent these reports by cable and in the pouch to Vientiane, where they were consolidated into final reports sent back to CIA HQS in Virginia.

One of the jobs Billy gave me was to take the raw information received from the roadwatch teams and type it on three-by-five cards, including the date, time reported, and the six-digit coordinates. Initially, I faithfully typed these cards, but over time it became tedious. I thought, *He read the cards everyday.* So I began to put in some bogus cards to give him a laugh.

For instance, the normal information said that a team of NVA soldiers with small arms was seen at thus-and-such coordinate. So I typed, "A team of NVA soldiers with short arms and long legs was seen at" a specific coordinate. Another one I added, "A unit of NVA soldiers was seen riding an elephant." They became sillier and longer, too. Several weeks went by as I created my amusing fabrications. I just figured Billy was enjoying them and then tossing them, not mentioning them to me because he didn't want to squash my imagination and fun.

Come to find out, he didn't read them, and only filed them every day. And of course, I hadn't recorded the dates of the funny ones, so I couldn't easily retrieve them, seeing as there were hundreds of cards. After I advised him of my mischief, Billy just left the bogus cards in the stack. Thankfully, they destroyed all the cards in the final shred when the war in Laos came to an end.

I created another job for myself. I taught English to the Lao translators and operations (OPS) assistants. I do not recall how I wangled this, but it remained one of the most rewarding roles I played while in Pakse. These men used pigeon English and phrases they picked up from the American men, often filled with colorful slang they heard repeatedly. Unknowingly, they used profanity in the class without understanding that it could be offensive to me. More than once, I almost laughed out loud when they said things like, "Mrs. Tamak, what is fucking word for this?" I think I helped them learn more useful phrases to get their points across more quickly and accurately during critical radio communications and expanded their vocabulary, but clearly their main focus was not to sit in my classroom.

Overall, I passed everyday frustrated over such a mentally routine and un-stimulating life. With John's endorsement, I requested a Fulbright Scholarship Program application, hoping I would be accepted to work in Thailand. I was in the process of completing it when Carl informed me that he had heard about my application. He asked if I knew that John could lose his CIA contract, if Fulbright hired me. "There's a list of organizations which CIA people are prohibited from belonging to. Fulbright is one of those. In fact, if you have been a member of one of these organizations, you must wait five years after that association before applying to CIA." He explained that this was to prevent these humanitarian programs from being contaminated. Needless to say, I tore up the Fulbright application.

It was a hard to be just John's wife. I was lost without my own identity. I struggled in the office doing the lowest, mindless jobs. I knew I was smarter and had accomplished more than many of the men I worked for. I was irked by their demeaning attitude toward me. John did not treat me this way, but we had so little time together. I learned to swallow my pride and accept that I was an appendage to his career. Carl's wife, Elizabeth, told me often of her professional struggles in the Agency, where women were not valued as highly as men. I understood what she was saying, but it did not reduce my frustration.

John and I lived on the compound for six months until December 1971 when we moved across the river to comply with Carl's orders to move couples out of the compound and away from the airport. I was glad to move since the stench of the tannery a block behind our Lao house had become nauseating to me. I could smell it regardless of which way the wind blew. I did miss the water buffalo who had become a daily acquaintance. I walked from our house behind the tennis courts and along a path to the Annex. The huge water buffalo had his favorite breakfast patch of brown weeds in the corner of a field. I spoke to him each morning as I passed, while he stood there chewing, his jaw moving in an exaggerated way from side to side. He never moved toward me. He was part of my familiar routine that I left behind when we moved, a loyal friend of sorts, who I never replaced.

The support chief located a nice French colonial house in a group of five or six other American-occupied homes near the soccer field and across from the Lao Army Officer's Club on the road headed north out of Pakse. The white stucco house stayed cooler inside than our Lao house. The high concrete fence surrounding the yard was strung with vicious concertina wire. We had a large gravel yard that was a very good alarm as we could hear someone driving into our yard by the noise of gravel under tires. Jim and Elsie had also moved from the house near the airport to a large house behind ours. A small flock of geese in her yard sounded an alarm by honking wildly, if anyone drove into her driveway.

A gazebo stood in the front inside right corner of our yard, where guards sat to get out of the penetrating sun and scorching humid heat. The guards discouraged petty thievery by the local population. Although the guards had weapons propped up in the corner of the gazebo, John told me not to count on them using them if we came under attack. In fact, he said to keep an eye on what the guards wore every day. Although issued khaki uniforms, John said, if they showed up one morning in civilian clothes, I should be alert to a possible attack by the NVA. Our guards could easily disappear into the crowds on the street, if they were wearing civilian clothes.

When my parents visited Pakse, my mother saw an unusual plant growing in the flower bed by the front porch. Glancing out of the corner of her twinkling eyes, she asked if I knew I was growing marijuana. Strange, I didn't recognize it, even though it was the most prominent and healthiest plant growing in the garden. We never let her forget that she had been the only one to identify the plant.

The house had a combination living room, dining room, and den with two air conditioners that kept the first floor cool. The support office had to construct a kitchen inside the house since the original kitchen had a dirt floor and was located outside the back door. We brought all the bruised banana furniture from our other house, which made resettling into our new home easier. We left our Lao house without furnishings as well as occupants, as no American ever moved into it.

John spent many evenings writing his journal in the den. He wanted to become a journalist before he enlisted in the US Army in 1967, having been accepted into the fine arts programs for journalism at Columbia University, Montana State, and Iowa State right out of college. His journal gave him the opportunity to practice and improve his considerable writing skills.

Beside the staircase to the second floor was a large bathroom. A bilious green bullfrog the size of a coffee cup made his home in the floor drain beside the toilet. There, he feasted on the mosquitoes and other insects. Occasionally, we heard him croaking, but he was usually silent, probably content with his private hunting ground. He seemed quite undisturbed by our comings and goings.

At the top of the stairs, previous Lao tenants probably had their parties in the large wood paneled open hall. Three small bedrooms, a small hall bathroom, as well as our master bedroom with bath were off this hall. Our master bedroom with our double bed, two wooden wardrobe closets, and a chest-of-drawers felt cozy. We never opened the shuttered windows over the bed. The attached bathroom ran the length of the bedroom, long and narrow. Over the toilet at the far end was an exhaust fan, actually just an open dinner-plate sized fan without a screen suspended in a hole knocked in the wall. Often, small birds flew into the bathroom through the idle fan and then panicked, flying around wildly. I became skilled at throwing a towel over the poor birds and releasing them outside unharmed.

The wobbly sink sat on a bracket on the outside wall under a window with familiar plastic covered screens. Someone had made a crude plywood vanity around the sink with a little gathered cotton floral print skirt below to hide the bracket and pipes. The maid loved to move our stuff around when she cleaned the bathroom, even married our toothbrushes together on the shelf. I never quite got used to having someone else in the house, but I always appreciated the laundry, kitchen work and cleaning she did for us.

When we moved in, the shower water sprayed from a head mounted on the wall next to the door and ran across the floor to a drain at the other end of the room by the toilet. No shower curtain. Interesting concept, but with water covering the floor the length of the bathroom, it meant standing on a wet floor at the sink and while on the toilet. John and I agreed we preferred a dry floor. We asked the Lao handymen who worked for the office to lay out a normal size square shower, boxed in by the width of a tile. Of course, we failed to mention a drain.

I bet the Lao laughed themselves silly, thinking about the water rising inside the shower floor to overflow the tile frame and run the length of the bathroom floor to the same drain. We explained we wanted the water to drain out of the shower. They chiseled a hole in the corner of the tiled-in square, allowing the water to still run the length of the bathroom, thus not having to wait for it to overflow. Finally, we managed to translate through gestures our point that we wanted the water to drain somewhere other than across the bathroom floor. They either finally understood or decided to be agreeable. To this day, I don't know where they drained the water, probably to the outside wall or into the cistern just outside and below the bathroom window.

We called the large open metal tank the cistern. A water truck came weekly and filled it. Open at the top, it also collected rainwater. Once I peered down into it from the master bathroom and wished I hadn't seen the green growth inside, not a pretty sight. It was likely good algae with natural organisms, but certainly not potable. After seeing that, I was fastidious and boiled water religiously, and then filtered it. We had no bottled water. All too frequently the water pump, which brought the water up to the master bathroom sink and shower, would quit due to power outages. It always happened when John was showering before dinner, leaving him soaped up. We laughed at his having bad luck or bad *pees*.

We instructed the maid to wash all the vegetables in Clorox when she brought them home from the local market. Amazingly, John and I kept ourselves relatively healthy, rarely getting diarrhea or stomach problems. Ironically, before I left Pakse, I found the whole gallon of Clorox untouched under the sink. Guess we developed immunity to the bacteria in fresh produce over time, even though they used "night soil" (human feces) as fertilizer.

As John knew from his showers, electricity was unreliable. After we lived in that house a while, the support chief asked me why our electric bill was so high. It wasn't hard to figure out. I showed him our power line outside the house where the electric line ran from the pole out on the main street to our house. He and I saw perhaps a dozen lines attached to our line along its route to our house. That meant that we were supplying all our non-American neighbors with power. We left the lines attached, and John and I heard no more about our electric bill. CIA provides a lot of "foreign aid" this way. Eventually, to solve the frequent power outages, the office installed a large diesel generator in our side yard, which serviced both our house and our neighbors, Roger and Lora, through the back gate.

Because John had to use the Land Rover for his work, he bought me a red bike to ride to work. It was ten miles round trip, riding along with the local traffic, crossing the one-way bridge, which spanned the Sedong River. The bridge had a traffic light at each end of the span. When one side was red, the other was green. I tried to position myself at the head of the line of traffic waiting for the light to change. The minute the on-coming traffic cleared the bridge, I began madly pedaling among the other bikes and *samlars,* moped-driven open carriages, racing as fast as I could across the bridge. My greatest fear was getting my front tire wedged in one of the wooden planks or being pitched over the handlebars, if I hit an uneven plank. But I pedaled like crazy and never looked right or left. I never had an accident. No helmet. Considering the temperature was over 90 when I left home around 7:15 a.m., I drip-dried when I got to work, as changing clothes didn't seem necessary.

I loved my bike even though it had no gears. I also loved seeing daily life on the streets: the women in long wraparound skirts carrying baskets on their heads or squatting neatly within the fold of their skirt by the side of the road to relieve themselves; the men leaning against trees or walls doing the same; barefoot children playing along the side of the street. I could also buy fresh warm French bread on the way home as I had a basket strapped onto my handlebars. The bread had black specks in it, dead bugs, but we picked most of them out. A warm loaf, however, was hard to get home intact.

John and I avoided malaria by taking weekly quinine pills. John and I were given a supply of pills to begin taking before we left the US. When we ran out of pills several months into our tour in Laos, I went to the US military medic by the office. I assumed the pills he gave us were the same dosage, taking two every Saturday, as we had the original pills. Soon I discovered that these new pills were twice as strong with a once weekly dose. I was alarmed when my ears began ringing, and I had double vision and dizziness verging on vertigo. I called the medic who assured me with a laugh that I wouldn't get malaria that week. A friend contracted dengue fever while we were in Pakse, a disease like malaria, high fevers and sweats, but much more serious, with the potential to return later without warning. She was very sick and weak for a long time. Diarrhea was also a common problem among Americans, but we had pills to stop it once it began. John suffered more frequently after he ate local food with his troops.

1 August 1971

It has been a while since I ate with the troops in the field. Always something new. Today's menu consisted of the usual sticky rice and hot sauce for flavor. Instead of the usual dried beef jerky and pork, I was treated to "river" food. Our camp was next to the Mekong, and I should have known better to refuse the sandwiches Noy offered to send with me. The two main dishes were straight from the river, "au natural." One bowl was filled with what best could be described as a green looking pudding with the consistency of baby food. It was a bowl of fresh algae, unboiled and uncooked, gathered from the river minutes before we sat down. The other dish was never explained to me. I stopped listening when I heard uncooked and "fresh from the river." Brown in color and with the same consistency of the green stuff, it apparently came from either fish or an area where fish spawned. It wasn't fish eggs, I've eaten those before. I apologized to my hosts and explained to them that, the last time I ate uncooked food, my American-trained stomach revolted for three days. Lomotil and tetracycline saved me from that experience with Lao gourmet dishes. Taking pity on me, my hosts quickly produced some fish soup and some dried water buffalo jerky.

Our entertainment in Pakse was getting together with other couples and watching movies shipped in by the US military. Films wound on large reels came in metal cans, each reel with a paper tape to retain the film on the reel. Each tape had a sequential number so you could watch the reels in order. Now and then, we watched the reels out of order because someone had put the wrong tape on the reel. It was interesting how many times we didn't realize this until the reel, or worse the movie, was over, depending on how much we had to drink during the movie. We also met for dinners, sometimes just couples, sometimes including the single men. Dinner conversation was limited, not having a lot of outside information on current sports or news to discuss. Mostly, the men talked about work; the women, about maids and complaints about life in Pakse. Evenings in groups became less enjoyable as time passed, and we heard the same stories and complaints over and over. That was why new people were welcomed so heartily for fresh topics of conversation and a positive attitude.

I remember one wine and cheese party at Jerol and Tom's. I don't recall any special occasion, if there was one. I remember telling a story, which brought the whole group to convulsing tears of laughter. I also could never live it down. "The other night while John and I were asleep, I barely woke, feeling something slowly inching up my thigh. Sleepily, I waited as it continued to creep up, wondering if it was a loving husband. Slowly, I reached down toward the moving creature. I came wide-awake as I realized a huge bug crawled up my thigh. I whisked back my side of the covers and jumped out, madly brushing the creature onto the grass rug. I could see it. I had smashed a huge black bug with my slipper into a crunchy blob. John never stirred. He slept on. My hero.

What amazed me about life in Pakse was that, with a significant war going on just up the highway, we continued our daily routines with little concern or disruption. We ate breakfast, lunch, and dinner. But we had no weekends. John worked seven days a week. The men knew better than the women about the toll the war took in human lives as their troops and Lao pilots in T-28 airplanes died regularly.

20 August 20 1971

I flew over nearly the entire MR IV area today. Beautiful real estate. Lush, green, abundant waterfalls, rugged terrain, clouds hanging low over the Plateau. Gorgeous. One can easily forget the NVA, Pathet Lao, our troops wandering under the triple canopy of the jungle, carrying their tools of trade, leaving their blood trails and bodies after violent clashes. One can only see the serenity and peacefulness in the greenness. The irony of it all is that neither side or sides is fighting over the beauty of this piece of geography, but over some nebulous, trivial ideology. Who needs ideology on a mountain top overlooking deep valleys and rushing waterfalls. The stupidity of man. If he would only learn to appreciate the simple things, remain ignorant of the subtleties of life. Let those with nothing better to do in life than worry about inconsequential things grapple with uncertainties. Unfortunately for us, it is usually those with nothing better to do who become our leaders.

On Christmas Day 1971, we were at home, a rarity that John took the day off, but he had promised me. I was busy at my favorite round coffee table working on a large jigsaw puzzle my cousin, Sharron, sent us, putting together the edge pieces and meticulously sorting other pieces into color groups. The phone rang. Gray Fox told John that one of the PM officers, Rattana, had gone up in a plane to check on his troops in the field and now his plane was missing. John left the house in a flash. Even though the Lao believed Americans had magic and couldn't die, John felt responsible for his fellow Americans and knew that death could find any of them. Thankfully, they found Rattana, the plane, and pilot eventually, all safe. The American magic held true. But the incident and Rattana certainly interrupted Christmas Day.

The next day, I instructed the maid (we had no common language between us) who came daily, that she was not to touch any pieces of the puzzle. She seemed to understand. Ah, what frustration to come home at lunch to find she had left the outline in tact but had put all the loose pieces back in the box. I wonder what she thought was the purpose of the puzzle, and why I might have divided the loose pieces into color matched groups. All the American wives vented pent-up anger, fear, and frustration about life in Laos by complaining about our maids. I just shook my head a lot. Other friends claimed their maids stole from them, but the items inevitably appeared later when they remembered they had hidden them when they traveled. They laughed sheepishly and admitted their false claims against their maids. But underlying anxiety filled our lives, and we looked for scapegoats release valves. The maids were just the misplaced targets of our fears. Placid on the outside, life in Pakse was normal and predictable, but somehow we knew life could always turn to lifelong tragedy for any of us.

CHAPTER 2

New Year's Eve - The War Comes Closer

John and I invited a mixed group of Americans over to the house, single guys and couples. The war was moving closer to the city, and the men were concerned that the NVA would actually enter the city. That last day of 1971, the closest NVA units came within seven kilometers, too close for comfort with the continuing presence of non-combatants, the American women. Carl had repeatedly asked US Ambassador Godley in Vientiane to allow the Pakse wives to be evacuated to Vientiane, but the Ambassador did not want to make the Lao military think we lacked confidence in their ability to protect the city. That night, the word came during our party. All wives were to pack one suitcase each and be ready to leave first thing in the morning. John was relieved since he couldn't focus on his troops and war tactics while concerned about my safety.

In one suitcase, I packed my clothes and our only treasures, my jewelry and John's camera. At the airport, we boarded a C-47 with our husbands and single men standing by Air Ops, watching. Noy, one of the single guys and a joker, kidded us that our husbands now could go to the bars with him to enjoy the local talent. Lots of laughing, and a few tears too. Also lots of beer, as I recall stashing a Heineken or two into my purse for the trip north. But, at this moment, the war became too personal, encroaching on my life. Leaving John was difficult, almost unbearable.

In Vientiane, the wives lived in motel-type housing, two wives to each room, near the US Agency for International Development (USAID) compound. This was not the optimum arrangement for keeping our morale high with all of us worrying together. Husbands called regularly by erratic phone connections and came to visit on a rotating basis every other week. When a husband showed up, the roommate wife moved in with another wife, giving the couple privacy. In fact, one couple conceived their first child during this time. I wonder if their thirty-nine-year-old son knows that. We loved ribbing them about this incontrovertible proof of their recreation during that visit.

Eventually, I was asked, along with Carl's wife, Elizabeth, to return to work as a skeleton staff at an up-country military site located not far from Pakse where Lao troops were trained. Elizabeth and I shared a small office in a wooden building housing the Pakse files. Also located at this site was a Lao military hospital manned by Philippino doctors. Carl gave strict instructions that Elizabeth and I were never to spend the night at this site. So, we commuted to Ubon, Thailand, every evening aboard a single-engine Cessna, where we stayed at a basic Thai hotel. Elizabeth hated the flight, but I enjoyed watching the countryside pass below, the rice fields and locals, sometimes a boy riding on the back of an elephant on a narrow path beside the rice paddies. The airstrip at the site was uneven packed dirt headed at a slight angle downhill, so the take-off and landing were bone-rattling rough.

Duties in the up-country office were uncomplicated: open the safes each morning and closing them at night, respond to the single sideband radio we tuned in daily. The radio was to be used for emergencies when we were instructed to call Gray Fox at Air Ops in Pakse. Occasionally, we received unexpected calls from US planes in the area. One afternoon, I heard our call sign from an American pilot overhead. But when I responded, there was a long pause before he replied. He repeated our call sign. I answered again. He said he was surprised to hear a woman's voice. He asked who I was, and I assured him I was on duty on the radio. Another afternoon Gray Fox called to ask us to prepare the site to receive a group of Cobra gunships that was going to park at the site overnight. Later, I must admit I was blown away, both literally and figuratively, as I watched these powerful war machines with the big guns mounted on the side land on our dirt runway. Such military might impressed me, as we watched from an open Jeep amidst the huge dust clouds kicked up as they landed. These troops on the gunships medivaced wounded from the field. We got them fed and bunked down before Elizabeth and I caught our flight for the night.

I remember some wonderful times there, too. John stopped in occasionally during the workday although he never stayed long since his troops were on the ground fighting around Pakse and on the Bolovens Plateau. He spent the night in Pakse since all operations emanated from there.

Sometimes, he flew in to have breakfast with me in the mess hall on the side of a hill overlooking the Mekong River. Songs by Creedence Clearwater Revival and Jeff Christie's 1970 song, "Yellow River," played over the mess hall stereo. Often, we heard the roar and then saw F-4s flying at our eye level in the mess hall as they slowly followed the Mekong River returning from Vietnam to cross back into Thailand where they were based. We could see the pilots' faces through their jet canopies. What a magnificent, powerful sight, evidence of our war machine as we watched it from our remote, pastoral setting in Laos. It impressed me to witness American military strength passing right before my eyes, a unique experience for an American woman to be so close to the sights and sounds of war.

28 February 1972

I am reading Stilwell's American Experience in China. I'm sure this experience was more interesting and exciting than the book. Marti returns to Pakse Wednesday, March 1, and it will be good to have her back, but I'm afraid the situation here is worse now than when she was evacuated, 1 January. Khongsedone got hit night before last with mortars, enemy was sighted across the river from Khongsedone and most of the inhabitants have left. Everything is quiet at

KM 21 although NVA are certainly still there. I swear I saw an NVA soldier in civilian clothes walking along the road near the airstrip. All I have to go on is my sixth sense. I even watched him for a while. Other than intuition, no other proof. But I think I know an NVA soldier when I see one. And I'm letting Marti come back to this. I ought to be shot if anything happens to her. "Retention of power without the strength or capacity to cope with multiplying troubles"...Stilwell's book. The entire China experience parallels Laos today. Haven't we learned anything? What a bag of worms!

The wives moved back to Pakse on March 1, 1972, when the NVA was pushed back a few kilometers from the city limits. Life returned to that strange normal of war being the reason we were there, yet continuing to live ordinary daily routines. Both sets of our parents came to visit us in Pakse in spring of 1972, and they were amazed at how normal life seemed for us. Once, sitting in our living room with the shutters closed, my mother commented on a distant rumbling noise. We told her it was "Lao thunder." Not a cloud in the sky. She didn't question it at the time, but, later when we were sitting in an elegant restaurant in Bangkok we admitted that Lao thunder was really the Lao-piloted T-28s, World War II fighter planes, bombing NVA targets just outside the city. Although our parents were concerned about the dangers we faced in Pakse, none of them voiced objections. It was the life we had chosen.

John's work frustrated him though.

14 March 1972

Fighting with Somsak again. What else? The alcoholic bastard throws more screw-ups into the game than do the Lao. It'll probably take me all afternoon to find the bastard, and then he'll be already drowned in scotch. He didn't get the weapons I thought he would pick up at the old KM 21 position. Now I'm short M-16s. Par for the course. The Americans are more frustrating to work with than the Lao. You expect incompetence from the Lao, not from the Americans.

16 March 1972

You pay, clothe, feed, and arm him, but you don't lead him. The Lao soldier can and will fight. Any soldier of any army will fight, if properly led. The Lao soldier will die, if he's shown how to die. We fight a convenient war, the eight-to-five variety. After a good night's sleep in the air-conditioned bedroom with your wife, you have your morning coffee, breakfast if you wish, read a little, jump into your Land Rover, and commute to the air strip. Donned in camouflage shirt, jungle boots, maybe an old flop hat, relic of Vietnam days, you check out a porter or chopper, and off to war you go, if the office says it isn't too dangerous for you. During the day, you play your role to the fullest. A few of us cheat and go where we aren't supposed to, where we might be shot at. But then, usually we're with at least a battalion of troops, and Lao battalion commanders rarely get killed. The better part of your day is spent with the commander. About 4 o'clock in the afternoon, you call for your chopper or porter to pluck you out of wherever you are to bring you home to a string of unnecessary meetings. But alas, eventually back home to a well cooked meal by wife or hired cook, cold beers, a good book, or a quick trip to one of the few night spots.

After our troops fail miserably, we wonder what is wrong. The entire project is wrong. We are fighting a "sort of war" but not really a war, not from our standpoint. From a Machiavellian standpoint, we're succeeding. We're pitting two different groups of people against each other with our only contribution money and whatever "advice" we can give. We haven't succeeded in winning anything, except criticism at home and from others with nothing to show for the criticism. We have succeeded in stalling; the experts call it "protracted warfare." We always succeed in inventing a new term for when we fail in something.

Our presence here, as I understand, is or was, it changes everyday, to thwart the NVA from re-supplying South Vietnam thereby increasing our chance of winning that war. Now, we have lost the war in the south. What are we here for now? To save the Royal Lao Government from NVA takeover, to create a buffer for Thailand and the rest of SE Asia. We have committed ourselves to our ears in Laos and won't admit we failed again. Are we looking for a gracious way out? We seem to be looking for gracious withdrawals from a lot of areas. And, if we are ready to withdraw, we're paying a heavy price. If we're here to win or at least do better than we have been, we better start looking for new ways, with new people. About the only thing I've heard from management lately is that we have been here for so long that the people who began this circus have reached higher places in our bureaucracy and can't admit that the show has gone sour because they were responsible for planting the seeds of failure. Their only recourse is to ask people here now, "What are you doing wrong?" We never had any problems." We're having problems because they didn't have any problems. Only thing I'm certain of at this point is that, when we're gone, the Lao will still be here.

One night as we slept soundly in our bedroom, horrific explosions shook the house and knocked dirt out of the cracks in the wooden bedroom ceiling into our sleeping faces. It was 3:00 a.m. We jumped from the bed, hearts pounding, and put on our bug-out clothes, including long pants and heavy hot boots. The electricity quit, and without air conditioning, the bedroom heated up quickly. We went out on the balcony off the bedroom where we felt a slight breeze.

27 March 1972

My first thought was of incoming, and I wondered why the enemy was firing so close to our house when they had so many more lucrative and important targets in Pakse. Rumbling explosions followed the first large one didn't sound *like incoming. The airport, I thought. They must be going after the planes and our ammo dump at the airstrip. A radio report on our ops net confirmed that it was the ammo dump at KM 8. The electricity in the city was out since the power lines from the dam to Pakse were near the ammo dump and probably had been cut by the explosions. Thinking that sappers were responsible, we sat dressed and waited for what would come next. To bide the time, we took our radio out onto the second story porch where there was a pleasant breeze in that sweltering night. And there was a grand view of the fireworks. The booms and fireballs and flares provided a magnificent fire show - although an anxious one. The final tally on what was lost went into the $5,000,000 range. An expensive show. The final investigation determined that carelessness on the guards' part and a festival in a neighboring village where flares were being fired for their celebration caused the destruction of the ammo dump.*

The ammo dump incident scared us both, making danger a greater reality and closer to home than it had been. We both had been mentally prepared to leave the house that night to follow the Escape and Evacuation (E&E) plan. It called for us to gather with other Americans at the soccer field behind our house to wait pick-up by a helicopter. Actually, we knew that was not a good plan as locals would overrun the field and attempt to get on the choppers, causing mayhem and utter failure in evacuating us. No such thing as a silent helicopter.

We had our alternate plan, although not office-sanctioned, to head down to the Mekong River and "borrow" a dugout for a quick paddle across the river. On the other side of the river were the wet rice fields that we would have to wade across to eventually reach Thailand, several miles west of the river. John estimated that crossing the river provided sufficient distance and barrier from NVA troops who might pursue us. I worried, though, about sloshing through knee-deep snake infested water in the rice paddies. But I would have chosen that option, if the other was to face the enemy at our front door.

During the week after the ammo dump blew up, thousands of unexploded shells were found peppered over a large area around the dump. US Army Explosive Ordnance Disposal (EOD) men, very brave or stupid, arrived to collect the ordnance into piles and detonate it. They knew their business well as they all survived this many-week process. One of these officers told an amazing story one night that reflected the Lao people's approach to life. The EOD officer had piled some of the ordnance and set the fuse, moving a safe distance away. Although he set it up a long way from the road, he still made sure that no one was approaching. After he lit the fuse, here came an old Lao man riding alone on a bike. The EOD officer tried to wave off the man, but he kept pedaling. Then, a deep gut-shuddering explosion. A huge cloud of dust obscured the area, including the road. Waiting and hoping for the best, the EOD officer stood still as the Lao man appeared, riding out of the cloud at the same cadence, never missing a stroke. The Lao did not believe in safety and caution. They believed in omens called *pee*s, both good and bad, that watched over them.

John had an operations assistant who translated for him and worked hard. They became very close. Every morning they flew out of Pakse on the Porter. There was an early 1960s aircraft known for its short-take-off-and-landing (STOL) capability, used almost exclusively by John and the other officers to monitor Lao troops on the ground and to resupply them with food and materiel. So, his ops assistant was used to a single-engine plane. One afternoon after he and John returned from a flight on the Porter, the ops assistant headed back to his office on the airstrip. A twin-engine Otter had just taxied in and parked near the Porter. As the ops assistant walked around the Otter toward Air Ops, he never saw the second whirling propeller and walked right into it.

His wife told John later that her husband was a hero, that he had died honorably. John couldn't get over her composure, but she explained that dying honorably meant having a wonderful afterlife. John and the others went to his funeral. His body was laid atop a funeral pyre, with flowers and food and great ceremony. They lit the wood under the pyre, but a sudden torrential rainstorm came and extinguished the fire, leaving it barely smoldering. The party went on, but John worried about his friend's afterlife. And he missed his loyal friend.

7 May 1972

The "Symington Amendment" could be the title of the last chapter in the tragic novel of American involvement in Laos. For whatever reasons, secret or public, the US has become involved in a "hot war" in Laos. The pros and cons can be and should be argued, and hopefully, analyses of the arguments will prevent a recurrence of another Laos in American foreign affairs. But the arguments for and against US involvement in Laos have become academic.

The involvement exists. The North Vietnamese exist. The fighting and dieing and all the other ugly paraphernalia of war exist. We set the stage and are now looking for a graceful exit, stage left. But there is no graceful way out of war. The Symington Amendment is taking away the props, but only of one side, ours.

The tragedy and irrationality of the Symington Amendment is that it is not taking enough away. By placing an unrealistic limit on military expenditures in Laos, our Senate is giving the Lao just enough military tools to die a slow death. The NVA will not leave Laos because an American senator cut American military support there, and neither will the Lao stop fighting NVA as long as we continue our military support. For the Lao to continue fighting and for us to remain within the limits of the Symington Amendment forces an unrealistic rationing of ammunition and equipment.

When Lao troops engage in combat against the NVA, Lao commanders will now be forced to decide whether the skirmish is decisive enough to warrant use of heavy weapons support, artillery, or air power. If additional support is required, the artillery commander will be forced to decide whether the skirmish is decisive enough for five rounds of 105mm fire, ten rounds, twenty or more. If he goes beyond his meager allocation, he may not have any ammunition when the situation becomes more critical. The US Air Force commander may have to use 500-pound bombs instead of napalm because the bombs are cheaper. The skirmish may not warrant the support available, and more Lao soldiers will die. Deaths could have been avoided, if ammunition had been available without limitation by remote Senate controllers.

It is not fashionable today in most American circles to discuss tools of war and how they should be used. The US gave the Lao the arsenal as well as the expertise in its use with no commitment of American troops or lives. Now that we have built this albatross, we should either continue the support we started or withdraw entirely. The Symington Amendment will not stop fighting in Laos. It will cripple the Lao military effort. Left without any support, Laos would quickly fall to the North Vietnamese, but at least it would be fast. Continued military aid on a realistic basis could keep Laos free until a political settlement is reached. But, to prolong the defeat into an agonizing death is criminal.

The ugly American is not always the arrogant American overseas. He can just as easily be the ignorant American at home.

20 May 1972

The noose is tightening around Pakse. Khongsedone has fallen. GM42 is still holding at KM 21, but it's only a matter of time before the NVA will bring pressure there. Two 85mm field guns, two 122mm guns, 12.7's, confirmed 14.5's and possible 37mm threat exists in the Khongsedone area. The NVA are serious. Even PS 18 is threatened.

Listening to Creedence Clearwater and rockets rain on Pakse…quite possible. The tension that was here in early January doesn't exist. Criteria for another evacuation was fighting at KM21 and the fall of Khongsedone. Both have occurred and yet no word of leaving Pakse. People go about their business, giving our precarious situation little thought. We cried wolf too often, and now that the threat is greater than ever, no one stirs. Ambassador Godley has stated that dependents will leave when husbands leave this time. An unrealistic statement considering the nature of our job. But, as always, decisions are easier to make when one is removed from the immediate area. I wonder if the Ambassador would have his wife by his side when he is forced to defend the Embassy from the NVA streaming through Vientiane.

Frustrating us even more is that, for once, we have a concrete idea of NVA plans and intentions. Our source has come through on most of the information. He has told us what the NVA will do and even how they will do it. Yet, we are powerless to react. Everyone we have is tied up keeping the status quo. The only help we could have received was immediately sent to Long Tieng to exploit an empty victory.

Amid all the gloom, I had one small satisfying moment. After having alerted GM 42 of a possible imminent attack, I discovered this morning that the General had actually moved, at night. Victories are small here and very personal. The GM has been doing a good job of keeping mobile and patrolling in the KM 21 area, which has prevented the NVA from pinpointing our positions. As long as we can keep them from directing accurate heavy weapons fire into friendly positions, we can keep our head above water. I'm sure GM 42 will eventually get tired of the constant mobile state, and they will make one mistake, which will cost us a battalion or even the GM. They've been at this cat-and-mouse game now for ten days. Malaria and bad drinking water are taking their toll. The soldiers refuse to drink the water brought out to them, preferring water from the nearby streams, which is more convenient but not potable. They must have started taking their malaria pills since the cases have leveled off some.

We should go on the offensive, but the Symington ceiling prevents any large use of ammo or air support, so all we can do is maintain our presence and hope the NVA don't push too hard. Unfortunately, wars and battles aren't won with wishful thinking.

This experience in Pakse reminds me of a living novel with us as the characters and the NVA, the skillful authors of a deadly plot.

One day, Jerol and I decided to catch a courier flight to Ubon to go shopping at the American Air Force Base Exchange. In the Air Ops office before we left, I chatted with a Thai man I had met before. He was preparing to head out on a helicopter with one of the Americans. They called him a "kicker" in the jargon of war planes; when the plane arrived directly over troops, he literally kicked supplies out the side door of the plane or through the trap door in the bottom of the fuselage. A happy man, full of life and fun to talk to, he was committed to his role in this war. But when we returned from our carefree shopping trip, we saw a fire truck on the runway. Gray Fox told us they were washing out the inside of the helicopter where this wonderful Thai man had been blown to bits while standing in the doorway of the plane waiting to do his job. How instantly life ends. How real the war was.

12 May 1972

I brought some flower blossoms back from the field today. I don't know the name of the flower, but it is treasured by my Lao troops. They gave me the blossoms with their stems in a clear plastic bag filled with water. Something is very sad about these blossoms. Lao soldiers prize them and string them around their necks with their Buddhas. The aroma of the blossoms is strong and lasts. The flower is to give the Buddha more power to ward off death and is also the flow-

er chosen to cover the dead soldiers. Several months ago, when BGR-20 was finally run off the eastern edge of the Bolovens Plateau, we managed to exfil about forty of them. They had been without food or water for over a week. The NVA had chased them all over the plateau for weeks. We relied on these troops to keep two NVA battalions occupied, and they did. But, at a high cost of life. When we finally did pick them up, I was flying over them in a Porter. I remember seeing little white things all over these soldiers as they trod along. When they got off the choppers that went in to pick them up, they were covered with these white flowers. It was beautiful to see them so decked out, and yet so tragic for those who didn't make it out. I brought the flowers in the plastic bag to Marti.

In September 1972, John's Lao troops went for more extensive training in an Agency-run training camp with Tony Po in Thailand. John departed Pakse with his battalions in what was referred to as a Group Mobile (GM), and I remained in Pakse. I felt uneasy, knowing that, if the NVA attacked Pakse, I would be left to my own devices, probably joining our neighbors, Roger and Lora, to evacuate from Pakse. While John was away three long weeks, work occupied my mornings. I spent the afternoons reading or sewing.

His final week away started out as usual. At least I could drive our right-hand-drive Land Rover to work instead of riding my bike. But, I was lonely and ill at ease at night without John, never certain whether I could actually fire the shotgun sitting in the corner of our bedroom, if I heard someone coming up the stairs.

On Thursday September 22, our deputy chief Ted came to our office door to ask my officemate whether he knew Ray in Long Tieng up north. He said he didn't. Ted told us that Ray had been killed the night before. I felt I had been kicked. I was shocked. I said, "I know Ray. He is John's best friend." I was devastated and went home early. I cried endlessly, alone. I couldn't believe that Ray was dead. I also couldn't believe an American had died. I wanted to believe as the Lao did that Americans didn't die. John arrived home the next day. I had become nearly inconsolable over Ray.

That night, John and I sat in our living room on the sofa.

He said, firmly, "Marti, this is war. These things happen. Ray was doing his job, but he was at the wrong place at the wrong time."

He then told me, "If this ever happens to me, be proud and strong. My family won't understand, but try and make them know that I am doing what I believe in." He also told me that I should give his family all the life insurance, because his three brothers and sister were still young. His parents would need this. He told me he knew I could make it on my own.

"These things happen. There is a plan, and Ray's death is part of it."

I tried to accept what he told me through my tears and fears, but I knew that it would be impossible for me to survive, if something happened to him.

CHAPTER 3

All a Dream - October 19, 1972

Three weeks later, I was sitting on the sofa reading. It was 7:30 p.m. and I was hungry. John was late for dinner even though he had often promised he'd try to come home earlier. I heard tires on the gravel driveway. The house was shuttered, so I couldn't see out.

I looked to the screen door where I expected to see John coming through the door.

But it was Bill, the new Chief of our office. My first words to him were, "John didn't tell me he'd invited you for dinner. Come on in."

The look in his clear blue eyes. Then he said, "Marti." He started again. "It's John, he's gone." Or "We lost him." Or "I have bad news."

His words were lost in my total rejection of what he was saying. I walked to the wall beside the kitchen door. Facing the wall, hands clutching my face, saying, "No, no, no."

Bill put his hands on my shoulder. I didn't want a hug. I was in instant shock and exquisitely alone. I didn't cry, I just kept saying "no."

Then I became part of the room again, so many people entering our home, all eyes filling with tears, watching me. It was the first of a thousand times I was to realize how difficult it was for them to look at me. Sadness for me, for my loss of a husband and best friend. Sadness for their loss of a true friend.

Bill helped me sit down. And Leon came in, John's closest friend. Leon tried to tell me how it happened. Leon had tears running down his cheeks, unembarrassed, unaware he was crying.

Everyone was sitting and standing around our lovely large round coffee table, watching me. It was like I wasn't part of the scene.

I remember trying to think. John will never come walking through the door. I had heard others say that they always expected their loved ones to come walking through the door. But this was real, not a dream. And it was forever. He had lost the rest of his life. How had he known when we talked three weeks earlier.

I sat there, so removed and unattached from this scene before me. Not crying, not hearing or seeing or feeling. Drinking a beer became my soft landing, my anesthetic. To keep my mind from shrieking and exploding. That night, and all the next nights when my mind shrieked, "He is gone!" My brain stopped that thought, just shut down to avoid the pain at the unthinkable.

Everything happening around me was observable, but I did not allow myself to get emotionally involved. It was a picture show of all those people in our living room. Bill, his wife Martha, Lora and Roger, and Leon, so many others. They told me they had the local Philippino doctor out in the car in case I needed a sedative. *What for? What could it change? Why would I want to forget these moments, the time closest to John's being with me, slipping farther and farther into the time called the past?* I didn't want to forget or to blank out this slamming shock. I needed reality. They stared at me.

Bill told me they had not been able to recover John's body. I looked at him strangely. John's body was already empty, a relic. He was gone. Why did they need to tell me about the shell of John? Why did they keep saying they'd get him out tomorrow? My mind began screaming—tomorrow? And then it shut down again. I couldn't think of tomorrow or next week or my life without John.

50

Then, Leon seemed to pull himself together and began to tell the story of that day, October 19, 1972, the day I lost John.

This was the big infiltration of John's GM. They were prepared to make a difference that day against the NVA units that had made a significant push south on the Ho Chi Minh trail toward South Vietnam. Leon and John had permission to go into the HLZ for the infil, even though the area was not as safe as the office would have liked. They went in on separate choppers and were on the ground as the Lao troops landed and dispersed. By mid-afternoon, as the infil was almost completed, they heard small arms fire in the distance. Leon and John knew it was time to get the hell out of there.

Leon boarded his chopper with his ops assistants. It lifted off low, beneath the tree line to avoid giving the NVA a clear shot at the chopper. John's chopper began to lift, but instead of staying below the tree line, it lifted up above the trees. It immediately attracted hostile gunfire and was hit. It tilted and came crashing down, catching on fire. John's troops, still in the area, rushed back to see the chopper engulfed in white-hot magnesium-fueled flames. They managed to pull John from the open door as well as his ops assistant and the pilot.

According to the troops on the ground, John was burned but not his face. Leon watched it all from his chopper that he ordered to return to the HLZ despite the very present danger. But they couldn't get close enough to really see what was happening, and they couldn't land because of so much gunfire in the area. Leon was frantic to get John out.

Leon cried as he told me this. Leon didn't accept that he couldn't change what had happened right before his eyes. He couldn't stop John's chopper from lifting up too high, or crashing down, or catching fire. He could just watch with utter horror, screaming into the radio to the Lao troops on the ground to get John out, to rescue his friend, TAMAK. How could this be happening?

When it was clear he couldn't help John, he told his pilot to leave the area so those on the ground could try to save John. But then, Leon's radio spoke the unspeakable to him. "TAMAK is dead."

Leon was devastated. He reported by radio to Gray Fox in Air Ops. Then he flew back as close as he could for one last chance to get John out. But the area had been overrun by NVA troops. John's troops managed to get away from the chopper, carrying John's body and those of his assistant and the pilot. Leon could do nothing but go back to Pakse. He was only keeping the area hot, making it more difficult for John's GM to get away. How could he explain that he was powerless to stop this from happening?

Later, I recalled the exact moment when John died. It was mid-afternoon and I was in the office van returning to work from lunch at home. The van was stopped at the one-way bridge crossing the Sedong River. John came to me; somehow I sensed it. Even now, I can't remember how I knew, but I was startled later to learn it was the exact time when he went down. When he died.

Leon was crying, looking at me so sadly, saying over and over that he did all he possibly could, but he didn't save John. He was horrified at his failure.

Bill told me John's Lao troops were carrying his body through the jungle that night and would find a place tomorrow where they could get a chopper in to pick him up. My response was the body was empty. No one should risk his life in this effort.

"What did I want to do tonight?" Martha, Bill's wife, asked. I thought: I want this all to stop happening.

I sat in the loveseat of my familiar bruised banana furniture and kept tracing the curves and cracks down the arms. I did not cry a lot, just kind of leaked when I let my mind admit what I refused to believe.

They asked me about going home and notifying my parents. I gave Bill my parent's phone number in Fort Lauderdale, but then it dawned on me they weren't home. They were in Pasadena, California, visiting friends, Merton and Alice. I gave them my sister's number since she knew how to contact them.

This was going to be awful. And then they asked about John's family and told me someone would go to their home to inform them. *Why couldn't we change this whole thing, stop all this from being true.*

Bill suggested I spend the night with Elsie and Jim. They lived down the lane. Someone went upstairs with me to gather things for the night. I saw John's things, our married toothbrushes, his hair brush with his blonde hair entwined in the bristles. His clothes in the wardrobe, his pillow and where we loved and whispered into the night. And where he kissed me tenderly good-bye, so early that same morning.

I went to Elsie's, encased in non-time, not looking back or forward, each view too painful for me to accept.

Elsie and Jim had a bar with air conditioning, a benefit of rank. I sat there and drank a few beers to pad me from the stabbing pain of reality. I talked about John. Finally, I went upstairs to a bed where I fell asleep. I woke several times but shut out my thoughts and drifted back to fitful painful sleep. I woke very early with a start. It was true. It wasn't a dream. What was I going to do today, tomorrow, forever? Where was our future? It had died with John.

Then necessary details spared me from dwelling on my pain. I had to go through papers and clothes and tell them what I wanted sent home. I sorted John's clothes—sending most to charity. Some with more emotional attachment were sent home, wherever that was to be.

But what should I do with his well-worn boots and the smell of him in his clothes? Can I take the smell of him home with me, the memory of his special touch in wonderful moments of our lovemaking? His snores, his voice, his thoughts, our conversations, and his love—how can I pack all that? Will I forget all of this when I leave this place where we laughed, cried, loved, planned our future, and lived each day together, even the last day?

I was afraid to look in the mirror because I knew half of me was missing, the best half. He had left that morning at 4:00 a.m. to prepare for the day's infil. He woke me to kiss me goodbye. If we had only known.

A group of Lao women appeared at the house. Their husbands had worked for TAMAK and they wanted to tell me how sad they were. They were really telling me how unbelievable it was that TAMAK had died. Americans didn't die; it was something that happened to the Lao. We sat in a circle of chairs and didn't say much because of our mutual language barrier. But I could see they understood my pain, and I shared their disbelief. How much I appreciated their visit. Later, someone told me this was unusual for the Lao to acknowledge the sadness of death by visiting this way. They believe in the continuation of a person as an eternal spirit.

I called our close friends, Dave and Barbara, in Thailand. Somehow, it helped me to tell them what had happened. John had been killed in Saravane in a helicopter crash. I was going home. The phone operator, who monitored the phone line, said, "Working?" several times to make sure we were still on the line. I said, "Yes." Later, I realized what an awful shock that must have been for our dear friends although the office probably sent everyone in the region a cable telling them of John's death. Like they had Ray's.

More details. Leon called. They couldn't get the body out. Maybe that afternoon. I told him it was OK. Later, they called and said they had recovered it. Leon told me that he had looked at John's face. It was the same, he said, his wonderful fumanchu moustache was only a little singed. They draped the body bag with an American flag edged with gold fringe.

They conducted an autopsy in Udorn to document his death and to prepare an official death certificate. That document devastated me when I received and read it. And every time after. It was in black and white. He died of third degree burns. Eventually someone told me he had also been shot with an AK-47. This document became my new reality.

As I stood in our living room, a distinguished man appeared. Hugh Tovar, the CIA Chief from Vientiane. Was this so important to him that he personally came all the way to Pakse to see me? He focused on me intently with his

54

clear eyes after hugging me compassionately with sadness in his embrace. He wanted me to know how devastated everyone was.

He said he represented the Director of Central Intelligence (DCI) who sent his personal condolences, regrets, and sympathies. I was astounded that the Director would be aware of John's death, reminiscent of the smallest bird in the field. Hugh came to tell me that. He didn't stay long, but I remember how he expressed his emotions so sincerely, and how he seemed to share my pain. I was grateful that he had come. I could see that it was not just me who had lost John. Over the years, I have seen Hugh many times. I always tell him how much his visit meant, and he hugs me. Again.

More details to save me. We had to finalize travel arrangements. My parents had been notified and planned to meet me in Los Angeles Airport enroute to Logan Airport in Boston, where John's parents would be waiting. The office decided that Elsie should travel with me. Someone gave her some Valium for me to take if she thought I needed it during this endless trip halfway around the world.

What were my parents, my sister and my grandmother thinking? And how were John's Mom and Dad, and his brothers and sister? There was no way to call and what could we all say to one another? Crying makes no noise.

That night, I hosted a party in order to clean out the freezer, which had been stocked in preparation for a party John and I were planning for Halloween. We had been ordering Kielbasa from the commissary to stockpile enough for the party. We also had lots of beer and liquor, also essentials for a great party. I asked Bill to invite everyone over, so we could celebrate John's life together. I needed to speak to everyone and say goodbye.

Some of the men didn't show up. Those who did had a hard time knowing what to say to me. But we all silently agreed it was good that we did this, being together, sharing our pain and sadness. There were so many stricken faces. Such profound sadness revealed what a wonderful friend John had been to all of them. They had all lost TAMAK.

The next morning, I had to pack what I thought might be useful or necessary for my days ahead. How was I to determine this when I had no clue what I was going to do in an hour, a day, a week, or a lifetime? It was October and probably cool in Massachusetts. My mind just couldn't visualize what the next few days would bring. It made packing difficult. Elsie helped me organize.

Our plane departed directly for Bangkok on Sunday. A group came to the airport to say goodbye, but later I couldn't recollect who. I realized my emotional exhaustion as I boarded that plane. We flew through wonderfully white billowy clouds in a deep blue sky, allowing me to think this was all a dream. But the trip was short.

We landed at the Bangkok Airport and taxied to a hangar away from the main terminal. A car waited to take us directly to immigration. Our Thai escort apologized that we had to go through this governmental formality, but it turned out to be quick and efficient. He led us back to the same car, then parked at the front of the airport, loaded with our luggage, and drove us into Bangkok where we spent a day before boarding our Pan Am flight to the US.

As usual, when John and I visited Bangkok, we stayed in a luxury hotel where everything smelled clean and fresh inside, yet outside it was hot and humid with awful raw sewer stench from the open canals called *klongs*. I needed to pull myself together and be presentable when I arrived in the US. Elsie and I went to my usual hair salon for a redo of the frosting and to have a real haircut since I had cut John's and my hair in Pakse. I looked in the mirror to see whether my face was all there. *Could this be me?*

Yes, it is and you are in Bangkok on your way to the scariest and most devastating experience of your life: a funeral for your young husband. How could an event so change my life and create a "now" over which I had no control. I had this unsettling ability to stand outside of myself. It was too painful being me.

On the way to the hairdresser, we saw a man lying dead in the street. A car apparently had struck him. Someone had covered his head with a small rug. It was the custom in Thailand that, if you caused someone's death, you were responsible for his burial and his family for life. So, this probably was a hit-and- run. Just like John's death, a lucky hit-and-run by an anonymous person.

The young petite Thai hairdresser, who had done my hair before, asked in her limited English whether we were in Bangkok for vacation. It was the first time I was faced with having to say out loud what had happened, that John was dead. Or I could choose not to, which I did. I found that saying my husband died was extremely shocking. Those who asked always blanched, and then fell all over themselves apologizing and offering condolences. I actually began to keep mental records of the reactions as they were interesting to compare in some maudlin way. Then, I would watch them watch me to see how I was coping with my tragedy.

The next day, we boarded Pan Am Flight 2 which flew eastbound around the world although we'd take it only halfway. We sat in First Class. I assumed it was consolation prize for what had happened. Elsie and I settled into our spacious seats, put on knit slippers, and waited for the hours to pass. I had no appetite to eat, but instead sipped beer. That had been my food of choice since the first day of this new life. It was the only thing I could swallow.

The plane landed in Taiwan, Tokyo, Guam, Honolulu, and finally Los Angeles. At each stop, Elsie and I went into the terminals, strolled around, commented on the local time, then re-boarded the plane. Invariably, we found the cleaning crew had taken our knit slippers. The stewardess gave us new ones, and we settled down again to withstand endless hours until the next stop.

Finally, we were on the approach to Los Angeles International Airport and my parents. As Elsie and I deplaned, I spotted my parents. Our emotional reunion was cut short by the fact that the airline was holding our connecting flight to Boston. They whisked us to another part of the airport, another airline, and another endless flight. We learned they had bumped a first-class passenger to accommodate the four of us on this Boston bound flight. I was looking for indications of how incredible this event in my life appeared to others. Bumping a first class passenger certainly ranked high to me at the time. But, of course, it was an empty indicator, meaningless in contrast to what had just happened to me. To John.

My mother recounted how she learned the news. A kind CIA security officer had the unfortunate duty of informing my parents of John's death. My father had been playing golf that day. Mother was phoned by a man who identified himself as a CIA officer who told her what had happened. She had to wait all day until my father came back to the hotel to tell him. The security officer advised her that he would meet them the next day in their hotel lobby and take them to the airport to meet Elsie and me. He told her that they would recognize him by a rolled-up TIME magazine under his arm as well as by the physical description he gave her. My folks were amused by his playing spy with the rolled up magazine.

The overnight flight to Boston did not offer the privacy I needed to tell my folks the details of what had happened. I was so afraid a news story about John's death would appear in the newspaper, given the fact that all our friends were still in Pakse, fighting the secret war. I had been instructed before I left Pakse, if asked, to say that my husband had been killed in a helicopter crash.

We all dozed the hours overnight as we crossed the country. Shortly before landing, though, I became very rattled and teary. Elsie revealed the Valium the doctor in Pakse had given her. She cut one in half and I took it, with beer, of course. I became calmer as we walked down the ramp into Logan Airport. John's parents, Lucie and Paul, were waiting tearfully. She was overcome with emotion. I didn't know how to console her. She wasn't consolable. I knew that. I was sad for all of us.

I recall with pain that long trip home, but even worse was the longer week that followed while we waited for John's remains to be returned for burial. All I pictured was a casket with rocks inside, and I referred to it in my brain as the "box of rocks." If I had pictured John lying inside, I might have fallen apart completely. The office told me that, after the autopsy in Thailand, they would arrange for transport on a military plane. Everyday I called HQS, and everyday there seemed to be a different reason for the delay.

Each day seemed an eternity. What there was to do was meaningless, as were all life's activities to me now. I had a hard time caring about decisions concerning the arrangements for the funeral and burial. The minister came from the church to talk about my preference for the service. The funeral home wanted to know how many limousines. The cemetery suggested I buy two, or even three, adjacent plots for his parents and me. I settled on two. I couldn't picture being buried there. That was a lot to take in. Then came a stream of people stopping by the house to pay their respects: John's high school friends, neighbors, and even John's lifelong barber. I was polite and conversational, but inside I wanted to hide and pretend all this wasn't happening.

During that week in John's family's home in Bellingham, Massachusetts, we talked about John the child, the adult, the son, the brother, the husband and fun-loving person. We looked at 8mm movie film his parents had taken when they visited us in Laos and Bangkok earlier that year. It was very hard for me, and probably something I shouldn't have watched. Eventually, I learned to avoid things that had the potential to cause me heart-wrenching pain.

I knew this week was the hardest on John's brothers and sister, all younger than John. They were each frozen in time in their own lives. Eriks was beginning his adulthood in the Air Force and had to be brought home. Paul was going to college in the area and was home when the CIA officer came to tell the family the horrific news. Kristina was away at the University of Massachusetts in her first semester of her freshman year, a difficult time anyway, made more so by being pulled home to tragedy. Bobby was in high school and watched his life transformed by the devastating loss of his big brother. They blended into the background in sadness, each one hurting but not able to speak outloud about it. They knew how special John was to his folks, how he had been an Eagle Scout, graduated from college in physics, and become a US

Army Green Beret. John's siblings could only stand in the background and offer memories of their big brother. He now sat atop a lofty pedestal.

Finally, on Friday HQS called and told us that the body was to be at the funeral home that night. The funeral and burial could be on Saturday. The funeral director came to the house that evening to collect a check from me, which he delicately explained included overtime pay for gravediggers who would have to work on Saturday. I welcomed these mindless details that distracted me from the depth of my sadness, In fact, the body didn't return until too late that night to plan the service for Saturday, so the funeral was rescheduled for Monday.

I had a sleepless Sunday night and woke very early Monday morning. Elsie gave me a Valium, as she could see I was in a constant teary state. I steeled myself as we entered the Peterson family's church, the all-stone Unitarian Universalist Church in Woonsocket, Rhode Island, adjacent to Bellingham. Just before the service in the narthex, the funeral director returned my original check and asked that I write another check before the service. He explained that the amount of the new check would be less, since it was Monday, I didn't have to pay for gravediggers' overtime for a Saturday burial. Talk about cash and carry, no credit.

I hardened myself to walk down the long aisle into the nearly-filled church. It was a large church. I looked down the aisle and caught my first glimpse of the steely gray metal casket draped with the American flag with the yellow gold fringe, the same flag that had draped the body bag when they brought it out of the jungle so many thousand miles away and a lifetime ago. My knees weakened, and my body shook uncontrollably.

A spray of red roses stood to the side. These were the flowers the florist had suggested the widow buy. I hadn't gone to the florist; it was just too hard to do. But I went along with his suggestion. Walking down the long aisle, clutching my father and mother, I looked at the casket and thought, "box of rocks." That's how I made it through.

John's family had filled the front pew when my family and I entered. I appreciated that Lucie and Paul, John's mother and father, needed this distinction in their hometown family church. I sat surrounded by my parents and Elsie in the second row. An old friend of John's family came up and began hugging my seventeen-year old sister-in-law Kris, crying loudly, obviously thinking Kris was the widow. Kris pointed back to me. The woman began the drama all over again with me, but my father quickly helped her return to her seat behind us.

I wanted to remember every detail, but I also wanted the funeral to be over. Hymns, Bible readings, all the formal funereal words. John's brother Eriks gave the eulogy, an act of unquestionable courage. When the young minister gave the benediction, I realized it was over. I had made it without sobbing out loud. We followed the casket from the church and watched as they loaded it into the hearse for the trip to the cemetery.

Mother, Daddy, Elsie and I climbed into the limo behind the family limo and hearse for what was to be the longest trip, an hour or more. It seemed like forever. Yet, we relaxed together out of view of others. We needed to let go of the seriousness of the moment, even laugh at the absurdity of the funeral director asking for his check and the mistaken widow skit. I watched cars along the way pull over to let our procession pass. I'm sure these onlookers wondered what celebrity or hero had died because so many cars followed behind the funeral procession, most filled with young sad faces.

The cars carried our many friends from Laos who had returned to the US before John died. And there were friends from college and from his hometown and my hometown. Pieces from our life together. They all had appeared at the motel the night before where we held an informal wake, which included a bathtub filled with beer and ice and several bottles. We laughed at the absurd things John had done, all the fun he was, and how we would miss him. It was perfect. I asked some of these friends to be the pallbearers, along with John's brothers.

At the church, these proud young men in dark suits and long faces accompanied their dear friend. At the cemetery, they stood on either side of the casket perched on the side of the hill. Did the other people at that gravesite suspect that among the pallbearers were CIA officers, all dressed in their trench coats on that gray windy day?

The funeral director led me to stand at the head of the casket, with my parents behind me, and the minister and John's parents beside me. As we waited for the crowd to gather around us, I noticed one corner of the flag on the casket had been flipped up by a gust of fall wind. I stepped forward to fix it. My father moved close to me, worried that I might fall or dissolve into tears. But I just unfolded the corner of the flag and softly smoothed it out. It was my only contact with that box of rocks. I refused to picture John's body inside.

The minister conducted a brief service. His words were standard for a very non-standard burial. I had asked him to say the Serenity Prayer at the end. With a strong voice I said it with him, just the two of us praying aloud. It gave me comfort, but I heard many around me crying. *God, Grant me the serenity to accept the things I cannot change; the courage to change the things I can; and the wisdom to know the difference. Amen.*

Then the pallbearers, these young men who lost a brother and a wonderful friend, began the ceremony of folding the flag. I wondered who among them was a Boy Scout who knew the ritual of folding the flag. I chuckled inwardly, hoping one of them knew what they were doing. When it was properly folded and with such love, they placed it into my arms. It was over.

CHAPTER 4

Finding a Path

My difficult trip home ended in Fort Lauderdale in my parents' apartment. Even though Mother made all my favorite food and Dad spent hours sitting silently beside me at the pool, I could find no remedy for the pain that tortured me, a physical pain in my chest and in my gut. And one thing worse, I couldn't picture John. The shock of his death wiped his image from my brain. I tried to remember John's hands, his strong hands with long fingers. Once in a while, I caught myself looking at a man's face and neck, trying to recall what John's skin looked like, the blonde hair on his arms, and his fumanchu mustache. Even his smell. But still, I never found a way to remember his face. Even today, I have to look at a picture to see him. How could the image of this man I loved so intensely not be forever imprinted in my memory? The shock I experienced seems to last forever.

Eventually, I began to eat again although small bites filled me up. My period, which had totally ceased, reappeared after several months. I stopped shaking, which had been incontrollable throughout the funeral experience, my hands trembling, my knees knocking. I had been uprooted from a wonderful life with a loving husband, a home, and a job, and tossed into an alone world. I floated in time without a connection to a day or a place. Of course, I knew where I had been and what had happened, but I had no clue what I should do next.

My mother's compassion was deep. She never shared her past experiences with death, but she seemed to understand my pain.

She'd say, "Let's go out for a ride. We need to get away from these four walls."

She was positive and optimistic. She believed in a God who was compassionate and kind. She believed there was a reason and purpose in all things, and she told me she was sure I could find my way. What else can a mother do when her child is so sad and hurt but fix comfort food and stay close?

My grandmother was a jovial and spirited companion.

She told me, "The good die young."

And then she chuckled and said that was why she was still around at age eighty-two.

They shared my sadness and tried their best to comfort me.

During those weeks in Florida, reflecting on my new situation, I wondered if I could ever find passion for living, working, being productive in a new life without John. John had been so committed to everything he chose to experience. He was deliberate and worked hard; he accomplished what he set out to do. He rarely opted for the easy way. He told me that sometimes he thought he disappointed his parents by not choosing what they wanted for him. After he was gone, his parents boasted with pride of all that he had accomplished.

He had goals. When he graduated from college, he applied to many highly ranked journalism graduate schools and was accepted at every one. But then he decided he had to prove and test himself in the face of danger by joining the Army. He enlisted for two years. He turned down Officer Candidate School because he didn't respect his peers in training. He chose to jump out of airplanes and train long and hard to become a Green Beret.

He volunteered to go to Vietnam, extending his service date a month to be eligible for a six-month tour there. He became a member of a reconnaissance A-team, a much respected group. He wrote letters to me about the legends he served with on the team, people who earned the Congressional Medal of Honor. He was given a free trip to Taiwan, another to Bangkok for his heroic accomplishments, including significant cash bonuses. But he never told me the details. He wrote me from Vietnam about fear and how he only found courage when he faced fear. He lived life either on the edge when deployed on a mission or without any worries, relaxed in his barracks, drinking beer, playing cards, taking hot showers. Ambivalent about the war, he acknowledged that he had made a commitment and served his time and adopted country proudly.

Why had he taken the hard and dangerous road to Vietnam, rather than the easy and safe one to graduate school? I was relieved when he returned from Vietnam alive, almost like I could finally breathe again. Now, we could begin our life together. After a two-month backpacking trip through Europe, including a stop in Donau, Germany where he was born, we married in a small ceremony with our families in attendance on December 26, 1969 in Fort Lauderdale. Not satisfied with our pastoral life in North Carolina where I taught in a community college and attended the University of North Carolina graduate school in Chapel Hill, he chose a new challenge: he applied to work for CIA.

With our past running through my mind, I alone had to figure out what my future was to be.

I evaluated my past jobs. I taught college in North Carolina, the blind in Virginia, young "disadvantaged" Spanish-speaking girls in Connecticut, and had a brief stint in the National Teacher Corps in Las Cruces, New Mexico. I had tried with mixed success to teach the Lao English. I loved teaching, but I didn't know whether I had enough emotional stability to feel in control of a classroom now after John's death. I had always used my sense of humor and flare for drama to make classes interesting and stimulating. At this point, I felt humorless and vulnerable.

I was also having a hard time tolerating everyday trivialities. After all, I had faced the ultimate reality, death. Why were people so consumed by vapid, empty issues of life? I kept encountering people who had everything going for them, yet they took the time to be negative. Didn't they know how much they should be valuing life and living? This I label my angry phase of the grief process. Instead of being angry at John—how could I be, when he was the victim, the loser—I was angry with strangers who had no clue what a devastating loss I suffered.

I went to get my driver's license renewed in Florida. The man at the desk, a nice man I'm sure, asked whether I was single or married. I looked at him, eye-to-eye. I said, "Widow." He said, "You're too young." *Bet your ass I was too young*, I thought. So was John. I told him in a clipped way that there was a war going on, Vietnam, and that my husband died there. Although it wasn't exactly accurate, it was true enough. Men died in war. He apologized.

Election year, 1972, was ugly. Anti-war candidate McGovern was running against incumbent Nixon. During the Democratic Convention in Chicago, riots broke out. Violent anti-war protests never made sense to me. They burned the American flag, the same one that covered John's casket. Talk about a personal attack on his patriotism and heroism. Why do war protesters believe that the families of men lost in war should side with them against the war? War protesters have no earthly idea of the pain of loss. By their actions, they negate the heroism of those who have died. I hated the protesters.

On voting day, after my father and I went together to vote, we stopped at the grocery store on the way home. I had a sticker on my shirt saying, "I Voted." As I waited at the entrance of the store, an older woman walked up to me. She pointed to my sticker and said, "Well, I guess we know who you voted for." I couldn't believe she'd said that, implying that I voted for McGovern, based solely on my age, I presumed. I looked at her hard and said, "No. I didn't." Her attitude cut through me. Why didn't I tell her what had happened? Oh, the things I wish I'd said.

I was adamant that John's contribution be recognized, even though what he did was secret. So, when asked about what happened, I just said proudly that he was killed in a helicopter in Vietnam. John's family had the same problem. Eventually, he was recognized in a ceremony when the VFW erected a monument in his memory in Bellingham. Often, I sidestepped reasons John's name does not appear on the Vietnam War Memorial in Washington, D.C.

It was a politically-charged time filled with negative images on TV of the war in Vietnam, of napalm attacks, of violent war protesters, and bombings in Hanoi. Daily kill-numbers were an essential of the nightly news, like the weather.

I was at a turning point. I no longer could live the life we planned. Now, I had to decide what my life was to be. I had the opportunity to start again. Deep inside, I had some positive anticipation of being able to create my new life, but this made me feel so guilty. Even the word opportunity made me cringe in its positive connotation. I didn't want to feel excited about starting a new life without John.

In the process of getting John's affairs with CIA completed, I made several trips to Northern Virginia to the office at HQS managing my affairs. They were kind and efficient. I never asked a question they didn't answer promptly, mostly translating government regulations that were difficult to understand. I had no idea what my income was to be, what money I was due, and how much I would need. When John's final salary payments and lump sum retirement refund were paid into our account, I was relieved to have income of sorts. John and I had saved a lot of money in Laos because we had nothing to spend it on, at least nothing we found appealing. He and I did not want a lot of things. He had his camera, and that was his most cherished possession, besides me. I always had whatever I wanted, but I did not yearn for things.

In December, CIA asked me to come to sign final papers. Going to Northern Virginia was a good diversion because I needed to stop doing nothing in Florida and loved seeing my old friends from Laos. But this time, there was a certain formality to the paperwork.

They said I had been approved to receive Workman's Compensation from the Department of Labor. The office had expedited this for me. The widow's benefit was substantial and tax-free for my lifetime, or until I remarried. By accepting this benefit, I waived my rights to any other benefit, such as those I would have been eligible for through Veteran's Affairs. CIA assured me that the Department of Labor benefit far exceeded those of the VA. I never doubted their advice, which turned out to be the best. The widow's benefit would be good income, but not sufficient to live on. John's predictions were true. In the past I had been capable of earning enough to support myself and lived on whatever I earned, a lot or a little. At this point, though, I was not sure where to live and what job to pursue. I recognized it was time to design my future, but I didn't have a dream or vision.

During this trip to Northern Virginia, I stayed with Jerol and Tom. They and their new son, Tommy, lived in Rockville, Maryland. Tommy was born on September 30, 1972; coincidentally, the day John died, I received Tommy's birth announcement. Tom had been one of the pallbearers at the funeral. From our days in Laos, I remained connected to both Jerol and Tom and trusted their advice and counsel. We talked at length about what I could do. Tom encouraged me to apply to CIA and specifically to the Career Trainee (CT) Program. I was naïve about CIA and unaware of the specific functions of a case officer. Tom spent time explaining the workings of CIA and why this could be an exciting career for me.

The CT Program was the fast-track training program for officer development for CIA. Although Tom didn't know details or qualifications for the program, it sounded interesting. Tom kept emphasizing that I should go into operations, like he and John had. But I had asked John so little of what his job entailed. In Laos, it was all paramilitary. And even though I was involved peripherally in his operations training, I didn't have a full picture of what a case officer did or what the role of CIA was. CIA was never highlighted in a civics class in high school, and I never studied political science in college.

That December while in Virginia, I asked the office to help me apply for a job, specifically the CT program. I was assigned a mentor, who had been Chief of Support in Vientiane while we were in Laos. Glenn was a wonderful jovial man with twinkling eyes and a devilish grin who seemed pleased to coach me as I launched my new life. He made an appointment for me with the CIA recruitment office.

The recruiter was a dry, humorless gray man, with a first and last name, probably an alias. I gave him my Personal History Statement (PHS), a duplicate of the form I had filled out in Vientiane eighteen months before. The recruiter began the interview by asking about my background, which kind of surprised me. Maybe the guy didn't have the imagination to start the interview any other way, as I thought that Glenn had filled him in on what had happened to me. I told him about the events of my recent life. I then led him back through my education, my work history, and my foreign travel. I was confident I had sufficient experience, including my CIA work for fifteen months in Laos, to qualify for the CT program. I added that I had studied three languages: Spanish, French, and German.

When he concluded the interview by saying he could offer me a secretarial position, I was outright offended. I barely thanked him for his time and returned to Glenn's office angry and disappointed. This recruiter could have cared less about me, my background, and my qualifications. He only saw a twenty-seven-year-old woman and matched me with a secretarial vacancy. Glenn was equally surprised by the recruiter's response and vowed to arrange another interview.

While in Washington, I decided to look for an apartment, knowing that I didn't want to continue living in Florida. Although Jerol and Tom lived in Maryland, I preferred Virginia, where many other friends from Laos lived. Off I drove one cold morning with the *Washington Post* classified ads to look for a place.

Eventually, I found an apartment complex near Fairfax Hospital, a good location near the infamous Beltway, which provided easy access to navigate the area. The rental office representative showed me a couple apartments, but the one-bedroom apartment seemed to suit my simple needs. I filled out the rental application, certain this was the beginning of step one into my new life.

Early the next day, the apartment manager called to tell me my application for the apartment had been denied, no reason given. I returned to the apartment, fire in my step, thinking it was some kind of misunderstanding. In fact, the reason was legitimate. I had no job and no apparent income. Great trip this was. No job. No apartment.

I called Glenn, who I hoped might help me out in this situation. He laughed and said his wife might not be too happy about his being my roommate, but he agreed to co-sign my lease. Together, we went to the rental office and soberly filled out a new application, which was approved, no questions asked. It seemed it was better to have a sugar daddy in the management company's judgment. Later, Glenn's wife and I met. She claimed that Glenn described me as plain and old. She and I laughed, knowing how devilish yet kind he was.

The evening before I returned to Florida to be with my family for Christmas, I went with Jerol and Tom and a few other close friends from Laos to a Christmas party. Everyone at the party was with CIA, among them some I had never met. One woman introduced herself and offered that her husband was temporary duty overseas (TDY).

She said, "And where is your husband tonight?" Many friends standing nearby heard her innocent question. Silently, I shrieked inside, *where has he been every night for the past two months?* But aloud, I quietly told her that he had been killed in Laos in October. She overflowed with apology and condolences. My friends quickly re-routed the conversation. This innocent question was repeated many times in the months to come.

And then another tragedy, the third in Laos. Another officer had been killed outside of Pakse. I flew to Texas to be with his wife, Kathy, a young friend whom I had met when she visited Pakse in September. At the time of her husband's death she was pregnant with their first child; she had conceived him when they came to see me in Pakse when John died. A life lost and one created. Looking back, I wonder how I found the strength to go to her, and why I thought I should do this. She never asked me why I had come and seemed to be comforted by my being there.

Christmas 1972 was a sad holiday. How happy John and I had been the year before on what was our second and last Christmas together. In 1972, the day after Christmas would have been our third anniversary. Somehow, I found the strength to write cards and, amazingly, I enclosed a copy of John's obituary in each one. I bet that was a shocker to those who hadn't heard before. I often look back at things I did like this and question my actions. I wondered later if that was appropriate, but at the time it seemed the right thing to do.

Sometime in December, my father suggested I buy a car. He knew I needed his energy to jump-start my life. Together we selected a white 1973 Pontiac Grand Am, and I added a red and blue pinstripe down each side, making it look very patriotic.

Now it was January 1973 and time to make my move to Virginia. I packed my minimal belongings and drove north. When I first drove up from Florida, I stayed with Jerol and Tom until I had purchased enough furniture for my apartment. My move to the apartment caused me more pain than leaving home when I entered college. Jerol had been such a strength to me, and leaving her was wrenching. But I knew I had to adjust to being alone and on my own.

In mid-February 1973, the US Vietnam POWs were released by North Vietnam. I was glued to the TV, crying as I watched each one painfully descend each step from the plane. My emotional response surprised me. I kept thinking: *Why are they returning and John is not?* And then the phone rang. My mother-in-law Lucie called crying and saying how upset she was. I didn't tell her I found myself deep in my own grief. I just consoled her.

I never understood why I could not admit my emotions to her. I let her have the spotlight and think she was the only one suffering. She and I had a difficult relationship before John died. Now that he was gone, I was unsure of how I should respond to her. I clearly remember her comment, that long week waiting for the funeral. She said I could replace my husband, but she had lost her son forever. I raged inside at this, wanting to tell her she had no idea how it felt to lose a husband, especially at age twenty-seven. She was fifty and had lived a lot of her life, but John and I were only starting together and had all our future ahead of us. Now that was gone. But I remained silent and never let on how she hurt me and how selfish she was in her grief. She never let me approach her sadness.

Jerol called next. She had been watching the return of the POWs. When she asked how I was, I dissolved. Her immediate response? To bundle up Tommy, now six months old, on that frigid clear February day, and drive to my apartment to comfort me. She stood beside me when times were tough.

With good friends, I passed in a haze through these first months settling into my new life. I enrolled in a sports club and went every day to work out and use the pool. I found that I could deal with my sadness better after strenuous exercise. I tried some challenging new activities too. I decided to learn to rock climb. The class met early one cold gray Saturday morning on the Maryland side of Great Falls where there are moderately high cliffs. First, we rappelled down the cliff. That was easy once I backed over the edge and then slowly lowered myself without getting raw rope burns on my hands or butt. But once at the bottom, the hard part came. We had to climb back up the cliff.

I found this the most physically challenging. For stability and a little rest, I tried to hang onto small trees growing out of the side of the cliff. The instructor kept telling me "no vegetable holds," knowing from experience that these small trees gave way very easily. So I learned to put my toe into a small crevice and push up with my thigh, not using my arms, which had very quickly turned to jelly from exhaustion. Thigh muscles are bigger and last longer. At the end of the day, I had some proficiency and definitely more appreciation for the difficulty of the sport. Although I didn't continue rock climbing, I figured out one thing: I was testing my determination to engage life by facing physical challenges. I grew more confident that I could cope better with difficult times. I also learned that to climb the cliff, I had to continue to take small steps one at a time to reach my goal, the future.

While building daily routines in Northern Virginia, I also progressed in my search for a career in CIA. After the debacle with the recruiter, Glen introduced me to Hal, a senior case officer. I remember my first meeting with Hal, an older, handsome and soft-spoken man. With sympathetic understanding that I needed a new beginning to fit my past, he offered practical suggestions on how we could advance my career goals. Because of my sociology degrees, he said it made sense for me to go into personnel work, but he also agreed I could recruit agents, as I clearly had the personality. I began to believe this might be exciting and fulfilling work for me.

At the same time he was scheduling my interviews for the CT Program, Hal had several other job leads for me. He arranged for me to meet Bob, who was returning from an overseas assignment. Bob's next assignment was in Europe. His pitch to me was that I travel there on my own, and he would hire me on a local contract to work as his girl Friday. This sounded a little sketchy. I'd have to pay for my airfare, bankroll a place to live, and then manage my own life while being available. Although an agreeable sort, tall, blondish gray haired and flabby, I had the feeling he wanted to set me up as a side interest, rather than offer me a career opportunity. I was twenty-seven and he was at least forty-seven. I was not interested in him, nor was I particularly flattered.

After I told Hal about what Bob had proposed, Hal was incensed. We agreed this was not a good offer. The next day and out of the blue, a woman at the Agency called and asked that I come in to discuss Bob's offer. So, I showed up as instructed with only that much information. I was surprised when she escorted me in to meet with Archie Roosevelt, the Chief of Europe Division in the Directorate of Operations. This was a big deal, Hal told me later. Chiefs at this level are powerful men, and Hal was amazed that my interview with Bob had come to Archie's attention.

Archie was a distinguished gentleman, somewhat diminutive in stature, but very dignified. He graciously welcomed me into his office and offered me his condolences. He told me straight out that he thought Bob's offer was inappropriate. He was sincere and seemed concerned about my future. He offered to tell Bob that I would not accept his offer. Archie implied he also thought Bob's intentions were to set me up to be his girl.

Meanwhile, Hal arranged an interview with a recruiter from the CT Program. I sensed he had to twist some arms, which was disturbing, given that both Hal and Tom had told me I was qualified on my own, setting aside my being a widow, to be accepted by the CT Program. I had a Master's degree. I was twenty-seven, not just out of college. I had work experience in the real world. I spoke three languages and had traveled on my own. Plus, I had fifteen-months Agency work experience in Laos. I was not a charity case because I was an Agency widow. It never occurred to me at that time that women were not given the same opportunities to succeed as case officers.

Although cordial, the officer from the CT program did not seem optimistic about my prospects of being accepted into the program. I left the interview less than encouraged. Later, when I met my classmates in the CT program, I resented that I had been made to feel less than qualified, as the others did not have many of the relevant and valued experiences I had. But in my CT class, there were only four women. Clearly, gender had more influence than qualifications in the acceptance process.

The application process was complex. I took a current events test that evaluated my awareness of the world and knowledge of international politics and personalities. The psychological tests included a question about whether I was sad at times. My answer obviously triggered special interviews with a psychologist, who asked about my moods. When I told him my husband had recently died, he judged my sadness to be acceptable. I apparently appeared reasonable and balanced as well as qualified. The CT Program finally accepted me to begin on 3 July 1973, John's twenty-eighth birthday, and the same day he started work for CIA in 1970. This was a positive omen, and I realized I finally had a future.

CHAPTER 5

CIA - July 3, 1973

As I drove down the approach road to the front of CIA HQS in Langley, Virginia, my heart beat up in my throat. All of a sudden, I was very sad and teary as I retraced John's steps. But I trusted myself and had confidence in how right and logical this new beginning of the next part of my life was, no matter how anxious I felt starting a new career.

Slowing to a stop as the guard stepped out, I handed him my driver's license. He checked my name against his list of visitors for the day and returned with my visitor badge and a map indicating where I should park. I followed the directions to West Lot up by the water tower in the back of the compound. After I parked, I grasped the map and followed the sidewalk down to the front of the building, a considerable distance in my heels on a hot sweaty Washington summer morning. My feet began to hurt trying to keep up with the pounding of my heart.

Coming down the slope on the sidewalk, I saw the huge portico over the stairs leading to the front lobby. I had been here before when I signed all the legal papers after John died. But this time I saw the huge building differently. I was to be part of this organization and not just a visitor. My friends from Laos worked here where I could find a safe landing spot after the extended trauma of the past eight months. Besides, this seemed like most stages of my life. I had not set out to go to Laos, to loose my husband, or now to become an employee of the Central Intelligence Agency. I had just followed others' advice and took the next step. Life without intention. Life by what seems to just happen.

I climbed the long flat gray granite stairs to the front doors leading into the main lobby. The doors were ordinary size, but the front hall was huge and impressive. The CIA seal inlaid on the floor in shiny shades of black, gray, and white marble was the classic TV shot of the Agency when the President was visiting. I felt proud of myself, soon to be a member of CIA. This was my life now, no longer just the wife of an Agency employee. The secrecy surrounding John's death took away some of the opportunity to express to outsiders my pride in who he was and what he had done. At least now I was the employee and took pride in my own accomplishment in getting this far. But I could also tell these people, who were in on the secret, about John's heroism.

My eyes settled on the stars engraved on the lobby wall. In a way they made me feel like I owned a part of CIA; his star was so personal to me. Later, I determined which one was John's. In the glass-encased book of names, he was listed as an asterisk, one of three nameless persons under the 1972 date. As I continued through the lobby to become part of what had been John's world, I had no time today to succumb to emotions that lurked just below the surface.

I approached the guard at the main desk and showed him my red "V" for visitor badge. He politely directed me to the Badge Office to the right up a short flight of stairs and down a hallway. Inside was a chair-filled waiting room with others who I presumed were starting work this morning with me. We spoke, those seated next to me, somewhat cautiously, as we did not know what we should reveal about ourselves. I was somewhat wary of telling my story, believing that being a widow of the organization might make me seem less qualified. I had gained that impression during my hiring process. I told generalities, like where I went to school, what degrees I had, and my work experience. The others seemed to do the same.

One by one we were called to an adjoining room to have our pictures taken for our official badge, complete an ID number, but no names. The man who took the photos was African American with an impressive handlebar mustache. When I received my last badge years later, he was still there. Perfect for the job, he had a bright smiling personality that brought out the best in each subject, even though the pictures were nothing more than mug shots.

Eventually, our group completed the badging process. Someone then led us down a hall to a conference room where we were greeted by the CT Program officials, among them my CT interviewer. We raised our right hands to be sworn in as members of CIA. I had never thought that I would be sworn in, but then again, I never thought much about what this new career would entail. It instantly occurred to me that John had probably taken the same oath on this very same day three years before, although he never mentioned it. Now I began the career that once had belonged to him.

They took us up on the elevator to our next briefing in an office that looked familiar, maybe from my previous trips to sign papers. An array of people presented health and life insurance options to us. This brought stinging tears to my eyes. I tried to predict what issues would jump up and bite me emotionally, but I hadn't anticipated this one. Seeing the life insurance options, knowing how young people deny the possibility of death or dismemberment, I wondered if John had thought about this or simply signed on the dotted line. He had faced some very real life and death moments in Vietnam, so he had experience with reality of young men dying. He told me that there was a war clause in the CIA's life insurance policy as CIA is a civilian organization, meaning if death were caused by an act of aggression in a war situation, the insurance would not be paid. Thankfully, John died in a helicopter crash. His family was better off now.

The morning had evaporated into these details and it was noon. We were directed to what was then referred to as the large cafeteria where we were to begin our habit of eating lunch as a group through the next six months. We pushed tables together and introduced ourselves around the table. Another woman in the group was named Martha, but she went by Martha Jean and later MJ. She was the youngest in the group, maybe twenty-three or twenty-four. She was from the Midwest and her father was a dentist. She spoke fluent French. Jerry (or did he say Frank?) was older and had worked on a contract prior to being accepted as a CT. Jim had been in Army Military Intelligence and was destined for a leadership role years later. Mike was young and fresh. Barbara was intense and quiet and spoke Chinese. Dennis was eager and a Soviet expert. Wes was fun, spoke Spanish and had traveled as a missionary. Carl was a lawyer, but preferred to be a spy. Eventually, though, he reverted to being a lawyer. Dan, also a lawyer, was a character, very friendly and intense, and drove a vintage Mustang. Bill was tall and lanky and a relaxed friendly person. The male Marty was blustery and not too interested in anyone other than himself. We constituted the next batch of CIA case officers, the spooks as outsiders called us.

After lunch we reported to a small compact theater on the ground floor for our mandatory security briefing. Over the years, we returned to this dimly lit theater to receive updated briefings, sometimes given by the original briefer. He was a stereotypical security officer. He wore oxfords, a gray suit and skinny tie, and had a regulation crew cut. Absolutely straight laced and by-the-books, his jokes were canned, revealing a limited sense of humor. His tone was military and his delivery, clipped.

The security briefing, however, provided an intense reality that serious enemies in the world actively tried to uncover our secrets, among them our identities as clandestine officers of CIA. In the briefing, he showed slides of the places where our enemies had hidden microphones: one imbedded in the official wooden carved US Embassy seal mounted on a wall in the US Ambassador's office in Moscow; another concealed in a block of wood and nailed underneath a wooden arm of a chair in a US Embassy conference room.

As I learned that day, foreign governments were clever in their attempts to penetrate US Embassies with these listening devices. They wanted to know the US Government's plans and intentions with respect to their country. They also wanted to determine the identity of CIA officers. The CIA case officers' mission was to recruit spies among the citizens of that foreign country. These spies provided secret information to CIA and the US Government.

By 9:00 a.m. on my second day of work, our entire Career Trainee class of July 1973 convened in a classroom in a building near Arlington. The CT Program officer revealed that each of us had been hired, according to our specialty, by one of the four directorates in CIA's organization: the Directorate of Intelligence (DI), the Directorate of Operations (DO), the Directorate of Science and Technology (DS&T), and the Directorate of Administration (DA). In theory, CT membership and training accelerated our career progression, and some thought this meant we had been designated as having the potential to be the Agency's future leaders. However, this was true for only a few.

Of the four women, three of us were hired to enter the DO, to be case officers, also known as operations officers in the DO Clandestine Service. They selected the fourth woman as an analyst in the DI, as she had almost completed a doctorate in Soviet Studies. All the women were hired at the rank of GS-8. A couple women challenged the CT Program as to why we did not qualify for higher GS grades. We all had at least a master's degree and had work experience equivalent to many of the men hired at higher grades although some of the men entered as GS-8s with similar education and experience. The CT Program insisted a numeric formula determined entry grades, and that was the end of the discussion.

CT Program managers provided an overview of our training. We started with a course called "Introduction to Intelligence" or CIA 101, its nickname. This course provided a framework for understanding the overall mission of CIA in relation to the US government's approach to world affairs and the balance of power. We had lectures on the mission of each Directorate, starting with the big picture and then narrowing it down to where we each fit in the organization. I found it fascinating as I had always considered what I did in Laos a mission in itself. I had little understanding of how CIA functioned in relation to the US government's positions and activities in that region of the world.

They peeled the onion for me. I began to see the broader picture. I am embarrassed to admit how little I knew about the intelligence process up until I joined the CT program. Not a student of world affairs, I saw most events as isolated news articles. The issue throughout my childhood was the competition for world dominance between the US and USSR. That I understood. After returning from Laos, I personalized this conflict as I came to realize the scope of the Soviet's influence in Southeast Asia in supporting communism there.

During breaks, we spent time introducing ourselves to each other. I became part of an amazing collection of people with outstanding qualifications and dynamic personalities. Some of them had extensive education and experience in the Far East, the Near East, the Soviet Union, Latin America, Africa, or Europe. Most of us could read or speak many languages fluently, totaling over a dozen foreign languages. Some had work experience in the business world or in other US government agencies and the military. Our ages ranged from twenty-three to thirty-three. We came from all over the US.

The DI officers tended to expound on their backgrounds, most providing far more detail than the DO officers, who kept their past somewhat hidden. The DI officers were hired for their existing substantive expertise. They were being indoctrinated into the organization through the CT program, but basically they had the area knowledge and skills to work from day one. After completing their training, they were assigned to offices where their expertise was immediately put to use. They faced the daunting challenge of learning to write in the DI style and to accept endless, tedious editorial criticism.

As DO officers, we also had to learn about CIA's organization and how the DO worked as an essential piece of the intelligence process. We were to learn how to covertly collect sensitive protected information on these issues by recruiting spies in foreign countries, all the while remaining hidden in the background of official US government organizations.

After we spent the hot Washington summer together in these classes learning about CIA, we were each assigned in fall 1973 to work at a HQS' "desk," which entailed our on-the-job training phase. In January 1974, those of us entering the Directorate of Operations, the new batch of case officers, were sent out of town for our Basic Operations Course, which we completed in June 1974. At this point, we were more than ready for permanent assignments overseas. Some of us entered intensive language training when this was required.

The CT program was logical and organized, and we all expected to be assigned overseas. That had become my goal, after all. Little did I know what the future held for me. Several years later, I became a popular speaker in the orientation of a new CT classes, an example of a female case officer who had succeeded. But I had to weather the assignment process first.

After graduating from CT training, I was assigned to a country desk to prepare for my first overseas assignment by reading all the ongoing operational cases being run in that Asian country. After working there two weeks, I learned that they had scheduled me for forty-four weeks of foreign language training for my assignment where they spoke the Queen's English. I was uncertain about my career progression, if I had to spend that much time learning a useless one-country-only language. So, I wrote a memo to the CT program and politely but succinctly stated that I refused this assignment. I suggested that my file be shopped around to other offices. Later, others told me that this was an audacious thing to do, that few people ever turn down their first assignment, or if they did, they rarely got a shot at better one.

My friend, Hal, again intervened, meeting with several Division Chiefs. Within a week, he came up with an unlikely but potentially very exciting opportunity. He had contacted SE Division, which was responsible for the Soviet Union and Eastern European countries. He met with Tim, COS-designate to Moscow, who agreed to interview me.

During the interview, Tim told me how difficult the Moscow assignment would be, especially because I was a single woman. In fact, he said I would be the first trained female case officer ever assigned to Moscow. Tim was also single, another first. He seemed amused at the prospects of the KGB trying to entice him with one of their female officers. The same might happen to me, Tim said, using a handsome man, naturally. We both understood the KGB's game.

Another area of concern, Tim said, was whether he would feel comfortable sending a woman out on an operation, no matter how well trained or experienced, if there were a possibility that she might be caught in the act and roughed up by the KGB. After reflecting, Tim said it didn't make a difference to him whether the officer was male or female. The KGB would hit a woman as well as a man, if the KGB knew it was necessary to make the arrest of that officer. We laughed, but it was true. He pointed out that the standards for operating in Moscow were stringent. The mandatory course that everyone going to Moscow had to take was the Internal Operations Course. He suggested I take this following my language training.

In September 1974, I began forty-four weeks of Russian language training, an intensive course of study eight hours a day, five days a week. To make life more challenging, I also decided to take Tai Kwan Do karate lessons, knowing that I needed a physical outlet for the mental stress of fulltime language study. Years later, I read that learning can be muddled by using the right and left brains simultaneously. All I know is that I enjoyed sparring with my fellow classmates in Tai Kwan Do because it relieved the unexpressed competitive stress in Russian language class, including occasional hostility toward my language instructor, my classmates, and my own learning inadequacies.

After successfully completing language training, I began the Internal Operations Course, reputedly very challenging as well as mandatory for an assignment to Moscow. The objective of the course was to learn to conduct covert operations, including executing dead drops, car tosses, signals, and personal meetings without these operational acts being detected by the ever-watchful KGB. The training also entailed determining whether we had a surveillance team following us, and if so, how to function so the team would not be aware we had conducted a covert act. They trained us to manipulate a trailing surveillance team by taking them on a pre-planned route around a series of corners or through dips and bends in the roads, which allowed us to deliver a secret package by means of a car toss without the team seeing this action. This was grueling training, requiring day and night forays throughout the Washington, D.C. area practicing our skills that included finding sites, covertly photographing, and then later sketching them.

The IO Course instructors, Bernie and Roy, were very effective trainers with reputations for being demanding. Bernie, white handlebar-mustached and flamboyant, and Roy, diminutive gray-man, quiet but highly intuitive, understood my unique challenge. Since I was not married, I had to take the course solo. They purposefully did not give me a co-trainee to work with because they wanted me to build confidence in my own abilities. Couples who went through the training had two sets of eyes as well as the opportunity to share operational judgments and to coach each other through package deliveries and retrievals. Although there were difficult moments when I thought I had "killed" my agent by revealing to our training surveillance team that I had done something operational, I passed the course and demonstrated my well-tested sense of humor and operational acumen. I was silently proud of myself.

After completing all my training, I had a two-month read-in time on the USSR Branch in HQS. I was assigned to Fran, a senior desk officer, who had complete knowledge of all the operations conducted by Moscow's CIA office over many years. She personally briefed me on an important Moscow agent file. The agent had not yet made contact in Moscow, but the decision had been made for me to familiarize myself with all details of this case and be prepared for the agent's signal after I arrived. Only bare minimum of information was kept in Moscow's CIA office, so it was important that I understand and absorb every detail. Even the true names of agents were not in the files in Moscow, an essential element of the highest security practices in the field.

To prepare to move to Moscow, I sold my car, rented my townhouse, and bought two-year's worth of paper products and staple groceries to be shipped to me. I also decided what limited household effects to ship. I had been through this drill before going to Laos, but there we didn't need to ship food or paper items. The Vientiane commissary supplied those needs. In Moscow, necessities were limited and costly. So, I used others' estimates of toilet paper, paper towels, sanitary products, detergent, soap, shampoo, and canned goods, all of which I figured would be hard to get or were my favorite brands. Among the latter was a case of Smuckers Butterscotch Sauce since I had read that Moscow's ice cream was the finest.

After I completed all these daunting chores, I signed out of HQS and flew to Florida to spend well-deserved vacation days at home with my parents before departing for Moscow. They had their concerns about my new adventure, but they stuck by me and offered support and encouragement. They shared my excitement as well.

CHAPTER 6

Moscow - November 5, 1975

It was late afternoon. The remains of the sun appeared as a streak of orange highlighter running along the horizon as the Lufthansa flight came in for an agonizingly long low approach to Moscow's airport. A cold sweat snaked down between my breasts as it suddenly became warm and airless in the plane. I felt like vomiting from fear, anticipation, even dread, and yet excitement as the wheels finally touched the runway, bounced, and rolled along smoothly. As we taxied to the terminal, the plane's headlamps reflected sand piled on the sides of the runway. No, not sand. I was seeing snow plowed into banks along the runway. Having flown from Miami via Frankfurt to Moscow, I was clearly stuck in the Miami mental photo album. I couldn't believe there were mounds of snow this early in November.

When we came to a stop, my plane mates simultaneously stood up to collect their things from overhead bins, jockeying to gain exit advantage. I suppose they wanted to get the best seat on the bus, even though all of us had to board the same bus headed for the same terminal. I knew the bus waited until the last of the passengers and crew deplaned. In fact, I was okay not rushing to get off. I didn't mind delaying the inevitable beginning of my new adventure.

An organized traveler, I had a small carry-on bag tucked under the seat in front of me containing the requisite clean underwear and toothbrush. I had stuffed my heavy pile lined camel coat in the overhead bin. A man helpfully handed it down to me, probably because I had jammed in around his carry-on luggage. I anticipated this bulky coat was a match for the frigid Moscow climate. I smiled, recalling how I thwacked everyone I passed on the aisle with my coat as I proceeded to my seat on the flight from Miami to New York. I'm sure a few wondered, why I was carrying this huge coat to New York in early November as it was barely cold yet. Little did they know my destination was Moscow. The passengers around me had thinned out when I stood up to put on my coat and collect my things. Feeling the bone chilling blast of arctic wind at the door of the airplane, I knew my coat and I were to be inseparable. After a short bus ride, we had a long walk outside to the terminal door. The cold wind penetrated down around my neck, freezing the droplets of dampness of my earlier sweat.

Over the door hung a sign: Sheremetyevo Airport, *MOCKBA*. I had arrived. I scanned the balcony over the entrance, but I couldn't see where they concealed cameras to photograph the potential incoming enemies of the state. I had heard the story that KGB officers were ten feet tall and capable of identifying every CIA officer assigned to Moscow. Apparently, they had not connected the Martha D. Peterson on my USSR visa application to the wife of John Peterson, a deceased CIA officer, because the Soviet Embassy in Washington, D.C. had not delayed my visa as they had others with previous experience with the KGB. I remained a nobody, I realized, as I quietly stepped into my new secret life pitted against the KGB in its Motherland, the Soviet Union.

An unusually strong smell of tobacco permeated the terminal. The smoke smelled sweet yet acrid. According to behaviorists, smell is an indelible memory. Years later, I can still identify these cigarettes and know that Russians are nearby. The terminal lacked melodic muzak and colorful ads welcoming travelers to the Union of Soviet Socialist Republic, USSR, or *CCCP*. Dirty tile floors and dingy scarred painted walls greeted us as we were herded toward the lines in front of passport control. I found my way into the line designated for non-Soviet travelers, overheating in my coat, which I quickly shed. I observed those ahead of me as they nodded to the official behind the glass. Although somewhat anxious, I knew nothing in my passport appeared suspicious. After all it was blank; this was my first trip.

I moved up. As I slid my official red passport under the half-glass window to the serious young Soviet officer, he asked me if I was assigned to the Embassy. Instead of saying in Russian *dah*, I said *yah*, the German equivalent. How frustrating to have spent forty-four weeks in language training, only to get the first word wrong. My previous overnight stay in Frankfurt must have awakened the German I had learned years before in college. No apparent damage was done, except my own annoyance at my careless, undisciplined error.

He held up the opened passport to compare my face with the picture without a nod or expression of recognition. Then, he laid my passport out of sight under his counter where I saw a huge loose-leaf notebook filled with what I suspected were watch-listed names. Suddenly feeling calmer, breathing more slowly, I realized my anticipation had been worse than actually standing here in front of the Soviet official.

As part of my preparation time working on the USSR Branch in HQS, we questioned our official travelers when they returned from the USSR about their experience at border controls. "Did the border guard make a copy of your passport? What did he ask you? How long did it take? Did he call over his superior to examine your passport?" We needed to know what standard procedures were at the airport and other Soviet borders, so we could anticipate problems when we covertly exfiltrated our agents from the Soviet Union. The officer continued looking down, and I began to wonder if my name appeared on a special list. But then, almost immediately, he looked up at me and handed back my passport. No comment, no smile, no recognition, no detailed questions, and no call to a senior officer. Done. I had passed this hurdle and had little to report on my first border crossing.

Ahead, I joined the crowd around the luggage carousel. I brought one big suitcase with enough warm clothes to last until my airfreight arrived in two weeks. As the conveyor belt started moving, my suitcase amazingly popped out of the chute, one of the first to appear. This seemed too easy, I reflected briefly, as I loaded my belongings on a cart and passed through the big swinging doors to an open hall where a large crowd waited for arriving passengers. I spotted a man with a sign, "M. Peterson." Clearly an American, he introduced himself simply as Rob. He had longish dull gray hair with a gray beard to match, but he looked younger than his gray hair, maybe in his early thirties like me. He was cordial, kind of dry, not overly friendly.

Rob led the way, pushing my luggage cart out to the waiting car, a big black mid-1970s Plymouth Fury idling at the curb to keep it warm inside. As we approached, a man jumped out of the driver's seat and greeted me enthusiastically in Russian. I replied appropriately this time. This cordial, smiling driver hefted my suitcase into the trunk and opened the rear door. Rob and I slid into the backseat, and the driver easily maneuvered us out of the airport.

Rob said he worked in the section that managed housing, furniture, maintenance, motor pool. He asked if this was my first assignment overseas. I didn't know whether he knew I worked for CIA. I also didn't know how our ranks compared, but I assumed his being an assistant to the chief of a section probably outranked mine. I also didn't want to say too much, knowing the Soviet driver was listening, and the car was probably bugged. The CIA office was going to make every effort to prevent the Soviets from identifying me as CIA. By not associating with my CIA colleagues, who were known or highly suspected of being CIA, I could stay uncontaminated.

Someone had told me that all the Soviet chauffeurs thought they were race car drivers. This one accelerated at whiplash speed out of the airport and directly into the passing lane, called the *Chaika* lane, of Leningradskoye Shosse. The left lane of wide avenues in Moscow was nicknamed for the long black shiny *Chaika* limousines, which ferried Communist Party and government elite around town. The *Chaikas* were allowed exclusive use of the left lane on any street to speed unimpeded to their important meetings. As I gained greater confidence driving in Moscow, I took the *Chaika* lane to by-pass traffic. My car had license plates that identified me as American, giving me some latitude, but, if an official Soviet car approached from behind, menacing me with flashing headlights, I immediately moved over. I didn't want risk their hitting me to make their point. That first night's trip in the *Chaika* lane to my hotel was a speedy ride.

I avoided looking out the windshield as we sped through the city, not wanting to embarrass myself by screaming out loud in sheer terror as the driver careened in and out of traffic. Clearly being the winner of this particular race, the driver pulled up in front of the Peking Hotel, where Rob said I had reservations for a few nights. A grim doorman appeared and collected my suitcase. Rob didn't bother to go in with me, but simply shook my hand and told me that the Embassy was a reasonable walk, pointing to the right. The car door slammed shut, and they sped off. That was quite a welcome. No dinner invitation, no care package for the evening, no suggestions about where I should eat. Nothing. Just *das vidanya, Tanya.*

A year later, Mary, a friend and colleague in the Embassy, and I formed a group called the M&M Club, dedicated to meeting and making sure newly arrived single women were personally welcomed. Mary's experience had been identical to mine. Just a ride to an unfriendly hotel, no dinner invitation, no interest in making the first day and night less hostile. We were proud that our joint venture, a welcoming force of two, had made a difference in the arrival experience of other single women.

I followed the doorman into the hotel lobby, alone and unsure of my decision to accept this assignment. The Peking Hotel lobby looked old and shabbily ornate with large framed pictures and a few chairs, but nothing Chinese. The only ethnic aspect, although I cannot vouch for its authenticity, was a Chinese restaurant off to the side of the lobby. It seemed incongruous to be in Moscow in a hotel called the Peking, given the rocky state of Sino-Soviet relations in the mid-1970s.

After checking in at the front desk without a glitch, feeling an overwhelming exhaustion, I headed to the only elevator, barely managing to lift my suitcase off the floor. Being used to Western self-service elevators, I was startled by an expressionless man who appeared right inside the small elevator. He manually closed the door and pushed the lever all the way to the right. I had a flashback to B. Altman's department store of my childhood in New York City in the 1950s. Now, that was a classy elevator ride, filled with wonderful perfume aromas and a very dapper uniformed elevator man who provided a colorful commentary about shopping treasures on each floor. But this was not B. Altman's. It smelled like stewed cabbage. The disinterested man brought the elevator to a slow stop on my floor, which somehow he knew without my telling him. This must be the foreigner's floor, I thought. I thanked him in Russian, *spacebo*, to no response.

The door opened to a small reception lounge with an older woman seated at a wooden desk. She held the title of *dezhurnaya* or hall dragon, undeniably in control of everything that happened on her floor. She kept all the keys, each hung on a large bulky key ring to prevent them from being carried out of the hotel. She knew from her key collection whether guests were in or out although I suspected this was not to expedite maid service.

I faced the unsettling reality that the KGB could enter my hotel room to search my belongings at will. In fact, to prove the point, the next day in my absence, they pawed through my suitcase. I knew my suitcase had been tossed because none of my things were as I had carefully arranged them. I had been told during training to expect this and never leave anything in a hotel room or my apartment that might cause suspicion or identify me as CIA. Knowing they had been in the room proved what I already knew. The KGB totally controlled my surroundings, and this confirmed that my life would be watched at all times.

I smiled at the hall dragon as she handed me my key and pointed down the hall to the right. I thanked her, again to no reply, and slogged my suitcase to my room. Opening the door, I groped for the light switch just inside. Dull ceiling lights came on in the short hall and the room ahead of me. I dropped my suitcase inside the door.

The furnishings were sparse. Twin beds, a nightstand with a dial-less phone, and a lamp, a large TV on a small table, no remote. No closet, but a large wardrobe standing against the wall with a cloudy mirror on the right inside door, three hangers, two drawers below, an ugly 1950s stuffed chair beside the window framed with dusty heavy drapes, and a dingy oriental rug on the floor. High ceilings with crown moldings. A musty smell tinged with residual Russian cigarette smoke. Tall windows with a brick wall view, evidence of Soviet paranoia, preventing a foreigner from seeing anything from this hotel room. A clinical all-white bathroom, the toilet seat wrapped with a paper tape, claiming in Russian that it had been sanitized. Waxed toilet tissue. A rough towel draped over an S-shaped pipe on the wall, actually the hot water pipe doubling as a towel warmer. A hot bath and a warmed towel the only creature comforts in the room. All tolerable for tonight.

The dull ceiling light gave the room the ambiance of a cheap motel. I switched on the bedside lamp, also pathetic. Reading would be a challenge. Dark outside, dim inside, the harsh and lonely reality of Moscow was sinking in.

I heaved my suitcase up onto the wobbly luggage stand. Hoping my hotel stay was to be brief, I decided to hang only the clothes I planned to wear the next day, my first day at work. Given the amount of snow I'd seen on the ride from the airport, I also pulled out my boots. At the time I packed them in Florida I laughed as I acted like Sarah Bernhart dramatically preparing for the worst, not imagining so much snow by early November in Moscow. I hung my nightgown on the towel rack in the bathroom to warm.

Sudden hunger pangs reminded me that I had not eaten since lunch on the Lufthansa flight somewhere between Frankfurt and Moscow. I thought about dinner. I could go down to the restaurant in the hotel lobby, but navigating a menu and ordering in Russian would be a challenge in my state of mind and more effort than I cared to make. Would the restaurant accept a charge to my room? Not having brought any rubles with me into the country in an effort to strictly adhere to the Soviet's import ban, I hadn't thought to ask Rob, my friendly greeter, for a loan, and he didn't offer.

Smart girl, I had slipped into my purse the small pack of rye bread rounds and the triangular foil-wrapped cheese from the lunch tray on my flight. I realized I might need a midnight snack. During my one-day stay in Frankfurt, I uncovered the bag of Macintosh apples my mother had stashed in my suitcase. I laughed, thinking how slick she was to sneak these into my bag. She knew how much I loved apples and how I had missed them when we lived in Laos. My mother was a sprite who loved to surprise me. And here she provided a part of my first dinner deep in the heart of the Soviet Union. Tears streamed down my cheeks as I sat on the bed to eat.

I switched on the TV and clicked through all three channels, each with talking heads chattering ceremoniously about some great communist accomplishment. During my time in Moscow, I occasionally watched emotional ceremonies on Soviet TV, where the host presented the coveted Lenin Worker Awards to sturdy Soviet women posed on tractors for producing the best crop of vegetables or hogs in their commune. They all tearfully accepted these awards. It was a human comedy to watch. But nothing amused me this first night, the TV noise sounded grating and unintelligible for the most part and not good company. The dreariness of the hotel accentuated my aloneness.

If this were today, I could have easily called home with a phone card to reassure my parents, as well as myself, that I arrived safely. But in 1975, calls from the USSR were extremely expensive and difficult to make, requiring an advanced reservation, so a KGB translator could live monitor the conversation, looking for spy talk, I assumed.

As I began to undress for my bath, it occurred to me that the KGB could be watching me. I wondered whether I should do a striptease, but silently laughed at the thought of making a fool of myself the first night. Out of curiosity, though, I casually scanned the room to see where they hid the camera. That vent up on the wall almost to the ceiling was a good place since it was high enough to provide a full panorama of the room. Embassy security officers found microphones embedded in the walls behind old iron radiators when they remodeled Embassy offices, so this radiator in the hotel room was instantly suspect. But what could they hear or see? I didn't talk to myself. And they could watch me all they wanted. I wasn't going to be that paranoid.

The hot bath comforted me before I slid into the hard bed with notably rough sheets. I was tired, yet keyed up, and had doubts about sleep this first night in Moscow. Surprisingly, I fell asleep. I startled awake at 2:00 a.m. when the phone rang. The KGB used middle-of-the-night calls to harass Westerners. I answered the phone, but no one was there. I hung up and settled back into bed. The phone rang again. As before, no one. I lay awake and wondered if the KGB had determined I was CIA. I looked up at the vent again. Sometime during this musing, I drifted back to sleep.

I woke tired, nervous yet excited about first seeing the city in daylight and facing my new and exciting role as a covert CIA case officer in Moscow. I was eager to be out on the streets, possibly being followed by goons, our nickname for KGB surveillance. But with my youth and confidence, I knew I could make a difference by attacking the Soviet Communists, somehow avenging John's death. I am not sure how clearly I understood my motivation at the time, nor did I hint at this when I had my mandatory appointment with a shrink in HQS, who was to determine whether I was psychologically balanced enough to take this stressful tour. But, the longer I lived in Moscow and the more damage we did to the Soviets, the stronger my conviction was that this was my fate, my way of evening the score. I saw it as my opportunity for payback although John would never return.

Wearing my great coat, boots, and gloves, I turned in my key to the hall dragon and proceeded to the lobby. I exited the hotel and looked to see whether, by some remote chance, a car waited to take me to work on my first day, but there were only pale green Soviet taxis. I knew from months of studying the CIA-produced Moscow map that the Embassy wasn't far. Interestingly, one of the CIA officers saw a copy of this map hanging in the taxi dispatch office in the Ukraina Hotel. No CIA or USA origin appeared on it. The Soviets produced no accurate or useful foldable map of Moscow at that time. They probably worried it might expedite spies getting around. Anyway, the taxi company hit pay dirt when they somehow acquired this map. Probably some American had left it behind in a taxi. The office had a good laugh over this. Navigating Moscow thanks to CIA.

I followed Rob's directions. As I turned the corner, a sharp wind took my breath. It was bitterly cold, probably in the teens. The sun had just risen, but, from November through January, it never lifted above eye level on the horizon, blinding me that morning. I'd gone a short distance from the hotel when a woman walked right up to me. She was not smiling, definitely not friendly. She said in Russian, "Where's your hat? It's too cold out here." I smiled at her and replied I left it in the hotel room. She insisted I needed one. I thanked her, as she abruptly turned and walked away. Old women of the Soviet Union were the keepers of others' health and well being, often scolding young mothers, American and Soviet alike, when their kids were not properly dressed for the cold. So, here I was, a well-trained under-cover CIA operant on my first Moscow morning, being reprimanded by a little old lady for being hatless.

I laughed to myself at my first exchange with a real Muscovite, but soon agreed with her as the walk stretched farther than I anticipated. At last the Embassy building came into view, a big characterless eleven-story yellow building sitting right on the fourteen-lane *Chaykovskogo* ring road, exactly like the pictures. It was an amazing sight with the American flag flying proudly above the main entrance, visible across all fourteen lanes of the road and from several blocks across the Arbat around the ring road in both directions.

Three Soviet militiamen were posted at the front entrances, big men, each wearing a *shapka,* the traditional Russian men's nutria or beaver fur hat, adorned with a large Red Star pinned front and center. Visiting American officials coveted these hats. Occasionally, they stole one and proudly displayed it back in their Washington offices. The militiamen also wore calf-length heavy gray wool great-coats and knee-high black- leather jack-boots like those worn by the German goose-stepping troops in World War II. The militiamen presented an intimidating barrier to the Embassy building. Any Soviet allowed to enter the Embassy had official papers that the militiaman examined closely. Those who tried to force their way in were dragged off by the militiamen to a "beat up" shack around the corner but within view of cameras monitored in the Embassy. However, the Embassy staff was powerless to help the hapless Soviet citizen.

I wish I had asked someone at HQS about the layout, so I knew exactly where to enter. But, assuming the sign saying "Embassy Chancery" was the main entrance, I followed a man who seemed to know, up half a flight of granite stairs and into the self-service Otis-inspected elevator. This took us to the reception desk on the ninth floor, an upside-down arranged entrance.

We opened the door into the small well-lit lobby where the Marine Guard stood behind a large raised desk with the American flag prominently positioned to the right. Charged primarily to physically protect the Ambassador, in reality he was the gatekeeper who determined who was enter restricted Embassy offices located behind his desk. He did not allow Soviet officials or foreigners' entrance.

I approached him and identified myself as a new arrival. He welcomed me warmly and picked up the phone to call the person listed as my official contact. Obviously, the person he called was expecting me because she showed up moments later. So far, so good. I was making progress and things were going as I anticipated. No questions asked that I was clueless about.

Kate, the secretary and office manager, a short blond with a warm, pleasant manner, greeted me cordially and gestured to follow her down a narrow flight of stairs. After making several turns, we came to an unlabeled paneled door. Past this door was a small anteroom with a cipher lock and a buzzer that I pressed. To my relief, Neal, someone I knew well from training, opened the door and escorted me in. I thanked Kate, and she silently returned to her office on the eighth floor.

Neal led me through the short hallway and up a ramp to another paneled door, also ciphered. The CIA office was in a box, easily inspected for any possible technical penetrations. Even the wiring to the inside of the box went through filters to prevent their use as conduits for any type of eavesdropping. I never walked around the box, but I know that Neal inspected it often to make sure it was clean. As Neal opened the door, I was amazed to see many of my CIA colleagues assembled to greet me. Most of them were familiar faces from months of language training and the Internal Operations Course. Only a few were new to me, but I instantly felt I was home safe.

Tim, the Chief, who was responsible for my being here, hugged me. He introduced me to those I hadn't met yet, in particular, Dottie his secretary. She was to be my rock and best friend although we could never appear together outside the CIA office. She kept me up-to-speed on what was happening in the office, including all the inner intrigue.

Dottie served in Moscow two years until the following summer of 1976. A year later, I shared rough times with her back in Washington, D.C. when she went through radiation therapy for ovarian cancer. She spent time with me recuperating, but eventually went back home to Florida where she died in 1978. I have always wondered whether her cancer was a result of the low-level microwave flooding of the US Embassy by the Soviets.

While I was in Moscow, the Embassy conducted monthly blood testing of all American officials and their families. Occasionally, they sent a child home whose white counts were too high, which made us wonder whether maintaining détente had more value than the lives of Americans assigned there. Eventually, the Embassy covered all the windows facing the ring road with metal mesh screening, which State Department technical staff advised would effectively deflect the microwaves. Over time, many cases of cancer could be attributed to this exposure, but to this day, no one has drawn any concrete conclusions.

Neal's wife, Lee, greeted me with a hug. She was my great training partner back in Virginia. She told me she had offered to bake cookies and deliver them to my hotel my first night in Moscow, but of course she couldn't contact me. Her thoughtfulness warmed me. I met Jack, Tim's deputy, and his wife, Susie, and the communicators and their wives. The rest of the office I had met at HQS before they left for Moscow the previous spring and summer of 1975.

All case officers were each assigned small student-size desks positioned along the walls. Several maps hung on the material-covered walls and were studded with colored pins and markers to designate operating areas in the city. A small stereo sound system with a variety of music masked our conversations in the unlikely event someone inadvertently brought a bug into the office. We left our purses and briefcases outside since they could be used to carry in listening devices. I recalled during my first security briefing in HQS that the security officer told us about a bug embedded into the sole of an officer's shoe when he sent them to the local cobbler. So, no one had shoes resoled in Moscow. But the office offered me the only place to talk freely to work colleagues and CIA friends, a place where I could be myself.

Tim invited the case officers into his office, a small room partitioned off at the end of the office. It had a door so private personal meetings or need-to-know discussions could be conducted. Inside, a small conference table barely fit perpendicular to Tim's desk, allowing enough room for chairs for all of us. At the end of the conference table hung a green chalk board for us to sketch sites and routes as we discussed plans for operational activities.

Tim said he wanted to bring me up to speed about CIA operations since I left HQS two weeks before. Each officer told me about recent patterns of his surveillance coverage, an occasional weekend off, close bumper-lock surveillance, and an incident where a wife had seen surveillance on her when she was out shopping. Jack wanted me to begin to determine how much surveillance coverage I had. He cautioned me that, without a car, surveillance teams would be difficult to spot. He told me not to be too aggressive in trying to flush out surveillance, not wanting me to play games, which might alert surveillance that I was aware of their presence. This would instantly make me a suspect CIA officer, since most other Americans in the Embassy generally didn't pay attention to anyone following them.

During the first months, Jack was friendly, but I had the feeling that he tested me constantly. Coincidentally or not, my desk sat right behind his. During our time in Moscow, we shared my desk. He swiveled his chair around and worked on my desk as well as his since the desks were small. He typed like a maniac, using two fingers in staccato rhythm, typing faster than most professionals. Occasionally, one of the keys broke off and flew out from the force of his strike. He and I came to know each other well, with great admiration and respect.

Over time, as I described my experiences on the streets of Moscow, Jack offered good advice, but he was also an excellent listener. He was intense and serious most of the time and very mission oriented. He spoke like a rapid-fire machine gun, his thoughts flowing out fast and furiously. In contrast to his in-control demeanor, he and his wife, Susie, who worked as our main site sketcher, frequently lost their car keys right there in our small office. We were amused by their fussing at one another over the missing keys. We loved ribbing Jack, and he laughed good-naturedly, rolling his eyes behind Susie's back.

Jack became my strong advocate and a tremendous coach. He taught me a lot about agent operations and ceaselessly pushed me to plan ahead for the next drop or pick-up. I remember coming into the office one morning, exhausted after a late night pick-up, holding the agent package triumphantly in my hand, and Jack saying, "Okay, now what needs to be in his next package?" He never let up or wasted time in lengthy congratulations. I didn't need a lot of stroking, but I could have used a little recognition for my contribution. He expected all of us to work as hard work as he did. He never took a break and always pushed us to find more sites and learn more about our operating environment.

At Jack's farewell party late in the summer of 1976, he revealed that he had originally vetoed my assignment to Moscow. He thought that a single woman could not endure the tough aspects of Moscow life or operate alone on the streets in Moscow. He worried that the KGB might target me for a recruitment attempt and send a tall handsome KGB officer to sweep me off my feet, like Tim and I had discussed when he first interviewed me for the job. But that never happened. Jack told me I had proven him wrong and become one of the most valuable officers in the CIA office. I was proud that he had developed such confidence in me. Deep down, though, I knew I had earned it, spending long and difficult hours on the street, alone.

Although well acquainted with most of the male case officers from our training before they came out to Moscow in the summer of 1975, I didn't know how they felt about working with a female case officer. I suppose I didn't really care. I intended to earn their respect by participating in operations as a full member of the team.

As I was one of the first women with full case officer training to be assigned to Moscow, the Moscow office wanted to determine whether the KGB considered me a threat. Even if the KGB somehow identified me as CIA, odds were good that they might not believe CIA used women actively in operations on the street because the KGB didn't. The KGB probably identified me as a clerk or secretary. The KGB's naïve view of women left me free to operate without detection.

From day one, I made every attempt to not fit the case officer profile. I had been warned by our trainers, Bernie and Roy, not to fall into the over-eager CIA officer trap by hitting the ground running when I arrived in Moscow. They cautioned me not to try to learn all about the city in the first week or to take illogical routes to find out whether I had surveillance coverage, all revealing traits of an ill-trained CIA officer. Most importantly, they told me to never challenge KGB surveillance teams by trying to lose them.

The social pattern I carefully crafted conformed to other single women in the Embassy, associating mostly with communicators and Marine Guards. I made a point not to be seen with any CIA personnel except occasionally at lunch in the snack bar in the company of other non-CIA employees. In fact, Tim, the CIA Chief, invited me that first year to his apartment for his big Christmas party and then immediately told me I couldn't come. We all laughed. But it was hard not being able to socialize with the people I knew and enjoyed.

After this introductory meeting in Tim's office that first day, I sat down at my new desk. I had so much to learn in the office. Jack showed me the files on the operational sites in Moscow and suggested I review them all before I went out to cautiously re-case those located near my new apartment when I moved in. Jack also briefed me on activities planned for the holiday the next day, the annual October Revolution celebration parade on November 7. I had finally arrived in Moscow, ready to face all the challenges we had discussed in HQS—then only in theory, now in reality.

I wanted to find out about my apartment and move out of the Peking Hotel. Jack listed my priorities. I needed to see Galya to be put on the list to purchase a car, a *Zhiguli*, which was a Soviet-made four-door Fiat sedan. She compiled this list and controlled most of the services in the Embassy as well. Rumors were she was the chief KGB officer in the Embassy, reporting directly to the KGB. In return, she had privileges such as more money and her own private apartment, allegedly sporting a padded leather front door.

To begin taking care of all these details, Kate had volunteered earlier to introduce me to the Embassy administrative section American assistant, Eleanor, who managed all issues concerning Embassy staff. I counted her as the most helpful person I ever met in the Embassy. I still remember how grateful I was to her for taking time to explain all the critical practical details about daily life in Moscow.

Eleanor took me to the commissary in the basement. From first glance at the front counter, I saw that the commissary stocked a full range of fine liquor, American cigarettes, and Carlsberg beer from Denmark, all at very reasonable prices. The rest of the inventory, arranged on shelves along ancient stone walls stretching down a long dimly lit hall, was outrageously expensive. The cost of shipment from the US had been tacked onto these prices. That's why we were all allowed to ship two thousand pounds of canned food and dry goods in household effects, which would deflect the high cost of living in Moscow. The Soviets also gouged Westerners by charging an exorbitant exchange rate for our hard currency dollars in Moscow. We had to exchange our US dollar checks for rubles at the Embassy cashier at the official rate, at the time $2.50 per ruble. On the black market the exchange rate was about $.50 per ruble, or a soft ruble as it was called in comparison to the hard ruble we had to purchase.

Vegetables, fresh or frozen, in the markets in Moscow were limited, especially in winter. That first winter I went to the market near my apartment and bought a preserved cabbage, which had been soaked in a barrel of brine. I only bought one because this putrid, rotten cabbage stunk up my refrigerator and my apartment for weeks. During this same trip to the market, I witnessed the butcher selling a cow's brain from the inside of the skull. I couldn't believe what I saw. Because protein and fat were in such high demand, they set the severed cow's head on a block, cracked open the skull and scooped out portions of the brain to be sold by weight. This was the most grisly thing I saw in any market, even those in the Far East where I thought I had seen the full range of gruesome groceries. The brain, as well as the globs of fat from the brain cavity, was rich protein ingredients for winter soups when fresh meat was scarce.

During my first winter, a large frozen foods shipment from the US via European commissaries arrived by truck. The cases of frozen vegetables and juices were stacked by categories outside behind the Embassy in the frigid courtyard. Kate and I went together to scan the precious commodities. The Soviet Embassy workers instructed us to designate on clipboards how many of each item we wanted, although there was a limit per household. At the end of that business day, I went and collected my boxes, wondering what the Soviet workers thought about us and our vegetables. They were probably green with envy.

Occasionally, the American Ambassador's support flight arrived in Moscow from Germany. This generally preceded a big occasion, and the Americans wanted to impress the Soviet guests with exotic foods. The plane arrived stocked with enough for the big party as well as a modest amount to sell to the American Embassy staff. It was a big event when we could purchase fresh green peppers and tomatoes, all kinds of citrus, an occasional avocado, and lettuce, all at reasonable prices. I eventually became so starved for salad other than Cole slaw, that I had a standing order for lettuce from the Helsinki department store, Stockmann's, delivered every other week to the Embassy. The cost for a kilo of iceberg lettuce (basically two small heads) was $9.00, an exorbitant price at the time but a delicious and essential extravagance.

At lunchtime Eleanor, had to go home to feed her kindergarten-aged daughter, Kimberly. So, I checked in with Kate who had offered to take me to lunch at the snack bar, a low windowless building in the courtyard. Each day, the snack bar offered a different lunch specialty, but over a period of time it became apparent that the rotating list of specialties was short. Regular items included hamburgers and fries, cheese sandwiches, pizza, soup, salad in the summer, and, of course, Cole slaw daily in the winter. Not inexpensive, the food was predictable and tasty. I learned it beat most food I could find in Moscow restaurants for a fraction of the cost.

Going to restaurants presented an ordeal hardly ever enjoyable. We had to have a prior reservation made by the Soviet workers in our Embassy. Then, with the requisite reservation paper in hand endorsed by the Soviet government service office called Miscellaneous Services-UPDK, we arrived at the restaurant, pushed in front of all the Soviets waiting in a long line outside the door, and waved our official UPDK document at the head waiter through the glass panel in the door. He then grudgingly allowed us entrance. Most food on the menu was unavailable, a menu of *nyet, nyet, nyet.* When we asked what they did have, we agreed to have that. Rarely delicious or even appetizing, we could count on it always being expensive.

Thankfully, Kate invited me after work that first day for an open-house in her apartment, which would shorten my evening at the hotel. The occasion was to celebrate the Soviet holiday the next day. After the office closed at 6:00 p.m. Kate and I went to her small one-bedroom apartment to set up for her party. During the evening, I met new people although I couldn't keep most of their names straight. Eventually, I came to know almost everyone by name in the Embassy.

The communications officers worked shifts, so those not scheduled for the evening shift showed up at Kate's party. Off-duty Marine Guards also attended. I met single women that night who became close friends. Someone brought Halloween masks of Nixon and Kissinger to the party, which stimulated all kinds of amusing commentary about current events. I admit I couldn't resist performing as Kissinger. Someone commented that I would fit in well into the Moscow party scene. In addition to meeting lots of new colleagues, I also had dinner, which made it a successful evening. Afterwards, someone drove me to my hotel, as it would have been a cold dark walk back to the Peking Hotel after a long first day.

Miraculously, even though it was a Soviet holiday, Eleanor had arranged for a driver to pick me up bright and early the next morning and take me to my permanent apartment at Vavilova 83, about ten miles southwest of the Embassy. My apartment was in the first of three high-rise buildings in a fenced compound with a guard shack at the gate, manned twenty-four hours a day by a Soviet militiaman. Labeled a diplomatic ghetto, my co-residents included foreign businessmen and correspondents as well as diplomats from many countries. Some foreign embassies in Moscow had housing within their embassy compounds. All other foreigners were required by the Soviets to live in one of many ghettoes scattered around the city.

The Soviets claimed that they fenced in the apartment buildings to protect the foreign residents, but the truth was very different. The Soviets effectively prevented their citizens from making contact with foreigners by limiting access to these compounds. The Soviet militiaman stopped and questioned each person they did not recognize. So when my driver pulled into the gate at the compound that morning, the militiaman quickly came up to see who I was. I smiled and greeted him in Russian. He was young and friendly, like most of those I saw at the gate during my tour.

My apartment was on the eighth floor, one of four apartments on that floor, all occupied by Americans. A small self-service elevator, but this one not Otis-inspected, accommodated the driver, my suitcase, and me. It smelled like stale cabbage and Soviet cigarettes. To get Soviet elevators to work, I discovered I had to jump on the slightly raised floor, which I assumed closed the necessary electrical contact to cause the elevator move. Or maybe this worked once for me in a sluggish elevator, so I always jumped when I stepped onto an elevator in Moscow. To this day I want to jump when an elevator is slow to respond. Odd habits die hard.

As my apartment door swung open into the combination living room/dining room, I was struck by the ugly 1950's Danish modern motel furniture, consisting of a tan tweed sofa and two matching chairs. The coffee and end tables, dining table, and hutch were abused teak. The only bedroom, to the left, had twin beds, one dresser and a wall of closets. The bathroom was at the other side of the living room/dining room, complete with sink, footed tub and, my new favorite, the lovely multi-use towel warmer/hot water pipe. Next door, the toilet barely fit in a separate closet-sized room not much wider than the toilet itself. Down the short hall the kitchen came complete with full sized washer and dryer, deep porcelain kitchen sink, and cabinets. After long cold nights out on the street, I turned on the dryer and leaned on it for warmth and comfort. The living room and dining room windows opened to a narrow concrete balcony that I only used occasionally as an extended refrigerator for beer and soda when I entertained in the winter. Everything in the apartment was utilitarian, rather than friendly or cozy. But I was extremely relieved to be out of that hotel.

I learned that, when the previous American couple moved out of this apartment, they replaced the well used furniture with brand new Drexel furniture. However, my US Embassy neighbors down the hall quickly appropriated the new furniture, replacing it with their collection of ugly motel-style Danish modern that they had tolerated for over a year. I guess that was fair, as I was an unknown and a lower ranking officer. My hand-me-down furniture was uncomfortable, not particularly clean, and made the apartment dingy and unwelcoming. Needless to say, I lived with the motel look because I didn't want to make a scene. I never told my neighbors I knew what they had done.

I came to learn that Moscow had a central plant that pumped heat and hot water throughout the city. The Soviet "water engineers" cut off the hot water to clean the pipes during the summer months, or so they told foreign diplomats. In the summer of 1976, during the forty-five days I was without hot water in my apartment, outside temperatures ranged from the low 40s F to the high 60s F. To bathe, I heated water in the biggest pot I could manage on the stove. I carefully carried the hot sloshing water in the soup pot down the hall and dumped it into my four-legged tub. I could never accumulate water deeper than my ankles, because the longer I spent heating more water, the cooler the water in the tub became. Looking like a large bird in a small birdbath, I splashed water all over myself, barely getting wet, although wet enough to get me sufficiently clean and thoroughly chilled. These were adventures of living overseas what the American public mistakenly pictures as a life of luxury.

Bill, a single officer in the science section who lived down the hall and across from my furniture-appropriating neighbors, must have heard us in the hallway as the driver was leaving. He came out of his apartment to introduce himself and invited me to go to Red Square that morning with him to see the famous October Revolution parade.

Bill had a turquoise Zhiguli like the tangerine-colored one I bought the following week. He gladly gave me pointers on driving the car, starting it, oil and maintenance requirements, and the necessity of studded tires in the winter. He told a story about a Japanese diplomat who was having trouble starting his Zhiguli in front of our apartment building on a very cold dark winter morning. He had seen Soviet truck drivers build fires under the crankcases of the ancient truck engines to warm the oil to get the engine to start. So he decided to do the same. But while in his apartment sipping his morning tea, the car caught fire. Then he discovered it wasn't his car, that his car was parked next to the burned out Zhiguli. It was a sad funny story.

My car always started. Of course, it probably helped that I followed Bill's suggestion and used winter weight oil. In Moscow, most private Soviet citizens put their cars up on blocks in the winter because there was no oil for sale for extra cold temperatures, or snow tires, or even windshield wiper blades. Americans who brought their cars with them from the States, like my neighbor's Mustang, or imported them from Europe, like another neighbor's Volvo, always had problems starting their cars in the minus 20 F temperatures. But my Zhiguli was totally reliable until something blew up in the engine after I had it a year. I promptly sold it as-is to an Egyptian diplomat, who shipped it to Cairo for repair and resale. Then, I bought another new Zhiguli, but this time it was a sedate navy blue.

Bill was highly intelligent. He told me he spent his summers growing up at science camps for gifted kids. His father worked as a nuclear scientist in Oak Ridge, Tennessee, in the 1950s. Bill worked in the Embassy Science Section and had a lively time trying to work with Soviet scientists on sharing scientific discoveries and experiments.

As part of these joint experiments, the Embassy Science Section arranged for an extremely low temperature magnet to be shipped from a physics lab in the US to Moscow for the Soviet scientists' work on their portion of a US-USSR experiment. Although huge, the magnet was very fragile. At the lab, they mounted it on a specially designed trailer, attached to a Mack truck cab that they literally drove into a huge US Air Force C-141 Starlifter airplane and flew to Moscow. The Soviets wanted the US Air Force to paint out the insignia on the plane, so the Soviet people would not know that the magnificent plane was American. The Soviet Air Force did not have a comparable model. But the US Air Force refused, and the plane with its full US Air Force insignia landed at Sheremetyevo Airport, Moscow.

Airport workers stood atop the cabs of their trucks along the side of the runway to see this amazing USAF plane touch down and taxi. The Air Force allowed Soviet officials to tour the plane, knowing that any highly sensitive equipment on board was not visible. A large crowd of us took the yellow American school bus out to watch this unique and highly patriotic display of American might on Soviet soil. One of the Americans in our group had a Polaroid camera, not available, generally unknown, in Moscow at that time, and took pictures of Soviets standing around the plane. The Soviets were absolutely amazed to see instant pictures of themselves.

The Soviet authorities demanded that the Mack truck be driven to the lab in the middle of the night, so that Soviet citizenry could not see it driving down Moscow's streets. Since it was painted in red, white, and blue stars and stripes from its appearance in the previous year's US bicentennial celebrations. It was a proud day, witnessing America's greatness in Moscow.

Bill enjoyed life in Moscow. Eventually, he bought a red two-seater Mercedes convertible that he adored. The Soviet KGB tracked him easily, as it was the only car like it in Moscow. Bill fancied himself a lady's man, dating every non-Soviet single woman he met on the diplomatic and business circuit in Moscow. Americans in the Embassy were prohibited from fraternizing with Soviets. Early on, Bill and I came to an understanding and did not date.

That morning of the parade Bill took an indirect route to central Moscow. This was useful to me as I began to mentally map out the different ways to drive from my apartment to work. None of the Zhigulis had a passenger door rear view mirror, which prevented my casual backward glances to spot surveillance. I wanted to turn around while Bill was driving to see whether anyone was following us, but I didn't want him to suspect I worked for CIA. My interest in surveillance might tip him off.

The parade into Red Square impressed me, a grand display of the Soviet's military machinery, brigades of goose-stepping soldiers marching in perfect cadence, and crowds of Soviet citizens carrying banners filling all the routes heading into Red Square. Bill told me that some sections of the Embassy had assignments during the parade. The American military officers from the Defense Attache Office had to determine what types of new armament were displayed. Others from the Political Section reported who showed up on the balcony on top of Lenin's tomb and in what order, providing Washington officials insight about whether the power-holders had shifted. Leonid Brezhnev was the General Secretary and remained strong during my tour. Yuriy Andropov was the KGB Chairman. Bill and I only made it to the outer fringes of Red Square by flashing his US Embassy credentials to police checkpoints. At this distance, it was difficult to distinguish the who's-who of the faces of these historical figures. But I was amazed to actually be there in a scene I had watched on the world news broadcasts each November in the US.

After the parade, we returned to the apartment where Bill fixed spaghetti, which was surprisingly very tasty. Even better than real food was having a new friend who gave me lots of information about living in Moscow. Still, I knew his city and mine were to be different.

The next day, Saturday, I left my apartment early to go out exploring on my own. Most important, it was my first opportunity to see whether the KGB would surveil me. The office had a theory that the KGB followed all new Americans until they made a determination whether the person was a CIA officer. Oddly, some non-CIA Embassy officers were CIA "wannabees." They taunted the trailing KGB team, trying to lose them by making quick turns or changing directions when driving, or picking up Soviet hitchhikers, who the KGB would have to track down, identify, and interrogate. Actually, these non-CIA officers were useful to the Moscow CIA office because it diverted KGB resources from surveillance coverage of actual CIA officers and swelled the number of suspected CIA officers the KGB thought they had to follow.

I walked down Ulitza Vavilova to the Universitet subway station, a long walk from my apartment. My subway ride to the Embassy required a change at Park Kul'tury onto the ring line, Kol'tseyeva, one that I came to know exceedingly well. I exited at one of the nearest stops to the Embassy called Krasnopresnenskaya. I decided to stroll along the Arbat, the most modern avenue in Moscow with tall glass and metal buildings. I followed a logical route for a new officer, heading for central Moscow, Red Square, the Kremlin, St. Basil's Church, the huge department store Gosudarstvenny Univermag-GUM, and the National and Inturist Hotels. I knew it would be nearly impossible to spot surveillance on this route, but after a few hours I planned to head home, hoping in that latter portion of my outing I could identify surveillance. At least I did not act like a type-A overachieving case officer.

As I walked, I noticed the local population, among them the broad pasty-faced Muscovite women, many young men trying to look cool in jeans, nondescript men in winter jackets and heavy boots, and badly bleached orange-blond women all walking along the sidewalk heading toward me, passing me, and waiting with me at the street corners. I did not get the feeling anyone was particularly interested in me or following me. As Jack predicted, this was the most difficult environment to detect surveillance since I was progressing in a straight line with a predictable destination. The KGB could track me by walking beside me, in front of me, or from across the street hidden among other pedestrians as well as in multiple cars passing me in both directions. Most of the cars looked the same, pale green taxis, many colorful Zhigulis, and lots of small white paneled trucks. I agreed with Jack that I could not determine whether I was being followed.

I stopped a few times to look into the storefront windows and out of curiosity entered a few stores to check out the merchandise. Bras were all the same massive size, style and color, no variety. If you weren't that size, you were out of luck. One style and size of men's shoes and a lady's dress in one size. I passed people waiting in long lines to buy whatever might be for sale. I knew they often had no clue what they were waiting for, but they hoped they might get lucky enough to buy something scarce or even useful. They carried string bags, called *avyozka,* the perhaps bag, to transport whatever they were able to buy.

I loved being out on my own, launching my Moscow adventure. I will never forget my view of Red Square that day, so different from being carried along in the throngs the previous day during the parade. I turned at the sidewalk beside the Lenin Historical Museum, seeing the somber, respectful line of people standing by the Kremlin Wall to my right waiting to enter Lenin's Mausoleum. And there I saw spread out before me Red Square. It seemed more massive than the day before when filled to overflowing with tanks and troops and faithful Communists. I could almost see the curvature of the earth looking across the square to St. Basil's Church. That's how big it appeared. Behind the Kremlin walls stood the glistening gold domed churches. To my left was GUM, the state department store of great notoriety, faced with gigantic billboard pictures of Marx, Engels, and Lenin, all underlined with

Communist slogans. Occasionally during my tour in Moscow, I walked through GUM, although not this day. Inside, it looked like a huge emporium with a glass ceiling and suspended walkways. The items displayed in the windows rarely were for sale inside. In fact, little was for sale inside GUM.

I walked across Red Square, following the lines painted on the cobblestones, having observed the militiamen rudely force pedestrians to stay within these lines. Control was the obsession of militiamen in Moscow. I was disappointed to see that, up close, St. Basil's Church was tarnished with paint peeling, but it still was beautiful, like an aging fairytale castle with faded gold, star-studded multicolored painted domes.

From the middle of the square, I had my first opportunity to observe the changing of the guard ceremony at Lenin's red granite tomb, emblazoned with his name etched in gold block letters. Two goose-stepping guards with fixed bayonets marched out from a gate along the Kremlin wall and up to the stairs in front of Lenin's mausoleum. After a few quick precise turns and sharp heel clicks, the two guards on duty switched places with the two fresh guards. Very snappy and impressive. With new guards in place, the old ones marched off. Dead Fred was well protected.

A never-ending line of faithful Soviet pilgrims waited to view his well-preserved corpse or wax replica, but, during my tour in Moscow, I never made the effort to see him. Larger than life-size posters of Lenin satisfied me. Watching their devotion, it dawned on me that they worshiped Lenin as a Christ figure. He had given them the script for life and had led them through the battle. Then, neither he nor his system deteriorated; all was enshrined in his body in this mausoleum. Occasionally, the legend had it that the Soviets took his body out to dust it off, but quickly returned to its place of reverence for the faithful to worship.

Leaving Red Square, I passed the relatively new Inturist Hotel, the pride of the Soviet Union's accommodations for Western tourists. A portion of it burned in 1977 while I was in Moscow. Horrified American tourists reported to the Embassy that the fire exit doors from the halls into the stairwells were chained closed. I assumed this was another effort by the Soviets to protect those foreigners from Soviet citizens, just like the guards in front of our apartments. I tried to take a picture of the hotel the day after it burned, particularly the charred streaks up the front of the building from the windows where the fire burned most intensely. But a militiaman jumped in front of my car window and angrily told me to stop and to leave. I did just that, not wanting to cause a scene. Without a picture, it didn't happen.

As I stood looking across the Moscow River at the British flag waving above the British Embassy, I realized the cold was getting to me, despite the fact I wore my heavy coat, hat, gloves, and boots. I also had become tired and hungry. I found the closest subway station and retraced my route back to my apartment. As I emerged from the Universitet subway station, I saw an ice cream vendor on the street and knew it was long past time to sample the ice cream. Although I didn't have the butterscotch sauce yet, I decided to buy a brick of ice cream, over twice the size of an ice cream sandwich, wrapped in paper-lined foil. The vendor had a typical list of flavors; all but one of them was *nyet*. So I "chose" vanilla. I slipped it inside my purse, so it wouldn't melt in my hands.

I trudged up the hill, having to walk partly in the street because portions of the sidewalk had not been cleared of snow, which was crusted hard and gritty dirty. I passed some of the dormitory buildings of Lumumba University on my left. Many African students attended this university and had full scholarships to be taught the path of true Communism. Bet those poor students were really cold, not being used to any form of winter weather.

I arrived at my apartment building and nodded as I passed my militiaman. The other case officers told me that the militiamen at their compounds received a phone call when a resident of interest arrived home or departed, hearing the ringing phone in the booth, corresponding to their arrival or departure. But when I passed his booth the phone didn't ring, a good sign. Or maybe I was too new.

Safe inside my apartment, I unbundled myself and set to finish unpacking. In the process, I discovered more closets that I had not found earlier. Actually, the apartment had an amazing amount of storage. Above the low ceiling over the hall between the living room and kitchen was a huge storage area, accessible through double doors above the dining room door and kitchen door. That's where I planned to store the Kleenex, toilet paper, Kotex, paper towels, and detergent I had shipped in my household effects. Behind painted cabinet doors, shallow shelves along the dining room wall were perfect for a single row of canned goods. The whole case of Smuckers would fit in there for easy access.

Almost tragically, I had been so busy exploring, I completely forgot my ice cream. Gingerly opening my purse, I was relieved to see that the ice cream brick was still in tact. I dumped the slightly thawed creamy vanilla brick on a plate and enjoyed every wonderful rich bite, defining the creamy in ice cream. It was the best I had ever eaten. That was dinner.

The office had loaned me a welcome kit for the apartment, which included the bare minimum for camping out until my shipment arrived. Sheets and towels, dishes, glasses, silverware, cooking utensils, and pots. Someone had also included a few canned soups and juices, instant coffee and peanut butter and jelly, enough to sustain me. This served the purpose as I had no dinner invitations for the weekend.

CHAPTER 7

The Mission Begins

In late October 1975 just before I arrived in Moscow, two HQS officers traveled TDY to Moscow to discuss a highly valued Soviet agent that the Moscow CIA office was finding difficult to re-contact. Jay, the USSR branch chief in the Soviet East European-SE Division, and Serge, a Soviet specialist and case officer, spent a week in Moscow conducting intensive meetings in the Moscow office to formulate new strategies. They also took long walks in Moscow and experienced what they described as harassing KGB surveillance. They gained a new appreciation for the rigors of operating in Moscow. Up until then HQS thought they knew better than the Moscow office and its case officers on the ground. But their admission gave Moscow greater leverage in making its operational proposals.

The sensitive agent had been recruited by CIA while on his first tour overseas. Now that the agent had returned to Moscow, CIA was eager to provide him spy gear to enable him to regularly pass us his valuable, unique intelligence information. By activating this agent in Moscow, HQS could assure CIA Director William Colby that Moscow's CIA office was in the business of running productive agents.

The agent, Aleksandr Dmitryevich Ogorodnik, code named TRIGON, was born in 1939 in Sevastopol. He was the son of a high-ranking Soviet naval officer, and as such, he was eligible for privileges in his educational choices and influential job prospects in Soviet society. Following his father's example, he graduated from the elite naval academy, but while attending the higher naval engineering school, he failed an eye exam, which effectively terminated his navy career. Shifting careers, he entered the Moscow Institute of International Relations. His first overseas assignment was to the Soviet Embassy in Bogota, accompanied by his wife.

CIA recruited TRIGON in January 1973 in Bogota. CIA's office in Bogota learned that TRIGON was involved in an illicit affair with a striking local woman who ran her own successful import business. CIA knew from experience that this affair made TRIGON an excellent candidate for a recruitment pitch. If he was willing to risk breaking the KGB's non-fraternization rules, the prohibition against dating a local, he was a maverick and might be willing to cooperate with CIA.

A CIA case officer managed to arrange a meeting with TRIGON's paramour. At first, she was tentative, believing the native Spanish-speaking CIA case officer was a local government official who was going to accuse her of some tax irregularity having to do with her company. During the meeting, it eventually dawned on her that the case officer was an American, and he had arranged this meeting with her for an altogether different purpose. Her relationship with TRIGON interested him. Her initial relief at not being arrested was quickly overtaken by a more base instinct. She smelled money.

Although seemingly naïve and briefly leading the case officer on so she did not appear too eager, she agreed to persuade TRIGON to meet with this US Government official as the CIA officer eventually identified himself. A shrewd businesswoman, she recognized the potential value of TRIGON developing a private relationship with this US official. She also knew that this presented TRIGON with an opportunity to avoid returning to the USSR.

In discussing the rules of engagement with the case officer, she insisted that TRIGON only be asked to work for the US government while in Bogota. She was adamant that TRIGON not be coerced to return to the Soviet Union. Although the CIA officer agreed with her during these meetings, he knew that it would be exponentially more lucrative if TRIGON continued his work for

CIA in Moscow. TRIGON's return to Moscow had the greatest value to CIA's intelligence collection program within the Soviet Union. What the case officer avoided telling tell her was that, if TRIGON did not return to Moscow, he would simply be a fugitive defector with instantly dated information. Although she played a significant role in his recruitment and his prolific intelligence production while in Bogota, the story for her would end tragically.

With great expectations, she set up a meeting in January 1974 between the case officer and TRIGON. The case officer dictated the meeting venue, a Turkish bath in a large downtown hotel. The first meeting lasted three hours. Clad only in towels, which negated the possibility of either man wearing a covert tape recorder, the two men got along well, although they looked like prunes at the end of their three hour meeting.

Initially, they sparred politely, each trying to disguise their real purpose in meeting, but their mutual goal became obvious: information for money. The case officer slowly eased into his offer. Intuitively, TRIGON knew he was being asked for secret information in exchange for money. He tried to appear thoughtful as he considered the offer, even though he knew he had come there ready to volunteer his services. TRIGON rationalized his acceptance of the offer by telling the case officer he wanted to change his system from within by cooperating with CIA. But in reality, TRIGON knew he had agreed to commit treason against his country.

I later wondered what TRIGON thought about that night, going back to his apartment, to his trusting wife, knowing that he had committed himself to a life of deceit and treachery. Either he was drunk with exhilaration, or he wretched with panic over what he had done. Whether he had second thoughts or not, he showed up at the next meeting, eager to throw himself into the game. He admitted to the case officer that he felt more in control over his life than he ever had. He no longer had to follow the path laid out by his father and the Soviet system.

After the thrill of the hunt and TRIGON's apparent satisfaction with being recruited, the case officer spent the next meeting with TRIGON explaining their shared mission. TRIGON was convinced that his cooperation with CIA could bring big changes to the Soviet Union. The case officer agreed that TRIGON's contribution was exceptionally unique. Flattered by this attention, TRIGON readily signed a secrecy agreement, vowing he would not tell anyone about his covert relationship with the case officer he now knew was CIA. With that, TRIGON began what was to become a highly lucrative relationship, in which he provided extraordinary documentary intelligence to the US Government in return for what was to be for him an infinite yet unspendable fortune.

Although case officers are given credit for recruiting agents, many agents are in reality volunteers, who seek out contact with an American official. They have a secret plan, or, at minimum, a fantasy to meet with a CIA officer, accept favors, and give CIA highly protected information. This behavior would get them executed if discovered. Eventually, the volunteer is willingly drawn into a more clandestine arrangement, meeting with the CIA officer in more obscure out of-the-way restaurants or hotel rooms. Deep down, they know they are being courted. Buried in their subconscious is a predisposition to accept an offer, having imagined how they could successfully commit espionage as well as how profitable the financial benefit could be. TRIGON was clearly aware of what was taking place in that first meeting in the steam bath, and the case officer confirmed the covert relationship in the second meeting. TRIGON did not hesitate and committed to cooperate with the case officer and the US Government.

One of the greatest difficulties CIA officers had in managing well-paid agents was preventing the agents from changing their lifestyle by becoming big spenders. The KGB kept watch over their Embassy employees and saw unexplained expensive purchases and spending as a red flag. They instantly put the employee through an extensive security investigation, even sending him back to Moscow. The KGB suspected their Embassy employee was either committing treason or illegally dealing on the local black market to his financial advantage. CIA warned its agents about this, trying to convince them to have CIA deposit a large portion of their pay in a CIA escrow account. But many agents were compromised and arrested because they couldn't resist enjoying their new affluence.

CIA paid TRIGON exceptionally well, in fact many times his yearly salary in the Soviet Embassy. He understood the dangers of reckless spending and let CIA hold most of his salary in escrow. He quietly invested the balance in emerald jewelry for his mother. He thought, if something happened to him as a result of his treason, his mother could conceal the jewelry, which had intrinsic value she could cash in later. He bought modest luxuries for himself, like contact lenses to improve his looks as well as his sight. Contact lenses were not available in the Soviet Union until many years later. Generous with his girlfriend, he funded her business expenses.

Although he claimed he wanted to work for CIA in Moscow, TRIGON considered not returning to Moscow and wondered about the course of his life if he became a defector. The case officer described TRIGON's life in obscurity, how he would have to change his identity and live in secret. After reflection, TRIGON convinced his CIA case officer and himself that he was a patriot and wanted to work to change the Soviet system from within and could only do that by returning to Moscow. He said he would continue to work for CIA in Moscow until he came under suspicion and was threatened with arrest. The case officer promised TRIGON that CIA could exfiltrate him immediately from the Soviet Union, if he suspected the KGB were onto him. Then, CIA could unite him with his girlfriend in the West where they could enjoy their lives and his escrowed money in obscurity.

In planning his return to Moscow, TRIGON and his case officer discussed which position in the Soviet government could produce the most critical information for CIA. They agreed TRIGON should seek a position that conformed to his ongoing career, yet simultaneously satisfy CIA's covert intelligence collection requirements. TRIGON understood that, the longer he worked for CIA, the more money he accrued for his future. Neither TRIGON nor his case officer believed that his life in Moscow was to be easy. But the physical and emotional toll on TRIGON could not have been predicted.

In an attempt to guide TRIGON's collection while still in the Soviet Embassy in Bogota, HQS developed a set of requirements, a prioritized list of what HQS wanted TRIGON to select among the documents he saw daily. His case officer discussed the requirements with TRIGON, but TRIGON opted for quantity. Within the first month, TRIGON had become an extremely productive agent, providing CIA stacks of secret documents he smuggled out of the Soviet Embassy at lunchtime and carried to the CIA safe-house rented and used solely for his meetings with CIA. The case officer and technical officer photocopied all the documents, which TRIGON returned later that day to his Embassy. HQS was impressed with his intelligence information. He provided unique insight into the correspondence among the Soviet Ambassadors assigned in that region. HQS had never seen such a collection of communiqués from the Ministry of Foreign Affairs (MFA) to all the Soviet Embassies in Latin America. Of particular importance, TRIGON's production gave CIA a unique perspective on the Soviet Union's relations with and attempts to influence the policies of the Latin American governments.

In anticipation of his return to Moscow, CIA technical officers began to train him on a new subminiature camera, the T-50, concealed in a fountain pen or lighter. He became amazingly proficient within a short period of time, and as a result, instead of carrying documents out of his Embassy, he now photographed the documents right at his desk with this camera. This improved his safety in contrast to using his 35 mm camera right in his office as well as taking documents out of the Embassy. The documents might have been missed, or he might have been caught with them, say in the event of a freakish accident. His case officer tried to convince TRIGON that he should not jeopardize himself by taking such chances, but TRIGON was overachiever intent on pleasing his CIA case officer. The miniature camera resolved most of these security concerns.

The CIA office also imported technical officers TDY to train and prepare TRIGON for his eventual return to Moscow where he was committed to work in-place for CIA. They trained him in the art of secret writing techniques, including embedding writing in his letters and developing secret writing CIA sent to him in letters and postcards. He also learned how to copy down and decipher one-way-voice-link (OWVL) radio broadcasts using one-time deciphering pads (OTP). They taught him how to disguise his dead-drop packages, so innocent people wouldn't be inclined to pick them up. CIA showed TRIGON how to retrieve dead-drops out on the local streets. He learned to find a fake brick in a pile of bricks or a fake hollowed log on the ground in the woods. We did not want to jeopardize his safety in Moscow by his acting suspiciously as he searched for our packages. A quick learner, he took great pride in his newly developed skills.

The clandestine meetings in safe-houses consistently lasted longer than planned because TRIGON craved attention. He wanted to practice the techniques he was learning and discuss the variety of documents he had access to. Ever eager to please, he thrived on praise from technical trainers and his case officer. He was a true competitor, wanting to out-perform expectations. His case officer worried that his colleagues might miss him at his Embassy, but TRIGON assured him that he had cleverly manipulated his co-workers to think he was doing errands for the Embassy or a similar verifiable alibi. He considered himself intellectually superior to others in his Embassy and claimed he did not receive the recognition he deserved from his comrades for his work.

By collaborating with CIA, he told us he took charge of his life, that he controlled his destiny. None of the trainers or case officers who worked with him found him arrogant or difficult. Instead, they admired his courage and found him bright, articulate and very likeable. In appearance, he was tall with an athletic build, dark, and attractive.

TRIGON proved he was willing to take huge risks spying for CIA while in Bogota. Now that he was on the verge of committing the ultimate act of espionage by spying against his government in the Motherland, he broached a very sensitive topic with his case officer. He wanted CIA to provide him an "insurance policy." He wanted to have an infallible means of committing suicide, if they caught him in the act, *in flagrante delicto*. In plain terms, he wanted an L-pill.

At first, the disapproval was unanimous by both the CIA office in Bogota and HQS. Even his case officer who knew him the best didn't want to entertain his request, thinking it immoral, unethical, not the American way. But the picture of this brave agent being brutally, slowly tortured to death tormented those who had come to know and respect him. How could CIA not honor his request, which, in extreme circumstances, would be warranted? At least it would give this courageous man control over his ultimate future.

TRIGON was adamant and finally persuaded his case officer to argue his case with HQS. As TRIGON departed for Moscow, his case officer told him HQS continued to weigh his request at the highest levels. If approved, he told TRIGON, we would deliver the poison when we re-contacted him in Moscow.

In late fall of 1974, TRIGON returned to Moscow, carrying spy gear concealed in his personal belongings. Technical officers hid a microdot in his personal papers, along with the first dates for future contacts in Moscow, his radio broadcast schedule and frequencies, miniaturized one-time pads, and a secret writing carbon. His case officer urged him to settle back into his normal life in Moscow without making any changes to his routines. TRIGON would have to withstand an initial security investigation endured by all returning diplomats since the KGB suspected CIA regularly approached Soviet diplomats, trying to convince them to cooperate. TRIGON's single most important mission for CIA: to find a position that afforded him the best access to highly sensitive information.

According to his recontact schedule, TRIGON agreed to make a sign-of-life signal for the Moscow CIA office three months after returning to that city. He had to stand inside the post office on the Arbat at a desk facing the window at 11:00 a.m. on a February morning in 1975. TRIGON was told that Jack, who TRIGON came to know well in Bogota, would walk by with his wife, who would wear a distinctive red hat.

On the specified day, Jack reported that he saw a man fitting TRIGON's build standing at the post office window during the specified time although Jack said he did not turn and directly look at the figure in the window because he suspected he had surveillance. The CIA office was elated that TRIGON had followed this prescribed script, demonstrating he was alive and hopefully free and not being controlled by the KGB.

Serendipitously, the next month a Moscow case officer spotted TRIGON's car, a black Volga, license tag MKG 123, parked at a signal site code-named PARKPLATZ. TRIGON had described this site to his case officer before he departed Bogota for Moscow. He could park at PARKPLATZ regularly within his normal pattern. More importantly, the site was on a route many CIA case officers could pass routinely on their way to or from their apartments out past Lenin Hills. No sketches had been made of PARKPLATZ, so the KGB could not imitate TRIGON's parking his car there by having read any instructions. The only way the KGB could know of this site or several others was to force TRIGON to reveal this. Although not part of his scheduled appearances to us, the Moscow CIA office saw this as yet another sign of life.

The next contact scheduled for late April was for TRIGON to make a marked signal, a dark smudge on a specific pole, which could be read by a case officer as he drove into work on his normal route. On the designated day, the officer saw no mark at the site. Several officers passed the site later that day on their routine commutes and concluded that due to snow piled on the sides of the road, TRIGON probably could not have navigated on foot close enough to the pole to make the mark, certainly not without calling attention to himself.

Moscow's CIA office began to second-guess the marked signal, thinking TRIGON might have made the mark on the wrong pole or may have misunderstood the directions. In any case, not wanting to pass up the first date in TRIGON's communication schedule, the CIA office decided to deliver a package at the site TRIGON described before he left Bogota. He hand-carried a sketch of this site concealed in a book he carried back to Moscow that contained his secret communications plans and sites. The CIA office planned to deliver a small piece of concrete with a message to him in the hollowed-out center.

During training in Bogota, TRIGON was shown a replica of this concrete concealment device, distinguishable with a black mark on one side. The instructions said to quickly put the package into his briefcase and take it home where he could smash it open with a hammer and later throw the chunks of concrete into the Moscow River. Since the contents in the package were not incriminating and would not identify TRIGON as the recipient, the CIA office decided to risk putting it down, even though he had not made a definitive signal, hoping TRIGON might go look for it. CIA eagerly sought to regain contact with TRIGON.

To prepare for the delivery to TRIGON, the CIA office held a long ops meeting to decide which case officer should make the car toss. The delivery route had to appear logical within the selected officer's normal travel patterns in Moscow. The last thing the CIA office wanted was to alert the case officer's trailing surveillance team that he was doing something suspicious or, worse, operational.

That night, the case officer, Jim, and his wife left from work and headed home taking the route from the Embassy to the bridge, down around a very tight left hand clover-leaf turn onto the *naberezhnaya*, the river road. The wife slowly and furtively rolled down the window, as few cars had electric windows in Moscow. Car tosses required precise timing, and Jim had to make an instantaneous decision. When Jim entered the curve, glancing back quickly in his mirror to gauge the distance to his trailing surveillance car, he gave his wife a silent signal to toss the package out the window. She aimed up on the curb just under short leafless bushes, landing it perfectly.

No matter how well a couple had performed in training or how many deliveries they made in Moscow, it was a heart-stopping moment when the decision was made to toss the package. If the case officer misjudged the following distance of the surveillance car, or if the wife bobbled the package over the windowsill and dropped it in the roadway, the surveillance team might immediately become aware of the package. If the team had approval from their KGB superiors, they could even stop the case officer as he attempted to drive away.

But, in this instance, Jim's wife delivered the package precisely as planned and Jim drove off, hoping TRIGON would come to find his package. If TRIGON retrieved the package successfully, he had to mark a recovery signal that night at another pre-selected site. The next morning another case officer looked for TRIGON's mark. But the signal did not appear. The CIA office concluded that TRIGON probably had not recovered the package.

So, now the office had a bigger problem: an unclaimed, loose package of spy gear. Having anticipated the possibility of this outcome, the CIA office had included in the package only what TRIGON needed to get back into contact, basically one-time pads and a schedule of dates, but nothing to identify him. If the KGB found the package, they might suspect it was intended for a CIA agent and be brutal in their attempts to prevent further drops by CIA officers by conducting close, harassing surveillance coverage.

CIA sent an officer to eyeball the drop-site several days later, hoping to spot and recover the package. When he returned, he painted an unsettling picture. The entire area looked like it had been swept clean. But the CIA office suspected what had happened. Annually, May first was a national holiday celebrating International Communism Day and Lenin's official birthday. As a Soviet tradition, the citizenry brought out their brooms and shovels to clean the streets the weekend before this holiday. Because this weekend came right after the delivery, the CIA office concluded that the package had been innocently swept up. Contrary to the CIA office's wishful thinking, TRIGON probably had no clue the package had been delivered.

The CIA office had failed to make contact with TRIGON on the only date and site he had scheduled when he returned to Moscow from Bogota. Now, the office had to rely on sending him a coded radio message with a new date and description of an alternative emergency drop. To make it simple, the radio message advised him to park his car on the first of any month at PARKPLATZ, the site that needed no description. The message told him to leave the fly window open on the front passenger side where the CIA officer would slip in a small package disguised as a car cigarette lighter. TRIGON had a limited number of deciphering groups on his one-time pad, so the message for him was very brief, hoping he would understand without a lot of details.

Another sighting buoyed the office's hopes. In July, Mike, a newly arrived case officer, noticed a black Volga stopped at a traffic light right beside him. He glanced over at the Volga, and from his vague peripheral impression of the driver, he said he thought it was TRIGON. As the Volga pulled away from the light, TRIGON's license tag confirmed Mike's initial impression. This sighting made us optimistic that TRIGON continued to live freely in Moscow.

It seemed that getting back in touch with him was easier planned than accomplished. The CIA office waited and watched on the first day of the next two months. To deliver into his car was a serious challenge, given that most case officers had near constant surveillance coverage. Although most agent drops were designed to be delivered while under surveillance coverage, this delivery had to be made by an officer totally without surveillance. Although extremely difficult to get an officer free of surveillance, the CIA office counted on either a case officer evading his surveillance team and later paying the price by having full-time bumper-locked surveillance coverage, or an officer would just get lucky and not have a surveillance team that night when he left his apartment to make the drop.

After two more frustrating no-show months, TRIGON's car appeared at PARKPLATZ on October 1, 1975. Ed, also a newcomer, had some gaps in his surveillance coverage. The CIA office counted on this when Ed left the Embassy that evening.

When he came into the office the next morning, Ed described the delivery, using his natural stand-up comedian talents, complete with dry wit and comical gestures. He replayed the evening for me when I was preparing to make the same delivery the following spring. Ed was short and appeared stout although he wasn't overweight. To add to his round profile was his mostly bald headed. He had a self-deprecating sense of humor and laughed easily, but he was a good ops officer who took our mission in Moscow seriously. As I became accepted, I found that he willingly coached me and offered good advice. He served a previous challenging tour, which gave his guidance more legitimacy for me. I learned in HQS that most case officers had opinions but not all had real experience.

Ed described his outing. He found himself surveillance-free after checking and double-checking to make sure. He assured us, though, that the delivery was not a cakewalk. After a seemingly endless approach on foot, he nonchalantly edged up to the area. TRIGON parked his car directly under a lamp along the curb without a single overhanging branch to provide natural screening. Ed described it as if he were walking onto a stage. He decided the best approach was to stagger and reel into the car as if totally drunk, a condition common to many in Moscow. As he bounced off the front fender, he rolled down along the side of the car, jamming the lighter through the slightly open window as he clumsily pushed himself erect. He heard the lighter fall with a loud thud, "almost startling the darkness out of the night," he said. As he groped his way to the back of the car, to his relief there was no one in the area who might have seen his theatrics. Stumbling down the block, he became aware of the bone-chilling night, the reason others were not out walking.

TRIGON finally had new spy supplies. Although only a small secret cavity inside the lighter, it accommodated a roll of 35mm film that contained the details of his new communications plan, designating future dates and drop site for him to deliver a package to us.

Then, the office's hopes plummeted as TRIGON did not signal for the next two possible delivery dates. The case officers continued to watch for TRIGON in Moscow, hoping to glimpse him driving around as a sign of life. The next date for TRIGON to deliver to us was in early December. It is an understatement to say the CIA office celebrated when we saw his parked car at PARKPLATZ, indicating he was ready to deliver the following day.

I had been in Moscow only a month when we saw this signal at PARKPLATZ. Since my acquisition of a tangerine Zhiguli, I had spent every weekend exploring the city and outlying suburbs where the Soviets permitted official Americans to travel without special permits. I often invited other single female friends from the Embassy since many of them hadn't bought a car and didn't have an opportunity to get out of central Moscow. My unsuspecting innocent companions enjoyed my field trips around Moscow, exploring parks and churches, the usual tourist sights the KGB, if they were watching us, would consider normal activities for newcomers.

I had an ulterior motive in ranging far and wide: I needed to determine whether I had surveillance coverage. It appeared that the KGB didn't care where we went, probably because we were all women on these excursions. During my first month, I had not detected any surveillance coverage. My male peers in the office doubted my ability since they had all experienced coverage from their first week in Moscow.

According to the CIA office's general practice, new officers had three or four months to familiarize themselves with the city before they were assigned any operational task. Knowing the city meant more than just memorizing the streets and avenues. We had to become intimate with the normal patterns of traffic and street activity, like where police vans usually parked or where truck drivers slept in their trucks at night. If we were operational and saw something strange or out of the ordinary, we had to make an instantaneous judgment about whether or not the KGB was staked out for a potential ambush.

This happened once when Mike was re-casing a car-toss site for another officer the day prior to a delivery. He spotted a large trash dumpster immediately at the bottom of the ramp to the ring road, clearly angled so someone hiding in it or behind it had a view of the location for the car-toss. Mike said his hair stood on end when he saw the dumpster. He concluded it had been put there to provide cover for a KGB ambush of our officer the following night. The bin had never been there before when other case officers made multiple passes along the highway. Although placed to the side of the road and probably not noticeable to others, Mike knew it was strange and out of place. He aborted the delivery to the agent. Later, we learned that the agent had been arrested by the KGB before the delivery date.

In addition to area familiarity, the most important skill we had to develop while driving was the ability to detect the presence of a surveillance team following us. As I spent hours, days, and weekends that first month driving around Moscow, often venturing to more remote areas, I never spotted a surveillance team following me. The CIA office considered this an anomaly, which they figured would not be my permanent or guaranteed status. The case officers thought I would eventually come under scrutiny and then have to endure constant surveillance coverage as they did.

The bottom line, I figured, was that the CIA office didn't think I saw the surveillance. They decided to test my alleged surveillance-free status by planning a moving surveillance detection run with Mike and his wife set up to observe my route. Mike was pre-positioned upstairs in the crystal *beriozka*, located near Novodyevichy Cemetery, on a Saturday afternoon. *Beriozka*, meaning birch, was the Soviet name for hard currency stores open only to foreign diplomats and businessmen who had foreign currency to spend. As he and his wife stood admiring a large display of Polish crystal, Mike surreptitiously observed from the large plate glass window on the second floor as I made the turn from a wide boulevard near Lenin Stadium onto the river road. He watched my tangerine Zhiguli, easily visible from his vantage point, as I made my approach, my turn, and then my drive away from him. Mike did not see surveillance precede me into the turn, fall in behind me from the *beriozka* parking lot, or follow me as I left the area. There was no parallel route where surveillance cars could have used to more discreetly follow me while staying out of my sight on this route.

Luck was with me that Saturday afternoon because the traffic was light; in fact, no other cars happened to be on the street as I passed the *beriozka*, making my surveillance-free claim easier to verify. Simultaneously, both Mike and I also secretly monitored the radio frequency used by KGB surveillance teams. We heard no broadcasts or miscellaneous squelches to indicate they were following me, or that I had become a target. Occasionally, case officers reported that their KGB surveillance team referred to them by a nickname. Our capability to monitor these KGB transmissions lasted until the end of my tour.

Mike reported that I was clean. I passed the first test. I claimed I had no surveillance and the CIA office seemed satisfied, at least for the time being. Although relieved, deep down I was confident in my ability to spot surveillance. The CIA office's lingering doubts, though, spurred me to be constantly vigilant, never wanting to miss detecting surveillance coverage while out on a critical operation.

The CIA office had been discussing many different delivery scenarios in anticipation of TRIGON making his signal at PARKPLATZ. Our deputy chief, Jack, lived nearest the site and had the best cover, his daily jogging, to pick up TRIGON's package. But the CIA office wanted an alternate. During one of the ops meetings, the Chief looked at me and asked whether I was sufficiently confident to go out on my own and determine conclusively that I had no surveillance. Then, he asked whether I could find my way on foot to the site where TRIGON was to leave his first package. I assured him I could. I knew I was only a back-up in case something happened to Jack. But the prospect to be called upon to pick up the package excited me. I managed to remain cool and composed, beginning to plan my route and how I would approach the site.

I never dreamed I would be called upon for an operational act that early in my tour. Also, I doubted TRIGON was actually going to deliver a package, given all the previously missed dates. What I hadn't told the CIA office at this meeting were my plans with another new Embassy officer, Shaun, for the same date as TRIGON's delivery to us.

Shaun had asked if I would go with him on an Embassy courier run to Helsinki. It was a wonderful opportunity for both of us to explore Helsinki, the closest western city to Moscow. Best of all, the Embassy was to pay for the train and one night hotel stay for each traveler. So, early in our tours, Shaun and I could see what Helsinki offered. Generally, it took over six months to reach the top of the courier list.

Shaun and I had quickly become friends. We arrived in Moscow at the same time and, more significantly, we had a mutual friend, a fellow graduate from my alma mater, Drew University. He had been killed on the flight deck of an aircraft carrier off the coast of Vietnam in 1967. Shaun had been standing next to him at the time of his death when the carrier came under attack by the North Vietnamese. Shaun suffered major burns but survived, enduring multiple painful skin grafts on his torso, arms, hands and face. We tearfully shared this tragic loss of our friend and the pain Shaun endured.

Unfortunately, this opportunity to go to Helsinki coincided with the date of TRIGON's delivery. Now that I knew I might be called upon to recover TRIGON's package, I had to bow out of the trip, not wanting him to suspect who I really worked for. I made an excuse that I hoped made sense to Shaun. Although disappointed, I was excited about being tapped for my first operational act. This wasn't the last time I cancelled plans because of operational requirements. I was in Moscow to be a case officer on the street, which took precedence over my personal life.

Case officers developed observable habits from their first day in Moscow, habits that KGB surveillance teams accepted as normal. Jack's jogging was such a habit, allowing him to run, many times without surveillance coverage. His team knew where he headed when he left his apartment early in the morning in his jogging attire. They also knew that, after a reasonable time, he returned to his apartment.

During the final ops planning meeting, we agreed that, even if Jack had surveillance, he would still pick up the package, since the site, located under a covered portico, allowed him to be briefly out of sight. At that moment, he could pick up the package without the surveillance team knowing anything operational had occurred.

The next morning, dark and early, as Jack ran his normal route, he passed through the portico where TRIGON had placed his package on a waist high ledge. Jack grabbed and pocketed the crushed triangular milk carton in one swift, smooth movement. He finished his run, never seeing any surveillance. After returning to his apartment and changing clothes for work, he departed for the Embassy at the usual time, following his daily pattern. The surveillance team that followed him to work did not demonstrate any unusual or aggressive attention. He immediately raced up to the CIA office and excitedly displayed the package to all of us assembled there. Neal opened it cautiously, not knowing what to expect.

Inside the milk carton were two pieces of paper, each with a child's pencil drawing, one of a crude sailboat, and the other with a freeform figure. But we knew that these were not simple drawings. TRIGON had imbedded secret writing on the paper. Neal gingerly carried the papers by their corners to his lab and applied the chemical developer. We waited for what seemed forever, our excitement mounting as we speculated about what he had written.

TRIGON's message was exactly what we wanted to hear. He said that, when he returned to Moscow, he passed the intensive KGB security checks. Obtaining a job in the Global Affairs Department in the Ministry of Foreign Affairs, he had access to incoming and outgoing classified cables to Soviet Embassies worldwide. In the last sentence in his message, he said he had a larger package of film he wanted to deliver.

We were exhilarated by his note. Tim fired off an immediate cable to HQS, so they could share our excitement about TRIGON's message. Instantly, the CIA office came alive with the urgency of the operation since the next pick-up from TRIGON was in two weeks.

The office selected Mike to make the pick-up late at night, based on the Chief's conclusion that Mike had the most logical reason for being in that area where the site was located. This package defined TRIGON's mastery. He protected this valuable package by using prophylactics to weatherproof the 12 rolls of 35 mm film. He tied the bundle up in a dirty rag soaked in diesel oil, making the package a drippy dirty mess, discouraging a stranger's inclination to pick it up. Mike recovered the package without difficulty and brought it into the CIA office the next morning.

Neal developed the film in the small darkroom. When Neal disclosed the contents, we were astounded that TRIGON had photographed nearly one hundred secret Soviet government documents. HQS analysts were going to have a field day reading these documents, clearly an intelligence windfall.

TRIGON photographed a personal handwritten note on one roll of film. First, he apologized that he had only recently found the October 1 cigarette lighter in his car because lots of trash had collected on the floor mat where the lighter landed. The next part of his note shocked the assembled case officers.

He said he knew that CIA was being seriously challenged by the US Senate hearings on alleged intelligence abuses. He worked hard to provide these documents "because I know CIA is in trouble." He took chances and carried documents home to photograph, returning them to his office the next day without anyone's knowing. He reported the KGB had investigated him when he first returned to Moscow, which delayed his getting this assignment in the Ministry of Foreign Affairs. But he knew this job would give him the access we would find most valuable. He had one co-worker, who often traveled. At those times, he would have unlimited access to all telegrams that passed through his office. He requested we pass him his miniature camera because he was afraid his neighbor in his apartment might hear the click of his 35mm camera when he photographed documents.

Sadly, he said, he divorced his wife because he didn't want to implicate her in his relationship with us. Finally, he wanted more jewelry to give to his mother to provide her with an insurance policy in the event something happened to him. He also said that, during the winter of 1975, he had been hospitalized in a sanatorium with pneumonia. At the end of his note, he asked that we deliver to him what we had promised, meaning the L-pill. He was willing to take the risk in collecting important documents for us, but we had to fulfill our promise to him.

The passion in his note amazed us all. He knew about the Senate hearings and thought his contribution could help our organization. He had analyzed his personal situation, isolating himself, so he could work for us without the distraction of concern for his wife, if he were caught. Jack, the only one in the office who had personally met TRIGON, was especially moved by the note. But the fact that TRIGON acted so aggressively in taking documents home horrified us as well. This action proved how committed he was to his work for us. Now, we had to decide whether we could keep our promise to him regarding the L-pill.

High precedence cables were sent to HQS, detailing the events of the past evening and a full translation of TRIGON's personal note. The photos of the MFA documents in Russian were cabled to HQS for translation and dissemination since the Moscow office did not have a native Russian-speaking officer. HQS replied immediately with congratulations. We were finally in communication with TRIGON. The next scheduled delivery to him was in January 1976. We had a lot of work to do to prepare our next package for him. The CIA office's operational focus, almost an obsession, became the TRIGON operation.

Photographs - Laos and Moscow

John's Lao photo ID, complete with his fumanchu mustache, July 1971.

John and I at a welcome dinner in friends' home in Pakse, July 1971.

A traditional Lao ceremonial *baci* welcoming John and me to Pakse, July 1971.

Our Lao French colonial house in Pakse, November 1971.

The gravel driveway in front of our house, which served as a door bell
to alert us to visitors, with the guard's gazebo in the left background,
and Jim and Elsie's house seen through the gates, November 1971.

Seated in the living room on our favorite bruised banana furniture, May 1972.

John discussing the location of the Lao troops in the field with his operations assistant. John always wore two-piece safari suits he had made by the local Pakse tailor. They were polyester, and washed and wore like iron. He had them in several colors since he had to wear a fresh one everyday because of the heat. March 1972.

The funeral pyre for his Lao assistant, killed when he walked into the propeller blades of a Twin Otter airplane. April 1972.

John and his Lao assistants calling in air support for the Lao soldiers on the day John was killed, October 19, 1972.

My apartment building on Ulitsa Vavilova 83 in southwestern Moscow.
I lived on the eighth floor of the 14-story building.

The US Embassy in Moscow on the 14-lane Garden Ring Road, also known as Tchaikovsky Street.

My Zhiguli, a Soviet-made four-cylinder Fiat sedan.

The stairs to the top of Krasnoluzhsky railroad bridge over the Moscow River where the dead-drop site SETUN was located. Among the men on the stairs was Keith Melton, benefactor of the International Spy Museum in Washington D.C., and other Americans who were given a tour of the drop site by their SVR (formerly KGB) escorts. Photo from the 1990s.

One of four identical towers on the bridge where I placed the SETUN dead-drop concealment device for TRIGON inside a narrow window in the tower.

A picture at the moment of my violent arrest on July 15, 1977.
The KGB was attempting to remove the SRR-100 device attached to my bra by
Velcro and the neck loop antenna around my neck. This photo appears in the
International Spy Museum in Washington, D.C. and the SVR/KGB museum
in Moscow and is included in many books on the Cold War.

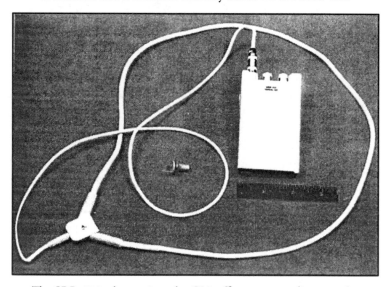

The SRR-100, the receiver the CIA officers wore to listen to the
unencrypted radio transmissions by the KGB surveillance teams
as they followed CIA officers throughout Moscow.

A photograph of Alexandr Dmitryevich Ogorodnik, the Soviet agent code-named TRIGON, who was recruited by the CIA in Bogota, Colombia, in 1973.

The infamous Lyubianka Prison where I was taken after my arrest on July 15, 1977.

My photograph, taken within an hour after my arrest. I was seated at a conference table in Lyubianka Prison where I was held for four hours by the KGB. They examined the concealment rock and its contents. The man beside me was an official of the US Embassy, who interceded on my behalf.

The photograph of the display in the Moscow museum called the Hall of the Federal Security Service of Russia, formerly the Chekist Hall of the KGB Museum of the USSR. Among the photos are my arrest, an approximation of the signal site DETI, a replica of the deaddrop package, the railroad bridge, and a CIA-produced sketch of the general area around the bridge. Photo from the 1990s.

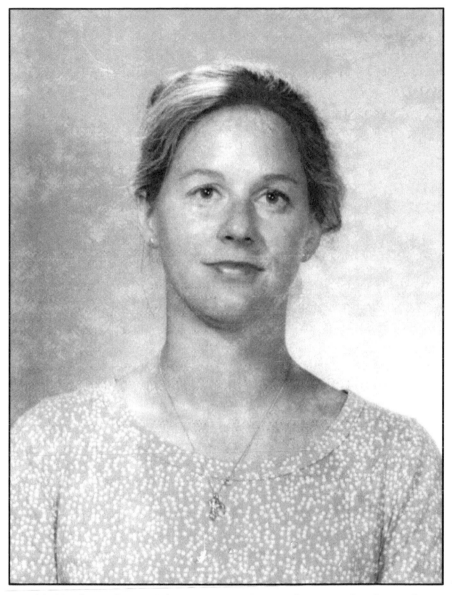

My ID photo taken on July 18, 1977, at CIA Headquarters when I arrived back from Moscow before meeting with CIA Director Stansfield Turner and the President of the United States, Jimmy Carter.

CHAPTER 8

Life in Moscow

Through that first winter, I began to feel at home in Moscow, but being alone was hard. I had few dinner invitations. Even my neighbors who "stole" my furniture never invited me over although they gave me a few starter geranium plants. The couple directly next door knocked on my door once and gave me some hot homemade soup when she found out from her husband that I was home sick. My neighbor, Bill, of course, invited me many times and I reciprocated.

So, to ignore my lack of invitations and to avoid my dreary apartment, I often stayed after work and went to the Embassy club for a couple beers, a slab of pizza, and some company. It was not great for my waistline, but at least I had a little social life. My apartment was not a cozy nest; I simply slept there, did laundry, and ate occasional dinners. The refrigerator reflected that. On Friday nights, the Marine Guard's bar was open, and I ended up there. Occasionally, I attended wine-and-cheese parties at girlfriends' apartments in the Embassy.

Ellen had interesting parties with very different people than those I was meeting in the Embassy. One night, she had a group of Western journalists over and showed a movie, which most of us had seen when it came out in 1966: *The Russians are Coming*. But the movie was funnier and even ironic here in Moscow. I probably drank more beer than I should have, but the movie inspired comedy routines and amazing conversations. That night was the first time I heard someone say, "Bring on the nukes!" meaning it was okay for America to bomb our Embassy in Moscow with nuclear weapons. Even though we would be at the center of the bull's eye and, potentially, the sacrificial lambs, this was the era when the Soviets were particularly prickly and difficult. We witnessed the harassment of Jewish dissidents and the persecution of famous Russian scientists like Nobel Prize winner Andrei Sakharov. Although the movie provided a meaningful diversion, the evening was sobering, especially hearing the journalists express their frustrations as they attempted to work in this closed, paranoid society.

One night in early January Shaun and I went for a long walk in the snow after work. We compared notes on our conclusions about life in Moscow. The winter of 1976 was one of the coldest in Moscow's recent history, with most nights bottoming out at minus 20F. As we walked it snowed harder, and felt like pouring down rain. The women, maybe forty but looking sixty, who cleared the streets did their best with their brooms made of tree branches lashed together. They wore heavy thick boiled-wool felt boots that kept their feet warm and dry, but their inadequate gloves made their hands white with cold. Full employment meant everyone worked, but many jobs were extraordinarily difficult, physically hard, and no one's first choice.

As we walked around the deserted inner city south of the Kremlin, we spotted a man lying on the sidewalk in the teeming snow. Barely moving and becoming buried alive in the snow, mumbling unintelligibly, he probably was drunk. Lots of people drank to excess in Moscow and, consequently, many froze to death. We weren't successful in finding a policeman to report the drunk, but interestingly we soon heard an ambulance siren in the distance and watched them pick up the man. I had been aware that we had a surveillance team following us that night. They must have called the ambulance. Shaun and I didn't discuss whether he knew noticed the surveillance team.

When I told the office about the walk, they told me Shaun was among the Embassy officers suspected by the KGB of being CIA. I knew he often picked up Soviet hitchhikers, which must have driven his KGB surveillance team crazy since the team assumed the hitchhiker was an agent. When Shaun dropped off the hitchhiker, the KGB team had to investigate who he was and why he was in contact with an American. I agreed with the CIA office that I should avoid associating one-on-one with Shaun because the KGB might assume I too was CIA.

Discouraged from having friends like Shaun, my sole focus in Moscow became my work. I was fulfilled because the challenge of my secret work satisfied me, but a little social life could have been amusing.

I spent every weekend out searching for new dead-drop and signal sites. The other case officers had to find sites while under surveillance, which was far more difficult, since they had to conceal their real missions. Case officers orchestrated outings with their wives, kids and dogs, working hard to make their destination and activity appear normal to trailing surveillance teams. As he drove, the case officer evaluated every turn into a park and every route leading to a church, up every hill or even around a slight curve. He had to determine if a package could be tossed out of his car in the gap before his surveillance team came around the corner or curve. He had to find a parking area, distinguished by a distinct sign or numbered pole, where we could tell an agent to place a package. Optimally, the location was near a church or a park, as either place provided cover for a case officer to visit.

Wives were adept at sleight of hand. While leaning over to help children and dogs out of the car, they accidentally dropped a jacket on the ground and simultaneously scooped up the agent's package. Once, a few years later in Leningrad, the KGB apprehended a couple when the wife bent down to pick up a package. In that case, the agent had been compromised before the date of the pick-up. The case officer could not know that the KGB had staked out the area, dug into foxholes, and prepared to ambush the case officer and his wife.

So when a case officer spotted a potential drop-site while out driving, he covertly took a picture with a Minox camera, palmed in his hand while he was driving. It was tricky to go into a cloverleaf turn and photograph the exact landing spot for the car toss package or to take a picture of an approach to the curbside drop-site without running into the curb. The officer had to capture the surrounding area in the picture, so he included the surrounding context or an identifying landmark to be included in the sketch for the agent.

Mike took one of the all-time classic pictures. He photographed a location for a curbside pick-up he had spotted when he was out with his wife, kids, and dog in tow. After the roll of film was developed, we all agreed he had taken a fabulous picture of the drop site near a church. It captured the background as well as the clearly numbered telephone pole, making it easy for the agent to locate the exact spot to put his package. To double-check the site before the sketch was included in TRIGON's package, I went to re-case the site. In Mike's picture, a guy-wire cut across the right side of the photo, probably a cable strung from the top of the pole down to the ground. Susie, who was responsible for sketching all sites for agent packages, had faithfully replicated the wire in her sketch. That weekend, as I drove by the site, I couldn't see a wire from the pole to the ground. I confirmed the number on the pole. Maybe the wire had been removed or was behind the pole. But there was no wire. After reporting my findings, or in this case lack of findings, we all closely re-examined the picture.

Someone figured out that the guy-wire actually was Mike's car antenna photographed through his windshield. Laughter reverberated throughout the CIA office as we all made fun of Mike. Mike hated to be wrong, but it was a mistake we all could make. We loved an excuse for good-natured kidding, especially with Mike who was a hardworking, serious, capable officer. Susie removed the guy-wire from the sketch, but we didn't let Mike forget it.

I soon discovered I had a significant advantage in casing operational sites by not having surveillance. Every weekend, I went exploring, becoming more aggressive in determining whether I had surveillance by passing by the logical turn to a predictable location, making U-turns, driving down dead-end streets, and appearing to be hopelessly lost. I had to be certain I had no surveillance.

Then, I began to take photos of potential clandestine sites with John's Nikon camera.

The irony of using his camera filled me with emotion. I recalled clearly when we bought it a lifetime ago in Hong Kong. John actually had a love affair with his camera in Laos. He packed it gently in his satchel along with his folding stock AK47 when he went out everyday into the field. Stealing spare moments in a local village or along the riverbank, he framed poignant photos of the native people. The sad eyes of the Lao woman holding her baby swaddled in a native scarf or the old man in the dugout, sad eyes too, wondering why this "round eye" was here, why he took his picture. John recorded the tragedy of these peaceful people as they witnessed destruction in their country situated in the middle of a war, but not their war.

When we bought this camera four years earlier, we couldn't know what was to happen, thank heavens. Now here I was in Moscow using the camera in a different war as I photographed places where spies were to deliver Soviet secrets to the US government. The Nikon lenses John chose were uncannily tailored to my needs. The telephoto lens allowed me to stand off and take pictures, so curious bystanders would not suspect my photo objective. The wide-angle lens took in the surrounding area and made it easy to simulate a photo of assembled girlfriends out on an afternoon junket, all the while making sure the photo included the specific curb line or lamp pole. To compare the Minox and Nikon photos was unfair, but I was proud of my 8" X 10" glossies.

Eventually, as the other officers' confidence in me grew, they gave me lists of possible sites they had seen but had not yet photographed. My pictures provided them with more than enough essential detail. I admitted I never gained proficiency at spotting potential sites, but I made up for this by taking effective panoramas of the sites the other officers found.

One Monday morning, I was chatting with Ed about his weekend. The weather had been cold with sleet and rain. He reflected thoughtfully as he described how he had been reading a wonderful book, relaxed in his easy chair in his den where he would have preferred to stay. He knew, though, that he had to go out to maintain his established habit of every Saturday afternoon driving to one of many *beriozkas* with his wife in order to observe his surveillance patterns. As he drove away from his apartment, his surveillance team fell in behind him. He told me, "Just once, I'd like to stay home on an ugly Saturday afternoon. Or, go out by myself and drive anywhere I please without being followed." I had a glimpse of what it must have been like for him and the other case officers. I was fortunate not to experience being followed constantly.

With the date for the January delivery to TRIGON fast approaching, HQS had prepared and pouched out the contents for our first package. The trick, Neal told us, was to fit it all into a crushed cigarette pack. It had to be the specific brand TRIGON had been told to look for in our radio broadcast. Viewing the contents spread out on Neal's desk, I whispered to him that he needed a shoebox-sized concealment device. I whispered so potential listening devices in Neal's area in a backroom right outside of the CIA office couldn't pick up my voice. I had no reason to be in any area of the CIA office. It would be stupid to be caught on tape in the CIA office spaces after all my hard work to remain uncontaminated by CIA people.

At the next day's ops meeting, Neal said he needed eight packs of this brand of Soviet cigarettes. He assured us that, with these multiple packs ripped up and glued together, he could fashion what appeared to be a single crumpled pack. Neal excelled at packing an amazing amount of oddly shaped items into very small, compact packages and then artfully camouflaging them, so they looked unappealing.

Obtaining these Soviet cigarette packs was an operation in itself. We had to buy them at tobacco kiosks without surveillance coverage since Americans never bought Soviet cigarettes. They were too strong and dry. The last thing we wanted to do was to raise KGB suspicions. Within a couple days, two case officers on separate outings at lunch found they were without surveillance, permitting them freedom to purchase the multiple packs.

Neal cut, glued, and crushed, eventually ending up with a package that was the size and appearance of a single crushed pack of cigarettes. It contained the miniature camera and cassettes and a role of kalvar film, a special 35mm film with miniaturized writing. The personal message on the kalvar film thanked him for his concern and praised him for his remarkable selection of documents.

We also included a personal message we obtained from his girlfriend in Bogota. The CIA office there had maintained close contact with her since we wanted to make sure she continued to be discreet and not tell anyone that she or TRIGON had been in contact with American intelligence. She had revealed to the CIA office that, before TRIGON had left Bogota, she knew she was pregnant. She did not reveal this to TRIGON, concerned that he would decide not to return to Moscow. She now faced supporting herself and her baby girl. However, she was still determined not to tell TRIGON this while he remained in Moscow, worried that he might take chances and get caught. Her plan, which she and TRIGON shared, was for him to work for a time and then escape from Moscow. Then they could begin their life together in anonymity with sufficient funds to live well. Moscow's CIA office continued to keep this from TRIGON, but it was a difficult decision.

The message for TRIGON on kalvar also included his new communications plan, including new site sketches and a schedule of deliveries. In the package was a critical re-supply of one-time pads on miniaturized sheets of very thin waylite paper. He used these numbers on the pads to decipher his radio messages. Neal managed to fit in a thin pack of small denomination rubles. Large bills were hard to negotiate in Soviet stores and could raise suspicions.

In a final review of the plans for delivering the package, the CIA office sent me to check on the site, which was called STENA (meaning wall in

Russian) to ensure there were no unforeseen changes in the area. When the site was first cased, the drop was to be a car-toss, located on the route to a *beriozka* off Kutuzovsky Prospekt. The site had been cased in the summer.

But now, in mid-January, the snow banks were steep and icy, piled up high along the side of the road around the lamp post. The package would have to be thrown far enough over the snow bank, so it landed in the dimple at the base of the pole. If it wasn't tossed high enough, the package could slide back down into the roadway in clear view of a trailing surveillance team.

Neal pointed out a second and far more serious potential problem. Could the miniature camera withstand the hard landing on packed icy snow? He had no room for cushioning bubble wrap in the package. Not wanting to make these decisions alone without technical advice, the CIA office sent an immediate cable to HQS. From the drop tests, duplicating the size and composition of the outer wrapping of the package and simulating the drop height and the hard surface, HQS concluded that the camera's mechanism might not survive the drop.

Based on this information, the CIA office decided and HQS concurred that I was to be the case officer to make this delivery to TRIGON. I could walk to the site and gently place the package at the exact spot at the base of the pole. Confident that I had no surveillance after two plus months, I was prepared to make this drop. My mission was imminent.

To signal that he was ready to receive our package, TRIGON was to park his car at PARKPLATZ on the designated night between 7:00 p.m. and 9:00 p.m. We were disappointed when several of us did not see his car there on our route home the night before the planned drop. The next morning, a marked signal site was checked and then, later that day, rechecked, but it was clear. TRIGON had not signaled to receive the package.

Knowing difficulties of keeping a car running in the cold winter months, the CIA office rationalized that TRIGON had put his car on blocks for the winter and couldn't signal at PARKPLATZ. We discussed looking for his garage since he had sketched its location when he was still in Bogota. But we all agreed that maintaining patience was the best course of action. We did not want to do anything that might cast suspicion upon him. We also knew he had alternate dates for this delivery in the coming months.

Then, the February date passed, as did the March date. Case officers visited the *beriozka* occasionally in order to check the site from a moving car. In preparation for the next delivery date in April, a case officer's wife was sent to look at the site and reported the snow was still high although compact and icy. We still had the same delivery problems at STENA.

Magically, on the night before the April delivery date, TRIGON's car appeared at PARKPLATZ. We concluded that, given the same conditions at the site, I would make the delivery at STENA. By now my surveillance-free track record had continued, and the CIA office had more confidence in me.

We had the final ops meeting the afternoon of the drop. I described what I would wear and the approximate route I planned to take, both by car and then on foot. We determined where I should park the car before entering the subway and proceeding on foot. The car had to be in a location where other foreigners parked for a period of time, so it didn't raise suspicion if a trolling surveillance team saw it. We went through my timing, including when I would leave my apartment, how long I would drive, length of the subway ride, and time required for me to walk to the site after exiting the subway.

The case officers discussed what would happen, if TRIGON did not pick up his package. The flipped back and forth through the pros and cons of my going back to check the site. What we didn't want was for me to run into TRIGON, but the thought of leaving this package on the ground with the miniature camera and all the directions for future drops was not acceptable. So, we agreed that I should return to the site after 11:30 p.m. to determine whether he had retrieved his package.

Finally we had to finalize my safety signal, the indication to the CIA office that I had returned safely from the operational activity. We wanted to cover the possibility that I could be in an accident or, worse, be arrested. If I didn't show up, the protocol was for Neal to call the MFA to report me missing. If they told him that I had been in an accident, the office could immediately start the process to get me medivac'd from the country. If Neal discovered I had been arrested, he needed to ask where I was being held. Bottom line, CIA could not leave me hanging out there without a pre-positioned plan. I knew they would eventually come to rescue me, which was a comforting thought.

After putting the crumpled cigarette package into my oversize canvas bag at the close of the meeting, I headed home to change clothes and begin my first operational outing. I had developed a litany of observable habits over these first few months. Sometimes, I went home after work to change clothes before going out for the evening. The guard at my apartment compound was used to seeing me come in, spend thirty minutes and then go out again. Some evenings, I came in later and stayed. Sometimes, I went out later and came back after a couple of hours. With no apparent surveillance keeping book on me, the guard was the only one observing my habits. So, I had a variety of behaviors that he recognized as my normal patterns. If questioned, his log reflected benign repeated activities.

I made this night appear normal. I changed into warmer slacks and a coat I had acquired at a clothing *beriozka* in town. An ugly calf-length gray tweed coat, made in Finland, it resembled coats worn on the street by Soviet women. I occasionally wore it to work and on Saturday market days. When I went operational, this coat helped me blend with others on the street. I wore a dark knit hat to cover the highlights in my hair and gloves to cover my manicured fingernails, both of which were uncommon among Soviet women.

As I pulled away from my apartment, I watched the militiaman standing outside observing me. He didn't go into his booth to respond to a call, nor did he turn to signal anyone in the observation post (OP) located in an apartment across the street. Ulitza Vavilova was traffic-free that night. I approached the intersection at the bottom of the hill. Normally, I turned left toward the Embassy. But this time, I turned right, heading to an area where I became more provocative in my route to flush out my surveillance team following me.

Although I was nervous about making this delivery, I had confidence that I knew the city and the planned route. While I drove, I thought through every step and the advice other CIA officers had given me. I also recalled something Richard, a former Moscow officer, told me before I left the US for Moscow. While standing in the USSR Branch at HQS, he told me about the stress of making drops in Moscow. He anticipated that I would have to tolerate some strong male egos in Moscow who might doubt I could do the job. He said all officers were anxious before performing an operational act. He suggested I not let the male case officers' bluster fool me. He added that even the most macho of them thought of taking a drink for courage before they left home. An interesting connection, he had been in training with John, and John always spoke highly of him. John said Richard wasn't like the other Ivy Leaguers who treated the knuckledraggers as lower class. Richard knew I had suffered, had overcome loss, and had pulled myself back up. I felt stronger as I considered his confidence in me. But I never needed a drink for courage.

No one followed me that night as I drove into Soviet neighborhoods and remote industrial areas. I snaked my way back to town where I parked my car and immediately ducked quickly into the subway. I confirmed I had no surveillance. I rode the subway several stops, changed trains and eventually exited on Kutuzovsky Prospekt. Walking toward apartment building blocks, I saw very few people out. I had my last chance to make sure no one followed me as I began my final approach to the site.

Although no professional KGB surveillance team followed me, I didn't want to be seen dropping something suspicious by an innocent little old lady looking out her window or a fellow pedestrian just happening by. The delivery had to be smooth, almost sleight of hand. Checking out the lamp post, I realized the delivery would be more difficult than I anticipated because the snow bank was wider, making it impossible to lean up against the pole. Given how fragile the miniature camera was, I couldn't gently lob the package over the snow bank as I walked past the pole. I decided on my tactic: I would stop, lean on the snow bank, blow my nose, and adjust my boot.

Lifting the package out of my purse along with the tissue, I let the package slide from under my purse a short distance to its soft landing precisely at the base of the pole. I realized that TRIGON would struggle to retrieve it without scrambling over the snow bank, but I was certain he'd think of something clever.

Relieved the package was in place, I started to walk at a measured pace in the direction of the *beriozka* down a hill and to the right. I scanned the area for bystanders. At a distance across a small park I spotted a man partially hidden behind a phone booth. As I turned the corner toward the *beriozka* and slipped into the shadows, I glanced back, but he had disappeared.

My initial thought was that he was part of a surveillance team. If so, he and the team would wait to see who came to pick up the package. But then I realized TRIGON might position himself to watch for a car to drive past the site since he knew this was a car toss from his training in Bogota. The chances of a car driving this route this late at night were slim as the *beriozka* had closed. In fact, the time planned for the car toss delivery at STENA was to be earlier in the evening when the *beriozka* would still be open. But since I had to place the package while on foot, I came to the site at the latest possible time to take advantage of darkness and fewer casuals on the street. I had until 10:00 p.m. to place the package, because TRIGON was instructed to come after 10:00 p.m. to pick it up. These details raced through my mind as I strategized what to do next.

I decided to leave the immediate area so that, if it were TRIGON, I would not spook him. I hoped he would check the site for his package, see it, and pick it up, thinking somehow he missed the car delivery. So, I nonchalantly walked away into another dark Soviet residential neighborhood. Moving was the best tactic. Standing still without an observable reason could cause suspicion.

I checked my watch. I had an hour and a half until my return to the site. I began walking down wide sidewalks, head down, passing only one old man, but making no eye contact. At nearly 11:00 p.m., I was cold and tired. I returned to the drop site. I checked out the area as I approached and saw no one. Instantly, I saw my package, lying exactly where it had landed. I stretched over the snow bank to pick it up, stashing it in my purse. Disappointed to have to recover my first drop, I made my way back through the subway to my car and the Embassy Marine bar. A CIA officer was among the crowd enjoying an evening with friends at the bar, but he made eye contact as I entered. He wanted to confirm was my safe return. Details would come tomorrow morning inside the CIA office.

I was exhausted as I rolled out of bed the next morning and headed to the Embassy. I was discouraged by the fact that TRIGON didn't have his package. We sat in the office discussing possible reasons TRIGON hadn't picked up this drop. If he was there and hadn't seen a car pass, we wondered if he did not even look for the package. Or maybe he was scared off by seeing someone walk up to the pole. Or all of the above.

And worse, he had no more scheduled delivery dates. So, in his next radio broadcast, we told him we were going to revert back to the option of delivering into his car at PARKPLATZ on the first of the month as we had the past October. This was an extremely risky delivery plan because it put an American officer in direct contact with the agent's car. Dead-drops were safer because they were completed without any identifying marks, anonymous in time and distance, unlike a car with a license tag.

Two weeks later was May 1. The CIA office was confident in my consistent pattern of not having surveillance. I was the logical officer to make the delivery if we saw TRIGON's car at PARKPLATZ. As before, the window of opportunity for delivery fell between 7:00 and 10:00 p.m. The later the better, given the fact that daylight lasted much longer at this time of year. Also, May 1 was a national holiday in the Soviet Union and fell on a Saturday when everyone would be out celebrating late.

I told the assembled officers during our ops meeting that I had a minor complication. My sister Mary-Alice had come to visit me in April and was planning to leave later in the month. I certainly couldn't take her with me on the street, and I could not tell her what I had to do that night without her. I didn't know whether she knew I worked for CIA, since I had only told my parents. But now was not the time to tell her. So, in the event TRIGON showed at PARKPLATZ, I decided to stash her for most of the evening with friends at Neal's apartment. She met Neal and his wife, Lee, during her stay, so it was logical. But, she looked at me strangely when I wrote her a note to tell her we were going to dinner at Neal's that evening, but that I could not stay. She was smart and did not question this.

Our plan was the same as before: If I had surveillance that night, I was to return to Neal's apartment, and he would make an attempt. On the way to the Embassy with my sister, I spotted TRIGON's car at PARKPLATZ. The plan was coming into focus. My poor sister looked a bit lost when I dropped her off at Neal's, but I was exhilarated, ready to begin my long route to determine whether I had surveillance. I was ready to make this delivery.

I remembered Ed's account of PARKPLATZ, and I replayed his description. TRIGON parked his car along the curb among other cars in front of an apartment building. I stood at a distance in the shadows and watched the area. I walked along the sidewalk near the river to observe the pedestrian traffic in the vicinity. As luck carried me, the courtyard nearest the car was empty. I crossed the street diagonally and walked close to the parked cars. As I passed TRIGON's, I tucked the lighter through the cracked window. Thud and it was done. Off I walked. No one seemed to notice me or to hear my pounding heart.

I retraced my route back to my car and returned to join my sister. In Neal's kitchen I enjoyed a nice cold beer with him along with a silent high five and congratulatory hug. I recall my sister said she had a great evening with a wonderful group of people. She has never asked me where I went.

The CIA office was ecstatic with the successful delivery, and we immediately began the process of planning for the next delivery in June. Included in the cigarette lighter message was a description of a new type of delivery called a timed exchange at a new site code-named LES, meaning *woods*. We took advantage of my surveillance-free status to make this delivery. I would put down a package for TRIGON at LES just before 9:00 p.m. An hour later, he would pick up his package, simultaneously putting down a package for me in the same spot. If he had nothing for us, he was to leave an empty crushed milk carton to let me know he had recovered our package. An hour later, I would return to recover his package or the empty milk carton.

This timed exchange required only one clandestine outing for us, which enhanced the agent's security. Because I didn't have surveillance when I went to this site, TRIGON and I re-used it, effectively making the delivery and pick-up even more secure because we both knew exactly where to find each other's packages, each in place at most an hour. We used this timed exchange delivery system several times at LES and later at another site called SETUN.

With the prospect of a major delivery to TRIGON, the CIA office and HQS discussed TRIGON's request for an L-pill. After hours of discussion, we were unanimous in our moral obligation to him. I had no experience with this, and wondered if this had been done for other agents. It turned out his request was highly unique, and HQS faced bureaucratic difficulties with the approval process. First, they had to figure out who needed to sign off on this, how high up in CIA, or maybe even higher. It may need to go elsewhere in the government. A flap over giving someone poison would definitely have an impact on diplomatic relations. They possibly needed get the Secretary of State as well as the National Security Council involved. There probably exists a Top Secret file somewhere containing this chain of approval signatures. In the end, approval granted at the highest level was not further defined in the cable to Moscow.

Then HQS had difficulties in designing and shipping the poison to Moscow. HQS crafted a small reservoir of poison which fit into the barrel of the large fountain pen. The pen appeared identical to the concealment device for his miniature camera. This fact ultimately proved to be significant. Hand-carrying it on a plane presented some concern about the pen leaking in a pressurized airplane cabin, endangering the courier. Finally, the technical people wrapped and double wrapped the pen, assuring a special courier that the pen was completely sealed inside the shipping package.

Not one of us wanted to provide TRIGON with poison, but we knew it was the right thing to do. His realizing in time, if he were under serious suspicion, concerned us most; simultaneously, we worried that he would take the poison prematurely, thinking he was on the brink of arrest. So, in preparing the pen for delivery at LES, we included a simple note stating we were committed to his mission and continued safety. In the end, we had fulfilled our solemn obligation to him in providing the poison. Ultimately, we had to trust him to determine when and why his final day had come.

A few days after the May 1 delivery, Tim called me into his office and closed the door. Although this was unusual and I had some trepidation, he assured me immediately that it had nothing to do with my performance. To the contrary, he said. He showed me an eyes-only cable from HQS that requested I return to HQS TDY to prepare to meet with a very high level Soviet agent. My role was to convince this agent to return to Moscow where he and I would meet securely under romantic cover, looking like lovers as we strolled in Moscow parks. I was very proud to be selected to participate in this high level and important operation.

My sister was flabbergasted when I came home that evening and told her I was going to fly back to the US with her the next day. We were busy that night, packing her up, and arranging my life for me to be away for two weeks. When she started collecting her purchases during her six-week visit, she noticed that the local grass broom she had purchased in Tbilisi was missing.

We had put it out on the balcony to freeze out any resident bugs. I assumed that someone had stolen it since it could not have blown off the eighth floor balcony. The KGB occasionally entered my apartment in my absence as I noticed things were out of place. We concluded the KGB was mortified that she would take this crude broom home to the US, which would misrepresent their country. Or, we joked, a KGB officer had stolen it for his mother-in-law.

I had no trouble getting a ticket on the twice-weekly Pan Am flight from Moscow to New York. In the mid-1970s, the Pan Am flight rarely flew full out of Moscow. By contrast, the Aeroflot flight was always sold out, taking Russians to visit family members lucky enough to have immigrated to the US. Russians didn't fly on Pan Am because the only way to purchase a ticket for that flight was with US dollars. The ticket on an Aeroflot flight was paid for with rubles.

Before I left work that evening, I told friends in the Embassy I was going home for a short vacation and that it would be more fun flying back with my sister. We always had to develop an effective cover story for trips like this. We did not want the KGB to correlate my travel with any activity that they might suspect was operational. Even though I was not suspected of being CIA, we didn't want to take chances. HQS preferred I return to the US using a benign family visit for cover, made plausible by traveling with my sister.

I took a large suitcase, so I could bring back vegetables and other luxuries I planned on buying. Mary-Alice and I looked like immigrants as we headed out into the apartment hallway with our two large suitcases and carry-on bags. The elevator door opened after the normal long wait. Knowing how quickly the doors shut, without any way to prop them open and no button to keep them from shutting, we rushed to shove in our suitcases and us in behind them. Breathless, we watched the doors close. I jumped up and down to encourage the elevator to begin its descent.

Feeling flustered, but satisfied we had made it into the elevator, we were unprepared when the elevator stopped sooner than we expected. Thinking we had reached the ground floor, I grabbed my suitcase and began to shove it out of the elevator the second the door started to open. But standing right in front of the elevator door was a teenage boy, who immediately lifted his two-wheeler to push it into the elevator. He hadn't anticipated an already crammed elevator and two women shrieking at him to get out of the way and let us off. Trying to push my large bag toward the open door, he tried to fit his bike in. As the doors began to close I jumped back in, and he ricocheted against the closing door out of the elevator.

Fortunately we were still inside and the elevator continued down. Mary-Alice and I were laughing hysterically, tears streaming down our faces as we unloaded us and our luggage from the elevator. We had a car waiting to take us to the airport, one of the few perks that I enjoyed. I am sure the driver thought we were exceptionally happy to be going to the US as we broke into fits of laughter all the way to the airport as we recalled our elevator caper.

I spent a week in HQS reading the agent's file and preparing my pitch to him. After thorough coaching from Ken, a senior officer responsible for this case, I succeeded in convincing the agent to return to Moscow and continue to work for us there. But he never returned to Moscow. Eventually, he defected and lived his life happily ever after in the US. I returned to Moscow, having enjoyed my break in the US. I felt satisfied with what I had accomplished. I had never considered myself a shopaholic, but I had a new appreciation for the expansive choice of things to spend my money on back home. I also loved eating out at nice restaurants with friends. I knew it would be difficult returning to my austere life in Moscow for another year.

While in HQS, I spent time with officers in the USSR Branch, describing the previous drop at STENA and the man I had seen at a distance. They also considered it possible that TRIGON never checked for his package because he hadn't seen a car pass, but they had no definitive answer either. Amazed that I continued to operate without surveillance, we all agreed the probable reason was that I was female, and so, not suspect by the KGB of operating on the streets.

Back in Moscow, I shared the office's excitement at the prospect of the next TRIGON timed exchange at LES. Mike and Ed joked, saying maybe I'd get it right this time and not have to pick up my own package again. With great relief, we saw TRIGON's signal at PARKPLATZ in mid-June, indicating that he was ready to deliver his package at LES, again located at the base of a lamppost.

Coincidentally, this site was originally also written up as a car toss, like the previous site, STENA. But we had warned TRIGON in the cigarette lighter that our officer, who might be a woman, would put down his package while on foot sometime before 9:00 p.m. and then immediately leave the area. We instructed TRIGON to come to LES at 10:00 p.m. to pick up the package and simultaneously leave his package at the same spot. Our officer then would return to the site to pick up his package.

To assure TRIGON that we had picked up his package, we told him our officer would mark a signal that TRIGON could read the next day, a smeared red lipstick streak on the side of a bus shelter on Kutuzovsky Prospekt. Although the lipstick signal would reassure him, we decided after I did it this once that it was far too risky to confirm future drop recovery. Someone could observe the bus shelter from a distance and there was no plausible reason to smear lipstick on the side of the bus shelter glass.

The day of the drop, we had the standard ops meeting to determine my route, parking location, timing, and safety signal. Even though we covered the same topics as in previous ops meetings, I was anxious and worried. I was to deliver the most important package TRIGON had received to date.

Neal meticulously packed the large log concealment device, making sure the contents were cushioned against possible breakage. We knew Neal was being overly cautious because of the poison pen device. He wanted to insure the fragile liquid reservoir could not be damaged during delivery. Instructions on the ops note on kalvar film directed TRIGON to keep this pen in a safe place. We concluded his note by saying we had confidence in his judgment.

Also packed in the log was an identical large pen that concealed his miniature camera. We instructed TRIGON to use this in his office instead of carrying documents home to photograph with his 35mm camera. Neal also packed twenty additional miniature film cassettes. Each cassette had a 120-page capacity, one document page per frame of film. Interestingly, our HQS technical office designed both large pens, so they continued to function as fountain pens. However, if the pen with the camera were examined closely, the camera could be discovered. The poison pen appeared to be unmodified.

Neal included a large roll of small denomination rubles, emerald jewelry, one-time pads, and the kalvar film with TRIGON's ops note, which expressed our relief that he was all right and congratulated him on his last package. We told him how impressed HQS had been with the documents he provided. Although we had discussed with HQS whether we should give him specific tailored guidance on what information HQS would find most valuable, we decided to avoid providing any clue in the package about what TRIGON had access to. If someone else picked up the package, worst case the KGB, we did not want to give specifics that might identify TRIGON. Basically, HQS assured us that any and all documents TRIGON photographed would be of great interest, given the access he had in his office.

Finally, Neal carefully placed a warning notice wrapped around the contents inside the log. It simply said in Russian, "If by chance you have found this log and opened it, you should not go any further. Take this roll of money. Throw the log and the rest of its contents into the river, as possessing this will put you in grave danger." We wanted to give some poor naïve Russian a fighting chance in case he picked up the log and tried to determine who it was intended for or the nature of the contents.

The large log looked impressively realistic when Neal epoxied over the opening with pieces of bark. In fact, no one would know from its outer appearance or heft that it was fake. Only TRIGON would know that it was his because it was lying beside the pole. It didn't fit into my purse as the crushed cigarette pack had on the previous drop. I didn't want to carry it in a plastic shopping bag because someone might snatch it, even though street muggings were rare. I decided to carry it under my coat tucked in the waistband of my pants, keeping it firmly at my side under my arm. I preferred its real tactile presence next to my body.

At 6:00 p.m. I departed from work, as I did most nights, drove home, and waved to the militiaman at my gate. I changed into my street clothes, including my spring jacket, which reached to mid-thigh and hung full, easily accommodating the bulk of the log without a telltale bulge. I packed my purse with my driver's license and several coins for the subway and for an emergency pay-phone call. If I had car trouble and realized I wouldn't get back to the Marine bar in time for my safety signal, I had Neal's home number to call. In that case, I would say something inconsequential and unalerting.

I drove away from my apartment and down Ulitza Vavilova as I had before and began my two-hour vehicular surveillance detection route. In the end I determined no one was following me. Sometimes, when a car fell in behind me I was startled into self-doubt, thinking maybe I just didn't know what surveillance looked like. But then the car would turn off, and I would make a couple of turns and be alone again on back streets, driving through an incongruous web of roads.

I never became blasé in my travels around Moscow prior to a drop. I was dry-mouth alert, checking side streets, and listening to the KGB surveillance frequency, rarely hearing even a faint transmission. Finally, the time came to wend my way to my parking spot and enter the subway. I dreaded the eyes in the subway, never knowing if the man across the aisle was an off-duty surveillance officer, who might find something suspicious about me, or might have seen my photo in a mug book of Americans. Although I tried to blend in with the crowds, I couldn't be absolutely sure. But this night, I was confident as I exited the subway and found myself alone out on the street.

It was light that night because June 21 was mid-summer, the longest day of the year. I strolled along Kutuzovsky Prospekt, judging the time it would take to get to the site and deliver the package by 9:00 p.m. Even with this amount of daylight, I discovered thankfully that the pathway into the park disappeared into dark shadows. The path, set back five or six feet back from the roadway, ran under a full canopy of large leafed trees. Although the dark provided cover, I found it difficult to see whether anyone else was in the park. It remained quiet, though, without street noise or sound of others walking nearby in the woods.

While still in the shadows on the path, I pulled out the log from under my coat and tucked it length-wise under my arm. I walked out toward the street and let the package slide down my arm and gently rest beside the lamppost. I left the park as I had entered. I knew I had at least an hour and a half until I could return. I crossed the wide avenue and slipped into the labyrinth of huge apartment buildings.

I had a lot of time to think about the drop for TRIGON as I walked. The only human contact he had with us was through the residual warmth of the log from its cradle under my arm. I wondered how he sustained himself, taking such significant risks working for us. He had to feel alone, one man against a mighty system. At least in Bogota, he could express himself when he met with our case officers in the safe house. But here, he had no one to share his fears, hopes, and dreams for a future. All he had to hang onto were our somewhat sterile words in the note in this package expressing satisfaction and congratulations. We could offer little human contact to sustain his commitment to his dangerous mission.

My gut felt empty, hollow, thinking about the pen with the poison in the log he was probably picking up at that exact minute. How could he know the precise moment just before he was arrested? And would he find the courage to use the pen? Or would he mistakenly suspect the end was near and use it prematurely? Was his request for the poison male bluster, a gutsy act, never believing we would come through for him? No, I knew he was a courageous man. He had thought all this through, and I kept our promise by delivering the poison. Still I felt sorrow as well as fear for him.

When I returned to the woods, I found a crushed milk carton exactly where I had left the log. As usual, he had smeared the top of the milk carton with a vomit-looking substance, actually the remnants of a mustard plaster, to keep a stranger from picking it up. I gingerly gathered it and put it in a black plastic bag in my purse. Victory was sweet. I had finally completed the first timed exchange in Moscow.

The recovery signal became the only glitch in this outing. I had to make a mark with the bright red lipstick on side of the bus shelter. On the way out of the woods, I glanced across Kutuzovsky and saw people waiting in the shelter. I had no choice but to make the lipstick recovery signal, no matter the conditions.

I strolled up to the shelter as if to wait for a bus. Leaning against the glass on the outside of the shelter, I slowly pulled the opened lipstick from my pocket. So intent on making sure the lipstick mark would be visible, coupled with nerves and adrenaline, I pressed too hard. The lipstick smashed into my fist. Still, I had left a blob of a mark on the side of the shelter. Not glancing down to see my handiwork, and not needing to wait any longer for my fictional bus, I turned and walked away, heading toward the city. On the subway ride back to my car, I had to keep my stained red right fist in my pocket. After this, we advised him by the next radio broadcast that we had recovered his package.

The next morning, I was ecstatic to show the package to those gathered in the Moscow CIA office and to tell them the amazing details of the previous night. The office buzzed with excitement and anticipation as Neal went to open the package. TRIGON had given us rolls of 35mm film, wrapped in prophylactics to protect them from the weather. One roll was his personal note to us. He revealed he had been sick during the winter and unable to make the scheduled drops. He also said that he put his car on blocks in the winter, so he couldn't make the signal at PARKPLATZ. The other 35mm rolls contained invaluable documents Soviet experts in HQS would spend months translating and disseminating. One of these documents showed the routing slip, indicating the relative importance of the document as it was routed up the MFA hierarchy. I liked the security of the timed exchange, and suggested we reuse this site again at LES.

CHAPTER 9

Meeting TRIGON - August 1976

In August, the office made elaborate arrangements for Jack to meet TRIGON face-to-face in a Moscow park. This was no easy trick since Jack had endured almost constant surveillance during his two-year tour. As described in the ops proposal cable to HQS, Moscow's plan depended on getting Jack out on the street without surveillance. The Soviets knew he neared the end of his tour and might try something dramatic or risky before he left, a tactic practiced by most intelligence services. If a soon-to-be-departing officer like Jack was ambushed and expelled, the office had his replacement trained and ready to arrive or possibly already present in Moscow. If an officer was expelled mid-tour, no one was prepared to replace him quickly, leaving the office down one person. In a small CIA office like Moscow in the mid 1970s, being shorthanded by one officer represented a severe disadvantage. For that reason, the office was relieved when Jack managed to elude surveillance and make this extraordinary personal meeting.

Jack later told me that one of the most significant events in his career was meeting TRIGON in Moscow. Our purpose in risking this face-to-face meeting was to personally tell TRIGON we had high admiration for what he had accomplished. Because Jack had developed a strong friendship in Bogota, he could encourage TRIGON and convey to him that we shared his unconditional commitment to our joint mission. Jack acknowledged to TRIGON that we knew he suffered being absolutely alone with no one to trust. Except for the CIA officers he might see in the shadows as he managed to steal Soviet state secrets and pass them in dead drops to us, maintaining his sanity and personal security had to be extremely difficult.

Jack described the meeting with TRIGON in detail. When he and TRIGON spotted one another, they first shook hands, and then forcefully embraced. Jack and TRIGON shared the high emotion of the moment. They both recognized that what TRIGON had committed to do as a covert agent in Moscow took amazing courage and bravery. They spent their first few shared moments expressing how wonderful it was to meet in Moscow.

It was clear TRIGON was nervous, with sweat beading on his upper lip and streaming down the side of his face despite the cool evening. His eyes darted. Watchful, worried about being seen with an American. After they walked through the park for a short distance, they found a bench where they sat out of sight from other paths.

TRIGON shocked Jack when he pulled out of his coat pocket a sheaf of original Soviet MFA documents as well as several 35mm film cassettes. As TRIGON began to hand them to Jack, Jack expressed serious concern that the documents might be missed, but TRIGON assured him he was to have destroyed them in his office, and no one would miss them. Jack quickly folded them and stuffed everything inside his inner jacket pocket, not daring to examine the documents out in the open. If the KGB detained and searched him, he would have no plausible denial for possessing these genuine MFA documents. One of the most significant dangers of meeting agents face to face in Moscow is being set up by an agent-gone-bad and ambushed by the KGB. But we had gauged that the potential gain from this personal meeting with TRIGON justified what we considered a remote risk. Up to this time, we had little evidence to cause serious suspicion about the TRIGON operation.

During their forty-minute meeting Jack articulated the CIA Director's heartfelt congratulations and appreciation to TRIGON. He confirmed that TRIGON had made a major contribution to CIA's rebuilding its reputation tarnished by the investigations conducted by the Senate committee. Jack told

TRIGON that the Director personally passed TRIGON's documents to the US President, and that only a small group of top US foreign policymakers knew of his work on behalf of America. Jack emphasized how his documents enhanced the US government's ability to understand and counter the Soviet government's attempts to influence international conflicts in unstable areas of the world. Jack said that TRIGON looked proud to have this kind of impact by cooperating with us.

Jack told him we were committed to his safety in Moscow and his future life outside the Soviet Union. To reassure TRIGON, Jack reviewed the exfiltration plan with TRIGON, promising him that we were prepared to whisk him out of Moscow the instant he thought he was under suspicion. TRIGON believed he had passed all the major security re-investigations returning diplomats are subjected to and now was convinced he was in the clear. But TRIGON told Jack that his office had been under suspicion the previous month, so he had thrown away his L-pill pen and all his other spy paraphernalia as a precaution. TRIGON reported nothing out of the ordinary happened to him, and the KGB apparently closed that security investigation.

TRIGON then asked Jack to re-supply him with the L-pill, concealed in the pen. Jack felt compelled to discuss the L-pill further, telling TRIGON we continued to be concerned about his using it prematurely. TRIGON reiterated that the L-pill was just for his peace of mind. He promised Jack that, if he found out about any other security investigations being conducted, he would not take any extraordinary risks in collecting documents. With this assurance, Jack told TRIGON that we would resupply the L-pill in his next package. Reluctantly, knowing their meeting had lasted too long, they shared a final handshake. Then each left by a different path out of the park.

Jack said it had been difficult to adequately express our concern to TRIGON about his safety as well as our appreciation of what he was under-taking on behalf of the US government. In meeting with such a courageous man, Jack later told me, he was humbled by TRIGON's simple focus on his mission for CIA. I envied Jack's meeting TRIGON. When TRIGON and I passed anonymously in the night, I wished I could speak to him. I would tell him of my admiration for him and how I understood the challenges we shared as we traversed the Moscow streets alone to make our secret deliveries to one another.

Our chief, Tim, was a wonderful man with a keen sense of humor. As the only other single officer in the office, he and I often shared the difficulties of living alone in Moscow. Once over a few beers during a short party after hours in the office, we started talking about dating in Moscow. We commiserated how it was impossible to slow dance at social events, even with an American, because we always wore concealed antennas and miniature receivers. We worried that our dance partner would feel the bulge of the apparatus strapped under our arms. Taking someone home and discreetly disrobing while removing wires and small metal boxes was impossible. Tim and I laughed uncontrollably as we shared these intimate facts. No one else understood our shared frustrations and why we were uproariously laughing and crying together.

Tim had ongoing problems with KGB surveillance. Not quite harassment, it was more like they enjoyed toying with him. As a clever storyteller, Tim emphasized all the hilarious details, making himself the victim in every funny anecdote. One Monday morning, he regaled us with stories of the past Saturday evening's outing to a restaurant. He and a large group of Americans went to a particularly wild Moscow restaurant where the Soviets always ended up singing and dancing, toasting the Americans they "coincidentally" discovered at the next table. In actuality, we assumed that when we made our reservations through the Embassy, the KGB arranged for either KGB officers or collaborators to sit next to us at a restaurant, in hopes they would overhear revealing conversations or at the least become friendly with the Americans.

For this evening out, Tim had asked Susan, an Embassy secretary, to go with him. The group had an uproarious time, probably drinking more shots of vodka than advisable, but honor was at stake in keeping up with the Soviets at the next table. Much too late, the American group spilled out of the restaurant and headed to their cars, saying good night. They were laughing and kidding Tim about the big fat Soviet woman who thought Tim was such a great dancer. Tim started his Zhiguli, but when he put it into gear to pull away from the curb, the rear wheels spun. He thought the wheels were on ice as it was winter. But when he leaned out his car door, he saw the pavement below was flat and dry. He tried again, but the wheels still spun.

He and the other Americans, who noticed his problem in attempting to pull away from the curb, discovered a large wire dangling down from the top of a defunct lamppost was wound around his rear axel. When he attempted to accelerate, he was actually pulling the top of the lamppost down on top of his car. The whole group screamed in laughter, knowing that Tim often had these kinds of unusual problems. They unwound the wire, and Tim drove off, laughing all the way home. After he finished this amazing story, we all agreed it couldn't have been anyone but his surveillance team screwing around somewhat good-naturedly with him. Tim easily laughed at himself, a wonderful and endearing quality in a leader.

After Jack left in the summer of 1976 right after the TRIGON meeting, we realized how intensely Jack had shepherded all operational factors involved in preparing TRIGON's drop package. Neal and I had to be vigilant so that we forgot nothing. The schedule for deliveries did not allow for mistakes. I worked nights and weekends, casing new drop sites. I reviewed all cables in the office at lunchtime and again at 6:00 p.m. if I was involved in an operation that night. I took ownership of the TRIGON operation and had to make doubly sure we reviewed every detail concerning the contents for TRIGON's package.

I didn't have a good feel for the new CIA officers and Jack's replacement. I wasn't convinced the new officers had the energy and drive to get out on the streets and learn about operating in Moscow. Maybe they were taking stupid chances and shortcuts, not being discreet as they scouted out new sites and re-cased old ones while under the watchful eyes of surveillance teams. The changes in the office were difficult to accept. I was intimate with most of the city and my operational environment, always alert to anything that might be out of place. When asked, I offered these new officers information about areas in the city although surveillance coverage was still not part of my on-street experience. I usually kept my comments limited unless they asked for advice. Learning to operate in Moscow took time, experience, and hard work. No one could tell someone else how to do this.

We were all gearing up for the next TRIGON package for delivery in mid-September 1976. It contained the new communications calendar as well as a resupply of his L-pill pen, that had been hand-carried to Moscow, and a new identical pen loaded with the miniature camera and cassettes. Neal worked hard to wedge all the contents into the hollow log again, the concealment device for the drop.

The night before the scheduled delivery date, TRIGON parked his car at PARKPLAZ. We were relieved to see that nothing had changed for him as evidenced by his making this parked car signal. I was eager to make this delivery at the exchange site LES the next evening. As I was the most experienced now in making these deliveries and pickups, I had developed a keen sense for being on the street, how to act naturally, and what was normal. But, when I thought I had a routine down pat, something popped up to surprise me.

CHAPTER 10

Ponytail

The night grew damper and colder as I made my way toward the World War II Victory Monument Park on Staromozhayskoye Shosse on the east side of Moscow. The fall days offered me benefit of earlier darkness as I walked along busy Kutuzovsky Prospekt. Nerves like I had experienced during previous drops to TRIGON over the past nine months besieged me. My gut turned upside-down.

Approaching the curb, I saw a car heading my way as it exited the one-way road that passed through the park. In my experience, few if any cars were in the park at this late hour, and I was immediately suspicious. Alert to all possibilities, it flashed in my mind that I might be walking into an ambush. Somehow, the agent had been apprehended, and now the KGB waited for me to walk into a trap when I placed the package at our secret site. This car was a scout car out looking for me.

Quieting my overactive, paranoid mind, I didn't look directly into the car as it approached. It wasn't slowing, a good sign. Stories about previous arrests included KGB officers jumping out of a slowing car and grabbing the CIA officer. The headlights on this car were off, standard practice in Moscow where only our parking lights were used. This was a holdover from World War II when the Soviets kept city streets dark to prevent German planes from delineating city boundaries.

The black car was a Volga, just like TRIGON's. I barely glimpsed the front license tag, black letters on white background. MKG- --. But I couldn't catch the numbers. Instant recognition flashed in my mind. Was it TRIGON's tag? Quickly, I glanced in the passenger window. I saw a female with a blond ponytail. The car's dim interior obscured the driver's identity, but he was a dark-haired man. As the car passed, I clearly saw the rear tag. It was TRIGON's. My heart double-timed on an instantaneous adrenaline high.

He shouldn't be here yet and certainly not with a woman in his car. He was over an hour early to be anywhere in the area. We had told him to follow our instructions and arrive on time, neither early, nor late. Of course, we never thought to tell him to come alone. That was too obvious to point out.

The tail lights indicated the car made a left onto Mozhayskoke Shosse, a major avenue. I crossed the street and entered the dark path that passed through dense trees and bushes, totally hidden from the street through the park. I was still trying to figure out why he had come early and driven through the park. I continued into the park as if nothing different had happened, but I was unsure. I had a real dilemma. Actually, more than one.

I had to relieve myself; nothing allowed me to ignore this. I walked off the path, and ducked under low hanging eye-poking branches, desperately searching for a remote spot. I always kept a wad of toilet paper in my pocket for these emergencies. It was hard to picture a proper, sophisticated American woman squatting in the woods in Moscow. That's why I silently laughed when a fellow case officer asked whether I was certain I had no surveillance following me.

Feeling better, I continued to worry about TRIGON's presence here. Why had he brought a woman with him and how did this change my plan to make the drop tonight? This is why I was paid big bucks, to make these critical judgments. HA, that was hardly true as I was the lowest in rank and pay among the case officers in the Moscow office.

I had to think. TRIGON must have brought her as cover for being out on a fall night stroll in the woods, but this didn't make sense. He couldn't explain to her why he was picking up a log in the woods, even though it looked like a real log. He lived in an apartment without a wood-burning stove, so he had no need for this log. As before, Neal had sealed it, carefully adding loose dirt and bark to make it even more natural looking.

If TRIGON left Ponytail, my instantaneous nickname for her, in the car, I couldn't imagine how he would explain to her why he walked into the woods at this hour carrying his briefcase. Maybe he had revealed to her what he was up to when she had become suspicious and challenged him. The most disastrous possibility was that she was a KGB plant directed to become romantically involved with TRIGON so she could discover whether he was spying for a foreign government. TRIGON was a notorious lady's man.

I had to decide whether to make this drop to him. This delivery was essential to the operation's continuation because it included the schedule for future exchanges. He hadn't received a new package since June when he returned his miniature camera and cassettes filled with photographs of Secret documents. This new miniature camera, again concealed in a large pen, was easily and openly pocketed, a concealment device in plain view. But I could not leave the pen with the poison to chance discovery by someone other than TRIGON, if he did not come to pick it up.

Approaching the drop site at the base of the lamppost along the road through the park, I stopped in the shadows and listened. Total silence. I reached under my coat and pulled out the log tucked securely inside my waistband. As before, I slid the log down the outside of my leg. With a slight thud, it came to rest at the base of the pole. I wondered if the light from this lamppost was brighter than most in Moscow, but decided that impression was the result of my adrenaline-fueled imagination. The package lay naturally in a shadow at the back of the pole away from the road.

I considered what to do now. Strategies for TRIGON's appearing as he had tonight were never discussed in the office planning meetings. I had to make this decision, based solely on my experience and operational instinct.

When I took the Internal Operations Course, Bernie and Roy consistently emphasized that the surest deterrent to discovery was to keep moving after making a drop. This action would drag a surveillance team away from the drop site. They taught me never to pause, turn my head, or fumble in my purse after I made a drop. Any gesture might make the surveillance team suspicious. But I had no surveillance team watching me. I was alone in the woods.

Another inviolable rule enforced by Bernie and Roy was never to use a site more than once. TRIGON and I had used LES twice. Because we could count on my never having surveillance, thus never exposing the drop site to the KGB, we had decided that re-using a familiar site with TRIGON eliminated the chance that he might not find the package at a new unfamiliar site.

As I started back up the path away from the log, I was convinced of one thing. I could not abandon this package with its precious, deadly payload. I had to be absolutely certain that TRIGON picked it up. If he didn't, I would retrieve my own package. Or, if a stranger picked it up, who didn't look like TRIGON, I would know the operation had been compromised.

I decided to stay and keep the package in sight. I broke the most sacrosanct rule. I wondered whether I could explain to the Chief why I made this decision. I would think about that later, knowing that I made the only right decision.

I walked off the side of the path to find a place to wait, hidden. I found a full non-prickly bush and backed into it, nestling under the low branches. I folded my legs under me, wondering how long I could sit in that position and how long before TRIGON would appear. I wiggled myself into the dry leaves to settle myself lower for more camouflage. My legs were telling me there was no chance of falling asleep.

Doubts flooded my mind. If TRIGON sees me, he will think I am a KGB stake-out, waiting to catch him as he picks up the CIA's package. I knew it would be disastrous if he spotted me. Scared off forever, he would likely not chance making another exchange with us. That would make my decision wrong and impossible to justify to the office. That would probably be my last decision in Moscow, knowing how important TRIGON's information was to the US Government's foreknowledge of the Soviet Union's positions on important issues.

An hour passed. I tried to breathe slowly, evenly, but my chest was taut. While I was beginning to worry about unseen forest animals attacking me, I heard the crunch of dry leaves barely five feet away. A man carrying a large briefcase passed me. It was TRIGON.

I watched him go directly to the pole and set down his European-style briefcase. After opening the briefcase's wide top, he leaned over. I couldn't see exactly what he was doing from my seated position, but assumed he placed his milk carton, and then picked up the log. He closed the briefcase. He didn't pause. He turned, walking briskly past me back up the path. When I could no longer here the sound of his footsteps, I began to breathe again.

I couldn't believe it happened just like that. And then he was gone. I waited ten minutes. I replayed the fifteen-maybe-thirty-second scene that had unfolded. It worked. He hadn't seen me. I knew it was TRIGON although I had never been this close to him.

Now, I could get up from the bush. At first my legs refused to work. Slowly, I stood, looking around and sucking in fresh night air. I fully appreciated the surrounding cloak of darkness.

Walking briskly to the base of the pole, I picked up his crushed milk carton. It was camouflaged with his signature disguise, the same mustard plaster, which dripped down the sides of the carton to make it unappealing to anyone who might think it was valuable trash. I quickly stuffed it into the plastic bag in my purse and left the park.

All the way home questions revolved in my mind. Ponytail's identity and the reason she was with him? His story to her about why he had to leave her in the car alone while he walked into the woods with his briefcase at 10:00 p.m. Primarily, I worried about what she knew.

Arriving home, I was exhausted. I changed into my flannel nightgown with some effort. As I lay down, I put the purse with its precious contents beside my pillow, looped my arm through the purse strap and fell asleep. It was early when I woke. As I stretched, the tug on my arm confirmed the past night's activity as reality, regardless of how nightmarish it had seemed.

Early that morning in the office, I described the past evening's events, and we discussed Jack's account of his meeting with TRIGON in August. We recalled that TRIGON had displayed anxiety, sweating and looking around nervously. These could have been indications that TRIGON was simply concerned for his safety in the company of a known CIA officer. Or, the meeting could have been set up by the KGB. TRIGON might have been concerned that Jack would spot TRIGON's KGB handler hiding nearby in the park during this personal meeting. Now, with the appearance of Ponytail, we were unsure of the state-of-play in this deadly game.

The most important part of the night, I learned, was that I knew without any reservation that TRIGON had picked up the package. As the events played out in this operation, this fact was to be the most significant.

We were all disappointed that the crushed milk carton was empty, as I had suspected from its weightlessness. We figured that, during the August personal meeting with Jack, TRIGON had passed Jack all the documents he had accumulated. Our greatest relief was that, with this delivery to TRIGON at LES, he was back in business with a new communication schedule for drops and deliveries. He now also had the miniature camera as well as the poison pen. The other case officers kidded me about being jealous that I had been replaced by Ponytail. Managing to share a laugh, I told them TRIGON was true to me, that she was just a decoy for his being out at night.

The analysis of Ponytail's appearance at LES continued in our dialogue with the USSR Branch at HQS. There Jack as Chief tried his best to support us as we wrestled with nagging unanswered questions. We continued to prepare to recover TRIGON's next delivery to us in October. Our intention was to proceed with TRIGON's schedule and to strongly suggest in our next package that he come to sites alone.

The next October pick-up in Lenin Hills was a one-way delivery from TRIGON to us. We designed the site, so we could service the drop while under surveillance. Having seen TRIGON's car at PARKPLATZ at 7:00 p.m., the CIA officer headed up to the site that same night. The large trees around the Lenin Hills park provided deep shadows to conceal his activity.

As he approached the package location down in a small hollow, he was startled to see the large log from our last delivery to TRIGON at LES. How clever that TRIGON had repacked the log, putting his film and note inside, and then resealed the log, using dirt and leaves, imitating Neal's technique to hide the opening. The officer reported the log fit in well, concealed by the dark among the leaves and tree limbs. TRIGON was a clever agent to reuse the log in such a perfect location, which was what we had come to expect from him.

The following morning, Neal carefully unpacked the log. Among the miniature cassettes, Neal found TRIGON's 35mm film containing his personal note, saying he had health problems, including losing his hair, enduring severe chest pains, and generally was unable to sleep. He asked for more guidance on the types of documents we wanted. He clearly felt the stress of his secret life. HQS recommended that we address these health problems in December's package by providing him mega-vitamins and a form of mild tranquilizer.

The analyst in HQS evaluated the documents he photographed using the miniature camera. To our relief, she saw no change in the types of documents or quality of photography. The same HQS technical officer who always developed the miniature film said his technique appeared to be consistent with his previous deliveries. We relied on HQS for such evaluations since we never saw the developed miniature film.

In December, Neal filled a smaller log concealment device with pharmaceuticals which HQS' medics thought might alleviate TRIGON's physical problems. As before, I delivered it at LES, where snow lay on the ground. The log blended into the shadow behind the pole. I decided to continue walking down the path after making the drop, instead of retracing my steps. After the last drop and Ponytail's appearance, I was uncertain where TRIGON had parked, as indicated by the direction he had entered the park. I wanted to avoid any possibility of running into him, so I continued down the path, passed into the area of large blocks of apartment buildings on Kutuzovsky Prospect. After I walked a long distance, I returned across Kutuzovsky to the far end of the path and then walked back up the other side. Enough snow had fallen to obscure my footprints. After an hour had passed, I assumed TRIGON had likely come for his package and left.

The park was still. Snow on the ground makes the world silent, almost like wearing earmuffs. At least the snow had stopped, or I would have been a walking snowman. Up the path on the opposite side of the street, I crossed over to the LES lamppost. I barely slowed as I came even with the pole, listening and looking to make sure no one was around.

Certain I was alone, I saw the lump of the milk carton, this time covered by a dark oily rag. I picked up the whole thing and slipped the mess into the small black plastic bag in my purse. I walked into the shadowy path and headed out of the woods. Now that the adrenaline rush of making the pickup was over, I was tired and getting cold. Ready to be home, I still had a considerable distance to walk before I could rest in the subway car. I saw no other pedestrians. When I exited the deserted subway, as usual I altered my route back to my car. Finally, I dropped into the car seat and immediately locked the door. I breathed long and deep in relief. I was exhausted. It was time to be home, tucked into bed. At least this delivery had been uneventful.

But again the milk carton was empty. Although we had hoped he would provide miniature cassettes with current information, we were satisfied that he had our package. Maybe the vitamins and mild tranquilizers would allow TRIGON to relax and recover his energy and stability. We tried to remain upbeat about TRIGON's welfare, but we worried about him.

CHAPTER 11

Concerns for TRIGON

The winter of 1977 was marked by extreme weather with temperatures dipping to into the minus 30-40 F in January and February. I spent free time on weekends cross-country skiing in the pristine forests surrounding Moscow. Enjoying the crystal clear days made Moscow winters tolerable. My friend, Ellen, and I enjoyed skiing together because we had about the same ability. We laughed uproariously when either fell or slid helplessly off the trail. We tried to get out to the birch forest skiing before noon, returning to my apartment by mid-afternoon since winter daylight didn't last long. On these clear blue-sky winter days, the sun appeared on the horizon at about 9:00 a.m., followed a low arc, and fell out of sight by 3:30 p.m.

From the Embassy, Ellen drove out to my apartment, and we easily loaded our skis into my Zhiguli between the driver and passenger seats extending to the rear window. We both had bought our skis from the Helsinki store, Stockmann's, our first year in Moscow. We simply provided the store's phone clerk our European measurement in height and shoe size on a Tuesday and they shipped our gear that Friday. It all fit perfectly, as if we had been personally measured, and was comparatively inexpensive.

We drove five to ten kilometers from my apartment, where we parked on the wide shoulder, put on our skis and slid off into the pristine forests. When we stopped on the trail to rest and appreciate the stillness and beauty, I saw the frost from her breath had painted Ellen's bright Irish red hair on each side of her face. We skied down the endless, straight paths of planted birch and fir-lined. Occasionally, we heard strains of Tchaikovsky, likely from another skier's transistor radio. It was idyllic and remote by contrast to the ugly, drab city life in Moscow.

On March 8, 1977, a Soviet holiday in Moscow known as International Communist Women's Day, we decided to take our final ski outing. Although tens of feet of snow had fallen throughout the winter, we knew our skiing days were numbered, soon to be followed by a long mud season in Moscow when everything dripped and melted, turning white snow to brown sludge. As usual, few people were out in what we now considered our own ski forest. Off we went, Ellen taking the lead. We had a favorite long straight run, white birch on our right and deep green firs to our left. It wasn't a steep run, but it ended in a gentle drop off, kind of a mini ski jump, followed by a smooth, somewhat speedy run down into the meadow. I watched Ellen several yards ahead of me slide effortlessly down the path.

Over the edge she went. But then, all I saw were skis and poles flying into the air. I managed to stop just before I dropped over the same edge. Below the lip at the path's end, the snow had melted into exposed dirt and mud that had brought Ellen to an abrupt, mud-covered stop. We laughed hysterically as she picked herself up, trying to brush off the mud, dirt and slushy wet snow. It was the last time we skied in Moscow.

When winter temperatures dipped to minus 40 F, I was surprised I could feel the difference from minus 20 F. I had figured cold was cold. But the moisture inside my nostrils actually froze at these lower extreme temperatures. When a group of us went to the American *dacha*, an old stone and wood house outside of the city in a village called Tarasovka about 50 minute's drive north from the center of Moscow, I had to bring my car battery inside overnight to warm it, so would start the next morning for the trip back to Moscow.

The *dacha* was a great place to escape from the rigors of Moscow life. Each American family (a single person, in this case, was considered a family unit) had a turn staying at the *dacha* for a week or weekend during a two-year tour. The summer was lovely at the *dacha* —long day-lit nights, paddling a canoe or small boat on a river behind the *dacha*, hiking through the neighboring village with old wooden houses and a single water pump in the village center. In the winter, we skied to the village, sometimes sledding down the slope from the *dacha* onto the frozen river. A Russian caretaker lived on the property and kept the huge wooden boxes outside the back door full of dry firewood to fuel the massive stone fireplace that heated most of the downstairs. Sleeping upstairs in winter was like camping out at the Arctic Circle although the *dacha* was furnished with many thick blankets.

I actually loved the winter in Moscow and was fascinated by the unique effects of the frigid temperatures. After very cold clear nights, very fine snow covered my car, even though there was not a cloud in the sky. Bill, my scientist neighbor, explained that this was a type of hoar frost that crystallized from the atmosphere when the air was too cold to hold the humidity. Fortunately, I enjoyed the winter and never felt the cold like others did, considering the hours I spent out on the street.

According to his schedule, TRIGON was to deliver a package to us in January 1977 at one of the ski areas out past my apartment. The actual site, VALUN, meaning *boulder*, was located down the main path beside "a prominent rock that would be visible even in the deepest snow," according to the casing report. We knew from our experience from the previous two years that TRIGON failed to show up for operational activity in the winter. He told us he had been in a sanatorium the past winter for a respiratory ailment. Thus, our expectations were not high for this delivery from him.

So, when we saw his car at PARKPLATZ on the scheduled Friday evening before the Saturday delivery date, we were surprised. I was selected to pick up TRIGON's package because I could probably count on not having surveillance, and the site was not far from my apartment where I had skied once or twice. When I awoke early that Saturday morning, I discovered absolutely torrential snow falling. It must have been accumulating at a minimum of two or three inches per hour, approaching white-out conditions. Not to be deterred, I donned my full ski attire, including bib overall down ski pants, and pale blue down parka with an attached down hood to keep the snow from drifting down my neck, as well as heavy black gloves.

I nodded to the militiaman holed up in his shack to keep warm and dry as I left the apartment with skis in hand around 9:00 a.m. to make a short run to determine whether I had surveillance. The site was designed to be serviced under surveillance because there was good cover to stop beside the rock to put on skis and adjust boots. So, even if I discovered I had surveillance, I could still collect TRIGON's package without the surveillance team suspecting I was operational. But, as always, I had no surveillance.

I likely appeared to be crazy going out in this blizzard, but the driving was not difficult. I had studded snow tires that had saved me from many slippery icy ditches. Soon, I realized I was driving almost entirely alone. Few cars ventured out on this snowy Saturday morning. Most were heading toward town as I proceeded in the opposite direction. I parked on the shoulder of the road, making sure I pulled over far enough so no one would hit my car. The car soon became a lump, fully obscured by snow. I would worry about digging out later.

I collected my skis and poles and entered the park. Coming around the bend in the path, I saw the rock but was amazed how covered it was by snow, as though snow had been poured over it like icing. Only the slightest indentation delineating where the rock ended and the ground began was visible. I figured the package had been in place for an hour at most as TRIGON had been instructed to put his package down right before 9:00 a.m. It was now 10:00 a.m. If he had been there, his tracks had been obliterated by snow.

I came around to the backside of the rock and leaned my skis against it, knowing this was where he had been instructed to place his package. I had hoped to see a slight bump, but the snow was smooth. I began to dig in the general area where I knew the package would be. We hadn't specified the concealment for his package at this site. I assumed it would be something crushed, like a milk carton or can, or a nasty rag or even an old ski cap.

The more I dug, the more certain I became that it wasn't there. But maybe the snow had disoriented me, and I was on the wrong side of the rock. I nonchalantly moved around the rock, disturbing the snow over a wide margin out from the base by dragging my ski poles and the toes of my boots. But there was no package. Inwardly, I was becoming frantic, hoping it was there, but doubting the more I dug. I kept looking around, but no one appeared in the woods with me. I figured I was alone out in this blizzard. By now, I had uncovered and sifted through every bit of snow at the base of the rock. The package was not there.

Realizing I had searched futilely for at least twenty minutes, I returned to the car. I quickly shoved the accumulated piles of snow off the windshield and back window and slowly opened the door. A big clump of snow fell from the edge of roof over the door onto my seat. Brushing most of it out, I slid into the dryness and some residual warmth. I actually was not cold, having worked up nervous energy digging. My concern about not having found the package caused a deep exhaustion. Being Saturday, I had no one to tell about this miserable, unsuccessful outing.

On Monday I told the office that TRIGON had not left a package for us. Logically, we reasoned the blizzard had kept TRIGON home, but we were deeply disappointed. We had not made the recovery signal to him on Saturday night in his neighborhood, so he knew we had not recovered his package, if he had left one. In the absence of our signal, he was to go out and recover his own package. Whether TRIGON made the delivery at VALUN was to remain a mystery.

LES was our next scheduled delivery site to him in February. We were relieved that there would be no ambiguity about where this package would be. Although I was becoming more concerned about TRIGON, he parked his car at PARKPLATZ according to schedule. Elated, I headed out to LES the next evening with new optimism. Maybe he was all right, and we could resume our regular exchanges.

Amidst the deep piles of snow, it was a peaceful night in the park. But, TRIGON had not been there. He had not taken our package, nor had he left a package at the base of the lamppost. No crushed milk carton, no oily rags. All I saw when I returned was our log, lying where I had put it. I had a knot in my stomach, the resumption of a gnawing unease that something bad had happened to TRIGON. I just couldn't explain this away since he had always left a package here. Now, we began to make excuses for TRIGON.

On the next scheduled date in early April, he again signaled with his car at PARKPLATZ that he had a delivery for us. The site for this drop site, named SOBOR meaning *cathedral*, was near an old abandoned church on the outskirts of Moscow where Mike had taken the infamous photograph of his car antenna. When Mike had originally cased the site, he had been under surveillance. Now on this approach, he could predict how surveillance would act as he came up to the church. Mike easily recovered the package concealed by the confusion of his family and dog getting out of the car.

The contents of TRIGON's package were even more worrisome. Several miniature cassettes were wrapped as usual in a prophylactic to keep them dry while they were exposed to the elements. Neal set them aside to pouch back to HQS. TRIGON's ops note on 35mm film included pages from notes he apparently had prepared for his January delivery, but he did not say whether he had actually delivered that package. In the note he prepared for this delivery, he said his health continued to deteriorate but without further explanation.

Neal pointed out that the quality of TRIGON's 35mm photography was poor in contrast to previous packages. Strangely, Neal found a piece of the 35mm leader clipped off and loose in the bottom of the film canister. Neal told us something I never knew. Film can be re-developed without deleterious effect to the film. Neal said he had never examined the 35mm film before he dropped it in the developer, so, in fact, it could have been developed previously and read by someone else. Neal sensed there was something very different about this package. We all concluded with growing alarm that we were compiling a list of too many unexplained issues.

We had exhausted the schedule of deliveries and now had to revert to slipping a package into TRIGON's car window at PARKPLATZ in mid-April 1977. This was the riskiest delivery process of all. If a case officer was observed while in direct contact with TRIGON's car, the contact was no longer anonymous, unlike an innocuous log in the woods separated by time with no direct contact between TRIGON and an American. Although I could complete this delivery again, Tim decided to test his new deputy, John's, mettle and send him out to deliver the package.

John had not done any operational act since his arrival eight months earlier. He kept to himself in the office and did not offer to go out on the street. He seemed removed from the office and operations, although he and his wife had produced several good casing reports for new sites. I thought he lacked nerve although his wife didn't, from what I had seen of her. John seemed content to have the title and sit in on the meetings, but he offered little substantive comment. He didn't seem to have the qualities necessary to face the risk of being a CIA officer in such a hostile, dangerous setting.

When we had the preliminary ops meeting to discuss John's plan to deliver to TRIGON at PARKPLATZ, John said simply that he would park a few blocks from the site after he drove what I considered a short and less-than-conclusive route to determine if he had surveillance. It was almost too much for me to contain myself, but I resisted and let Tim suggest that parking so close might compromise the site and the agent. This was especially true if John had not determined without a doubt that he had no surveillance. John countered that he had adequate cover for him and his wife to walk down to the river for a stroll and to pass TRIGON's car when he would make the delivery by sleight-of-hand. Tim calmly stated that wouldn't work. I was screaming with horror silently, knowing that John would drag a surveillance team right to TRIGON's car, thereby sealing TRIGON's fate.

It finally became clear to Tim that John just didn't understand the risks of operating in Moscow. John must have figured, if he didn't see surveillance, he didn't have it. Surveillance was often very difficult to smoke out. It took time, distance, and special techniques to spot surveillance, all of which he seemed to have somehow missed in his training. He also apparently thought that, if the cover for an operational act made sense to him, surveillance would just let him go without paying attention.

I was annoyed to see someone being given a challenging assignment to Moscow without taking our ultimate responsibility for our courageous agents' lives seriously. John just didn't get it. We held TRIGON's life in our hands. This was not some diplomatic game. This was a deadly serious commitment we had made to all of our agents. I genuinely feared what would happen when Tim left that summer and a new Chief arrived who might think John was sufficiently experienced in operating in Moscow. But, for the moment, I focused on was my overwhelming concern about TRIGON.

Another experienced officer was selected to deliver the package into TRIGON's car, being very cautious, scanning the approach and the surrounding area around PARKPLATZ for a KGB stakeout or some indication that TRIGON's car was being watched. These indicators might prove he was under suspicion. We all sighed with relief, hoping we could get this operation back on track. We wanted to come through this long dark winter and re-establish reliable two-way communications with TRIGON.

We were amazed and relieved to find TRIGON triggered a delivery at LES a short four days after the successful PARKPLATZ delivery by parking at PARKPLATZ again. LES had become a routine delivery although I was still anxious about TRIGON's well being, given the anomalies in his film in his previous package and his self-reported declining health.

With great relief our timed exchange at LES appeared to come off as usual, successfully. TRIGON retrieved my package and left a crushed milk carton at the same spot for me.

This time, however, Neal was even more concerned when he discovered that the quality of TRIGON's photography, all on 35mm film, was worse than in the previous package. TRIGON had been consistently meticulous in his photography, all framed perfectly, with sequential pages of documents. But in this package, several photographed pages were incomplete, blurred, or only partially legible. Most pages contained portions of documents, some uncentered and out of frame. I was beginning to doubt that TRIGON was going to survive. Nothing seemed right. TRIGON, who had been so predictable, had become erratic. Maybe it wasn't TRIGON anymore, but someone trying to replicate TRIGON's covert work with us.

We had to confront the possibility that TRIGON was under KGB control and that they were reducing the amount and quality of useable documentary information in these packages. If so, the KGB was trying to string us along while giving up very little or, in fact, no intelligence of value. We decided to proceed as if he were going through a bad patch. Still, deep down we were aware that TRIGON may have met his end.

In the April PARKPLATZ car window delivery, we included sketches for a new site for TRIGON's next timed exchange in mid-May called SETUN. The site was located in a narrow window inside a stone pillar on the Krasnoluzhskiy Most, a railroad bridge near Lenin Stadium. The bridge spanned the Moscow River with a pedestrian walkway running parallel to the tracks. The site could not have been serviced under surveillance since there was no plausible reason for an American to walk across this bridge. I hadn't re-cased it before I used it, because it was a straightforward site with no chance for misreading where to place the package.

As usual, during the ops planning meeting, I ran through my schedule and route leading up to the emplacement of the package. I felt more apprehensive about what might happen that night as I headed home to change clothes and start my extensive surveillance detection route.

After driving three hours throughout the far reaches of Moscow and determining I had no surveillance, I parked by a theater on a side street near the center of Moscow where other foreigners frequently parked. I entered the metro and sat quietly on the subway car, casually observing fellow passengers. No one seemed to notice me. I made two subway line changes and exited at Lenin Stadium. As I walked toward the river and the bridge, I appreciated the quiet night. Thankfully, there was no sporting event that night at the stadium.

I approached the bridge along the sidewalk next to the river, scanning the bridge's walkway across the river and down side-streets near Novodyevichy Cemetery. Confident I was alone and unobserved, I climbed the forty-plus steps to the top of the bridge. The bridge had four pillars, two on each side of the river, one on either side of the railroad tracks. They looked like guardhouses with large decorative balls perched on the top of each one. Inside the walkway through the first pillar, the narrow window was at shoulder height in the right wall of the pillar.

Inside the pillar, I quickly pulled the package out of my purse and pushed it into the window as far as my arm extended. Pitch black inside the window, no one could see the concealment device, a dark piece of concrete. I immediately returned down the stairs and left the area, walking into a Soviet neighborhood behind Novodevichy Cemetery where I would wander until time to climb back up onto the bridge, hopefully to find TRIGON's package. When I returned to the pillar, my heart was beating fast as I reached into the dark window. With great relief, I touched the crushed milk carton exactly where I had left TRIGON's package. All of a sudden the evening had become more peaceful as I retraced my long route back to the metro and my car.

I was high the next morning when I arrived at the office with TRIGON's package, thinking we were back on track. But my optimistic hopes crashed when Neal brought in TRIGON's ops note on the 35mm film. TRIGON said that the KGB had been inspecting his department again. He had decided to cooperate with the KGB in his office, hoping that, if he agreed to inform on others, it might take the heat off of him. He provided no documents in his package. We had to face the horrific truth that TRIGON's situation was deteriorating. Our fears of the worst-case scenario were coming closer to reality. He could be under the KGB's control, especially because he enclosed no documents.

In our package at SETUN we gave TRIGON a date for our next exchange at LES, June 28, 1977. We confirmed LES was the site, not providing a sketch since he knew it intimately. We did not ask him to park his car at PARKPLATZ the night before the drop date as we assumed he would be there.

Right after lunch on the day of the exchange Tim called a brief ops meeting to review my plan for the night as well as to thoroughly discuss potential problems I might encounter. No one would admit we had serious concerns about whether TRIGON had survived. The indicators were not good. I also made sure that my after-action safety signal was clear. I wanted the assurance that, if I were arrested, someone would take action to rescue me at the earliest possible hour.

At 6:00 p.m. I collected the package from Neal. Armed with his sober "good luck," I headed home. The young militiaman greeted me as I ran past him into the building to change clothes as it had started to rain torrents, unusual for Moscow. As I drove away from my apartment, I figured I was going to get wet that night. After spending two hours running a surveillance route and parking on a back street, I entered the subway. It continued to rain as I walked the familiar sidewalk along Kutuzovsky Boulevard to the park. I wore a plain dark rain jacket that I knew blended in with the attire of Soviet women on the street that night. Although it would have made sense to carry an umbrella, they were not common, and I didn't want to call attention to myself.

The package was a log, similar to the previous one we had used at LES, but thankfully this one was thinner and shorter. As before, I tucked it in the waistband of my pants and held it tight against my body. I wanted to transmit my personal message to TRIGON through the residual body warmth in the log, the only piece of my humanity I could provide him as we passed anonymously in the night. It was my small effort to fill the void of his lack of human contact in these impersonal exchanges. My rain jacket fit loosely over the package.

This night, TRIGON did not pass in his car with Ponytail. In fact, no traffic traveled through the park. I walked into the woods, passing the bush I had crouched under so many months earlier. But tonight, it was different because of the rain. The noise of the steady rain seriously restricted my ability to hear whether anyone lurked nearby. I had always counted on hearing the crunch of broken sticks or rustling leaves to alert me to someone's presence. I stood still in the darkness of the path, reassuring myself that no one was in the woods with me. I also knew that I had arrived later than usual. I had to get the log in place and leave the park, so I would not run into TRIGON. I didn't want to cause him to abort his pickup and delivery.

I let the log slide down my leg. It landed in the shadow behind the pole. I immediately exited the park and crossed the broad boulevard to lose myself deep in the neighborhood of multi-entrance, immense apartment buildings where I spent the hour before returning to the site. At each turn in the path wandering around the apartment buildings, I concluded that I walked alone. It continued to rain. This calmed me as I began my return to LES. Maybe TRIGON had just had a bad spell and could now begin to rebuild his confidence with this new package from us.

I reached the park at the designated hour and slowly made my way down the familiar path. But then, I saw something that stopped me cold. All my spy training alarms went off in my brain. A small Soviet delivery van sat parked under the street light on the opposite side of road. I hardly breathed. I scanned the path for people lurking in the shadows ready to grab me. I stood in the darkness and stared at the van through the dripping branches of bushes and trees. The front windows were fogged up, and the cab light was on. Oh, to have superwoman's ability to see inside.

. Luckily for me, the rain had almost stopped, making it easier to hear noises in the woods surrounding me. I saw no one around the van and no one was on the path. With caution, I slowly continued down the path past the van and past the LES lamppost, not daring to go near it. I remained in the darkness of the path, figuring I would walk farther down and wait before returning to see whether the van had left. I would not go near the lamppost until I knew it was safe. I was extremely apprehensive, wondering why this van had appeared and whether TRIGON had safely recovered the log and left me a package. I had never seen a van, or in fact any vehicle, stopped on this road. It was hard to believe this van was here by coincidence, that it had parked here tonight while I was out making this delivery to TRIGON.

I continued down the path to another path intersection. Startled to my core, I jumped back as I almost collided with a tall man carrying a flashlight the size of a baseball bat. By his reaction, he seemed genuinely surprised, too. He wore a long dark raincoat and a military hat with a shower-cap-affair over the brim and the top. We made no eye contact but continued in our individual directions, me down the path and he out onto the road. I walked with purpose for a long distance, not daring to look back. When I finally decided to stop, I moved into the edge of a large bush off the path to conceal myself in case he came down the path looking for me, armed with his flashlight.

I waited, heart pounding, ears alert, eyes straining. All remained silent, deadly still, with just a few drips of remnant rain. Minutes became half an hour when I finally decided to cautiously cross the road and walk up the path under the trees on the other side of the road. I inched my way up to where I judged the van had been parked. I started to breathe again. It was gone. I was alone again.

Adrenalin pumped through my system as I collected the nerve to cross the street, cutting close beside the LES lamp post. I spotted my log exactly where it had landed. I bent over enough just to pick it up. Under the trees on the path, I never slowed but headed out of the park, repositioning the log under my coat inside my waistband. I was devastated to have recovered my own package. TRIGON had not been there that night, making the presence of the van and the man in the raincoat truly ominous signs. There is no such thing as a coincidence in espionage.

I entered the Marine bar that night after changing out of my wet clothes in my friend's apartment. I'm sure my face revealed to Tim that the outing had not been successful. Little could he know how horrifying it had actually been. I joined a group of friends standing in a circle drinking beer. One of them playfully stepped on my toes. When I kind of winced at the pain and pushed him away, he jokingly said to the group, "Gee, it looks like you've been ridden hard and put away wet!" Everyone laughed and I tried to look like my jovial self. Little did they suspect the truth of that statement. Inside, I was weeping, sober, incredibly sad. After drinking a beer, I drove home, keeping the log next to me in the bed. Sleep came from exhaustion but certainly not peace of mind.

I woke early and headed to the office with a heavy heart. Tim and the assembled case officers were shocked as I recounted the harrowing events of the previous evening. No one could share my deep distress, verging on abject grief. I had been responsible for this brave man, and now I was sick with worry about what might have happened to him.

His radio broadcast became our sole means of communication with TRIGON. In the briefest message possible, we told him to park at PARKPLATZ on July 14 or make a marked signal at the new signal site early the morning of July 15. We would deliver that same night, July 15, at SETUN. We only had two weeks to prepare this new package.

CHAPTER **12**

The Final Chapter

We were anxious about whether TRIGON could copy our radio broadcast and whether the instructions were clear to him. We always instructed him in our packages that, if his car were inoperable, he should resort to the back-up marked signal. We knew he hated making marks. I fully agreed with him, having only made that one lipstick mark on the glass side of the bus stop. I appreciated how blatant it felt, right out in the open, especially because anyone could see what I had done, no matter how discreet I tried to be. The mark remained. And the KGB could stake out the mark signal site to see who came near it and might be "reading it."

So for this delivery on July 15, TRIGON was to park his car at PARKPLATZ on the evening of Thursday, 14. That evening between 7:00 p.m. and 9:00 p.m. several case officers, including me, passed PARKPLATZ on our normal routes home. But TRIGON had not parked his car there.

As the alternative to PARKPLATZ, he would mark the signal site, called DETI, meaning *children* in Russian. We instructed him to make a red mark on a "child crossing" sign mounted five feet up on a lamp post. The lamp post could be seen along a route I often drove to work, so I could read the marked signal within my well-established pattern. A sketch and instructions for DETI had been included in TRIGON's May package, delivered on the bridge at SETUN.

On Friday, July 15, at my regular morning commute time, I headed toward the office on my route past DETI. From more than two blocks away, I saw the red mark on the sign. It looked as if it had been stenciled, cherry red, drawn evenly inside a definite outline. My heart in my throat, I continued past DETI, not daring to look up at the mark or to slow, in case the KGB hid nearby, watching to determine which American drove past the site.

In the office our new chief, Gene, and the other case officers waited in hushed anticipation.

"I saw it. It was very red, and looked like someone stenciled it." Leaving no time for anyone to speak, I continued. "Since I am leaving in the next few months, it probably makes sense for someone else to get the experience by servicing the drop tonight."

My rationale, of course, didn't make sense. I had been the only officer to service site SETUN, and I could make the drop with complete assurance that it was in the right place. Also, if I were arrested, the CIA office's personnel strength would not dip because my replacement could arrive in Moscow within a week of my departure.

Weary with worry, and hoping that Gene would agree, I offered to coach another seasoned officer on the drop-site location and ways to approach it. I knew it made no sense, but it was worth a try. Gene simply said that I was to make the drop.

At this point, we were all into wishful thinking. We hoped that TRIGON had intentionally made the marked signal, so it would be absolutely unmistakable. This was our most important, and most desperate, effort to re-contact TRIGON. We had to deliver his camera, film, and new sites to him. But there was a political aspect to this delivery as well. Since this was the first operational act under Gene's management of the office, he was not going to express doubts to HQS. He had to be macho. He sent a cable to HQS, describing the mark and giving Jack a feel for our operational plan, including my safety signal. Gene wasn't asking for authority to make the drop since, as Chief, he had that power. He just wanted HQS to know we had serious concerns.

Deep down, we all suspected that the KGB drew that red signal. They wanted to guarantee we saw it and would come to SETUN that night. Interestingly, no one verbalized this doubt at our ops meeting. I didn't want to seem unwilling or to lack the courage to make this drop. I didn't want to give Gene any excuse to doubt me because I was a woman, especially after the twenty-one months I had worked in Moscow, making risky drops and pick-ups.

If I didn't show up by 1:00 a.m. at the Marine bar, the office would presume I had either been in an accident or, worse, had been arrested. Tim and I went over this scenario multiple times, and I assumed that the procedures would be the same under Gene. According to the script, if I was a no-show, Neal would notify Soviet authorities in a non-alerting way, saying only that I was missing. Our hope was that, if I had actually been in a car accident, Neal could find out the details of my location without associating me with CIA, so I could continue working without KGB surveillance. In the event of an arrest, the Soviet authorities would advise the Marine Guard where I was being held.

By 6:00 p.m., HQS concurred. HQS would never believe that an agent operation had ended without some definitive and observable act. And we had an unspoken commitment to make every possible effort to retrieve an agent's package, regardless of probable consequences. I had never refused an operational task. In this case, I was committed to TRIGON, the man, who had worked so bravely and tirelessly for us well over two years.

I quickly reviewed my delivery schedule and plan for the night with the assembled case officers and Gene. I had done this so many times before, but for some reason it felt different now. Tim wasn't there. Jack wasn't there. They had known a lot about the Moscow operational environment. The other case officers asked all the right questions and, in the end, they trusted my judgment. I had no assurance that Gene had confidence in me. He figured I was a young female trying to be a case officer. He was never to know how difficult it was to work alone in Moscow, to walk those cold, dark, forbidding streets alone.

Changes in office management are always hard to accept. Later, I served with a wise Division Chief who explained this succession problem. He told me that the two dumbest people are the guy who holds your position before you and the guy who replaces you. And, if we are smart, we keep our comments to ourselves.

I left the office that evening feeling uneasy as well as excited at the prospect of successfully delivering to TRIGON. Before I left, Neal helped me bury TRIGON's package in my navy Stockmann's canvas bag under miscellaneous groceries and personal items in case the militiamen glanced in the bag as I walked out to my car parked as usual on the side street next to the Embassy. As I left the office, Neal gave me his thumbs up at the door, our routine sign that he had confidence in me and that the night would go well.

It was a clear, gentle warm night that July 15. Of course, it was broad daylight at 6:00 p.m., being only three weeks past mid-summer. Traffic was normal, as I headed home to my apartment complex. As usual, I parked on the curb and greeted the militiaman at the gate in Russian, smiling broadly. He smiled back. Little did he know what this ever-friendly, smiling young American woman had been doing for the past two years. I heard no phone ring in his shack as I entered the compound, a positive sign. I was to re-examine each step of that night later, looking for any clue that they uncovered my true identity because I had driven by the DETI signal that morning.

I quickly laid out my clothes for the evening. Black wide-legged pants, a white black-and-brown floral patterned blouse that the Lao tailor in Pakse had made, straw-soled leather platform sandals, and a navy blue wool hand-knit sweater, a gift from Meg, a Swedish girlfriend, years earlier. The outfit didn't match well, but I wanted to look more like a Soviet woman fashionable than fashionable. I took out a brown leather purse and shook it to make sure it was empty. I often used this purse on operational outings because the concealment devices Neal packed fitted perfectly as did TRIGON's crushed cans and milk cartons. But I also used it other times when I went out in the evenings because it was smaller than my daily work purse.

Inside the purse, I put my Soviet issued driver's license, which proved I was an American in the event of an accident. Or worse, an arrest. I also included several five-*kopek* coins for the metro and a couple of ten-*kopek* coins for the pay phone in case I had to call Neal, if my car broke down or some other innocuous event prevented me from returning to the Marine bar by 1:00 a.m. It was impossible to obtain these small coins out on the street, so I made sure to save them from my occasional shopping.

As anticipated, the concealment device fit in this purse. It looked like a piece of concrete, somewhat smaller in circumference than a dessert plate and about three inches thick. I put it in a plastic bag to keep the crumbly debris Neal packed around it from rubbing off in my purse. The debris made it look realistic when it lay in the drop site and also filled in and camouflaged the screws holding the lid on. These screws turned in the opposite direction than normal, which our techs called "reverse threading."

I was all set, except for taking off any jewelry that defined me as a non-Soviet. I removed my nail polish the night before since manicures were a distinct give-away for a foreigner. My hair was long with grown-out highlights. I pulled it back into a rubber band at the nape of my neck to minimize the streaks of light blonde color. I wanted to blend in when I entered Soviet public transportation as I made my way to the site. As far as I could tell, I had passed before without being singled out or noticed. Tonight, it was even more important that I look anonymous within the local population.

I nodded to the militiaman as I opened the door of my navy Zhiguli. Heading down Ulitsa Vavilova toward the market at the foot of the hill, it seemed I was on my way to the Embassy for a typical Friday evening with friends.

This time, though, I didn't turn left at the market but continued straight, beginning a route that ventured farther afield from any logical destination. If the KGB were following me, they would conclude I was not going to the Embassy. I drove into industrial areas and old neighborhoods out in the far reaches of Moscow, passing the few remaining wooden houses the Soviets had done their best to replace with gigantic, sprawling apartment complexes.

Eventually, after two hours running an erratic and seemingly destination-free route, an intentional and obvious attempt to detect surveillance, I wound around in a spiral to the central part of Moscow.

During our ops planning meeting, I had told the office I had found a small unnamed street just off Gorky Street in the vicinity of restaurants and theaters frequented by foreigners. My goal was to park where it wouldn't look out of place or be suspect. The last thing I wanted to do was call attention to my car or to me by association by parking in an area far from where foreigners generally visited. I didn't want a KGB officer or militiaman to stake out my car and identify me as a person of interest. If they became suspicious, my long-protected, hard-earned cover could be blown. So, I parked in plain sight, but in a place that would not call attention to my car among other foreigner's cars scattered throughout the area.

When I left my apartment that evening, I placed my blue Stockmann's bag on the floor of the passenger seat. I had a ritual every time I went out on an operation. I packed normal clothes in the bag, this time pink slacks and a deeper shade pink top. Before I went up to the Marine bar as my safety signal, I usually ducked into a friend's apartment to change, so I looked like typical me when I joined ongoing social activities. I also packed a Carlsberg beer for my private celebration when I returned safely to my car. A sip of beer, no matter how cold or warm and a slow deep breath. This custom always amused and calmed me. This evening, I hoped I could celebrate as I had before.

During my long ride throughout Moscow, I reviewed everything I had seen and done while living in this city. I had attended the Bolshoi Ballet several times. I had visited the Kremlin and Red Square. I had visited the Ascension Church in Kolomenskoye often, my very favorite historical place, built in 1532. I had traveled four hours with friends to Yasnaya Polyana to visit Tolstoy's remarkably intact home, now a museum, and his grave down a wooded path where local newlyweds traditionally made a pilgrimage on their wedding day. Zagorsk's St. Sergius Monastery, one of the few in operation in the Soviet Union, was about sixty miles from Moscow. Very young, bearded, black robed Russian Orthodox priests walked around the grounds of the ancient churches with their gleaming blue and gold onion domes, visually transporting visitors back to the 13th and 14th centuries. It was astounding that these treasures persisted in the Soviet Union. I tallied up my visits to the few public museums as well as attendance at many operas, ballets and concerts. No, I had no regrets and nothing left undone.

Satisfied that I had no surveillance following me, I parked the car on the side street off Gorky Street. Locking the car, I moved quickly away, hoping no one noticed me. It would not make sense for an American to park a car and enter the Soviet metro.

I passed through the turnstiles and entered the metro. Over time, I had become knowledgeable about all the metro stations and changes made in the various stops. But at this station, they had added a new spur. I inadvertently entered the new line. The minute the train arrived at the second stop, I realized I was not on the route I had planned, which unsettled me. By the third stop, I determined this train came to the ring line just as my intended line would, just further around the ring.

I sat on a side bench facing others across the train. I looked down at my hands, purposefully not making eye contact with anyone. I focused on people's pants, shoes, and the bags. If someone on this train were following me, I could spot these tell-tale signs again when I changed trains. Surveillants changed hats or jackets, but rarely changed shoes or bags when they wanted to alter their appearance.

At the Garden Ring station, I exited that train and made my way to an adjoining line. I saw no one making the same switch although I knew surveillants could be waiting to replace those who rode with me on the first train. Eventually, the next train came, which took me to Lenin Stadium. When I stepped off the train, I was pressed back by throngs of people on the platform, all waiting for trains. I edged my way to the right and headed toward the escalators up to the street where I had planned to begin my foot counter-surveillance run. As I fought my way against the tide of people to the bottom of the UP escalator, it became clear that all the escalators were set to come DOWN to accommodate the crowds apparently leaving a soccer match at the stadium.

Turning around, I began to walk with the crowd. I headed to the other end of the platform and the other escalators, hoping these were going in both directions. In the process I used this direction change to my advantage. Changing directions 180 degrees very abruptly is a known counter-surveillance move. The maneuver enabled me to see someone watching me or quickly ducking out of my field of vision. In this case, I might have spotted a surveillant as the only other person fighting the flow of the crowds. But no one followed me, or at least no one had walked against the masses. Maybe they just stood watching until I made the discovery that these escalators were not going to serve my purpose.

I came out of the subway onto a quiet street, far different from the other mobbed exit. I had never been on this side of the metro station, so I walked a several blocks to orient myself. In the process, I also made some tricky, yet transparent moves, like sitting on a park bench or tying my shoe. But no one was anywhere near me, walking by me or in front of me. No cars passed and no one stood watching me from dark doorways. So, I became more confident that I had no surveillance and could proceed alone to the delivery site, SETUN.

Because I arrived too early to make the drop, I decided to walk along the sidewalk that overlooking river in the opposite direction from the railroad bridge where the site was located. When it was time, I turned around and headed back to the bridge. Although the metro had been packed, the street near the river seemed eerily deserted.

I was not alarmed when I saw three men with typically well-fed bellies, all in white shirts that glowed in the early evening twilight. Looking inconspicuous on an evening walk, they strolled across the street from the sidewalk near the bridge and took the small entrance into Novodyevichy Cemetery. This famous cemetery, where Krushchev is buried as well as the Cosmonauts, fills the entire block. I mentally registered this group's behavior as non-threatening.

It was 10:15 p.m. and barely dusk. Moscow never gets dark on summer nights. And this night was particularly clear. I noted that the corner had brighter streetlights, probably because it was near the stadium. But other than the three men, no one else was in the area. I prepared to place the package at SETUN.

I proceeded across the street to the bridge and climbed the forty-plus steps to the top pedestrian walkway. Walking confidently on the metal-grated walkway to the pillar to put the package into the window just as I had before, I became momentarily rattled by the deafening noise of a train behind me. Its headlights illuminated the full span of the bridge. I stopped, waiting until the train passed. Ironically, by using the train's headlight, I had the benefit of being able to see that no one else was on the bridge. So far so good.

I moved forward and entered the pillar, opening my purse to dig out the package. I carefully handled it so as not to disturb the crumbly dirt. Sliding it into the narrow window, I pushed it in at arm's length. It was pitch-dark in the window, so no one could spot it and think it was trash of value. After all, no one wanted a chunk of concrete. Satisfied that it was in place, I walked halfway across the bridge, looking down at the dark waters of the Moscow River. All was quiet.

As I had done before, I returned back through the pillar and headed down the stairs. I knew I had an hour's walk in the neighborhood before it was time to return and pick up TRIGON's package. Four steps from the bottom, I spotted the three men in white shirts re-emerge from the cemetery. They quickly crossed the road and headed toward me.

As I reached the bottom step, these men grabbed me forcefully by the arms, one on each arm, one in front of me. My question was whether I was going to be raped or mugged, or worse. They smelled bad, a stale male sweaty odor, their bodies pressing on me to restrain me.

At that instant, a van appeared from under the bridge. The passenger doors flew open and out came ten or twenty men. I thought of the circus car with an unending stream of clowns. But these weren't clowns. They were goons.

I came to two possible conclusions. They knew about TRIGON, he had been arrested, and this was a set up. Or, I had led these men to the bridge, and they saw me put down the drop. But that was impossible. No one could have seen me. No one was there.

So, armed with this small amount of reasoning, I began to speak loudly. "You can't hold me. Let go of me. I'm an American. You must call the Embassy. The number is 252-00-11." How absurd that I knew the number, and recited it in case someone wanted to write it down or even call.

Immediately, I was red-hot angry and did not want to be restrained. I hadn't been held like this since I was a four-year-old child. In my rage, I kicked out and landed a solid blow on hard bone. It was the shin of the white-shirted man in front of me. With that, he reached down and picked up my feet, suspending me in air. So, here I am restrained by two men holding my arms with the wounded man holding my legs. I didn't figure they could continue holding me up for long, but it served to keep me under control for the moment. I remained in mid-air for a few more minutes.

Later, we heard reports that I had hospitalized two KGB officers with a kick to their groin. This is what legends are made of. I strongly denied the story, although some say it would have been the natural reaction.

A large distinguished man in a dark suit, clearly in charge, told me in English to be quiet. He was polite but forceful. I repeated what was to become my mantra: my name and the Embassy phone number. From his perspective, I was causing a scene. However, in my mind, I was attempting to warn TRIGON to stay away, if he was still alive and hiding nearby.

With the man in the suit taking charge, the man holding my legs slowly lowered them. The other two were still holding me by my arms, their odor unabated.

After they grabbed me, I reflexively clutched my purse to my chest. Typical female reaction. But with that move, I inadvertently caused the arms of the two men holding me to come into contact with the sides of my chest. The man to my left said excitedly that I had something concealed under my arm. The man in the suit directed them to find out what it was. They first wrenched my purse out of my hands and then dug into the front of my blouse, untucking it, roughly unbuttoning it in order to retrieve the unknown object at my side.

I'm sure they had notions that it was a concealed weapon. I knew too well that it was a radio receiver in a small handcrafted pouch attached to the side of my bra with Velcro. What a great invention Velcro. This was the first time I had ever seen it and had an opportunity to use it in this spy game.

The official photographer began to take pictures with a large flash camera, including pictures of the KGB's rough hands searching me. It's natural not to want your picture taken in such an awkward, humiliating setting. A mental picture flashed through my mind of convicts ducking under their shirts when faced with cameras, and I identified with these hapless criminals.

But the photographer captured this violent moment on film. I looked angry, pulling away as their hands groped inside my blouse, my fist pulled back as if to let fly a left-hook.

Finally, they retrieved the small receiver, which we used to monitor the KGB surveillance frequency. They discovered it was attached to a loop of plastic coated wire, the antenna, plugged into the receiver. To take it from around my neck, many rough hands tried to lift the neck loop over my head. The one who ended up with the neck loop immediately decided it was a transmitter and started to speak into the junction of the connecting wire to the neck loop. I momentarily smiled to myself, thinking how ignorant they were technologically. Of course, my amusement was short lived, considering my dire situation.

They searched through my purse and discovered my driver's license. Then, they dumped the purse upside-down and shook it. I knew the small spare ear piece battery that I kept in the bottom of my purse probably was lost in the dirt and grass as well as the coins. Their carelessness eliminated my facing questions about what batteries including why it was in my purse. It was satisfying, knowing they did not have a clue why I wore this equipment and its usefulness to me. But it was a small victory, given my pain at what I now was beginning to realize.

TRIGON had been caught.

Even more harrowing than having strange men molest me was to have TRIGON's package appear within moments. They held up the concrete concealment device next to my face and FLASH! A picture of me with the goods. A picture of me with my blouse gaping open and male hands pawing and grabbing. Pictures of me with all the goons.

I had to put all this together. They had knowledge of where the package was, but I knew no one saw me put it there. This made me that they had forced TRIGON to confess. Or, they had his package with the directions to SETUN. Amazingly, fear about my current situation was not my dominant emotion; it was anger, and abject concern for TRIGON.

At the time, I realized that anger was not a useful emotion when trying to reason. I needed to determine how this had happened and what was going to come next. Slowing my adrenaline-spiked brain, I had to begin mentally recording what they were saying, how they were responding, what they were planning and, most importantly, what they knew. The worst to happen to me was to be declared *persona non grata* (PNG) and to be expelled from the Soviet Union. Not a disastrous outcome. I was ready to leave. But the most devastating question remained: What had happened to TRIGON? Most likely, torture and death, or worse, a long brutal imprisonment.

As part of my training, I had been given one lecture on what happens if you are arrested. The speaker stated that when Americans are arrested the US Ambassador makes an official protest to obtain a release. Then the Soviet government expels the individual. But what I should do at the moment of arrest, what language should I speak, were questions not addressed in the lecture. My guidelines came by the seat of my pants, by instinct and judgment at the moment.

I spoke English because I knew exactly what I was saying. I began to almost enjoy repeating my mantra as it became clear that it irritated them. But I knew that the Moscow office and HQS would want to know everything: what these goons said, what they did, what they seemed to know, what they looked like, and what names were used. The KGB's had apparently not known I spoke Russian by talking in front of me about various aspects of the arrest. This afforded me the opportunity to hear information they might otherwise not have revealed. They didn't know who I was or where I worked. Apparently, they had no book on me. At least, those at the arrest site didn't. Now I started my brain's tape recorder and my language skills were put to the test.

There was no female KGB officer at the arrest, so I concluded they did not anticipate I was to put down the drop. I had to be one of only a few Americans who drove by the signal site DETI that morning, so they didn't have many candidates to expect at SETUN. But now I wondered. Maybe they knew nothing about me, and this was the first time they had connected me to CIA.

One lone militiaman stood among the throng of goons. A young man, younger than I. He wore his uniform, so no one doubted he was the Soviet official. Everyone else at the arrest was a concerned citizen, offended by whatever this American woman had done. They all wore civilian clothes. So, the young militiaman represented the government and became the arresting official. I assume he was told not to do or say anything, to just be there. And that is all he did. Well almost.

After the pictures were taken, and still holding me by the arms, they moved me into the middle seat of the black van. I realized that this van was identical to the black vans in Stalin's era of horror that backed up to apartment buildings in the middle of the night. Innocent people were thrown in and taken away, never again to be seen, heard from or spoken about again. This was a chilling reminder of the gruesome past as the van pulled away from the bridge.

Seated to my left was the young militiaman. To my right was one of the original three men who had held my right arm throughout the arrest. They continued to grip my wrists. In the front seat, the driver, and in the passenger seat, the photographer. Behind me in the back seat sat three men, all unknown.

As the van passed Novodevichy Cemetery, I decided to calm myself and focus on what was happening. I put my head down, closed my eyes, and took a deep breath. Immediately, they thought I had fainted. Someone behind me patted my shoulder in attempts to waken me. I noticed that, when I relaxed, my seatmates also relaxed their grip on my wrists. After three or four breaths, I lifted my head to see what route we were taking.

Glancing down, I saw that my watchband on my left wrist had popped open in the melee. Following my eyes, the militiaman looked down. He gently adjusted and clasped the watchband. I realized then that we were actually holding hands, this young man and I. So, the devil made me do it, I squeezed his hand twice. Damned, if he didn't squeeze back. I'm sure he was amazed that this young woman had been arrested. Could she really be a spy?

We made a few turns, and it became clear we were headed to central Moscow. One of the men behind me said, "Should we pick up her car now or later?" How did they know where my car was? Did they just find it by chance? Was that what he had said, or did I misunderstand his Russian? This is still a minor mystery after all this time.

I was amused during the ride to hear the small earpiece I still wore P-I-N-G-ing every time we passed under a fluorescent streetlight, to which it was sensitive. In Moscow, there weren't many streetlights even though it was a law that cars drove at night with parking lights only. I also noticed that the van's turn signal made the earpiece ping. These were little known or useful facts, but a mildly amusing diversion at the time.

We came into central Moscow and around Dzerzhinsky Square, the location of Lyubianka Prison, the dreaded prison where citizens, picked up in these black vans by Stalin's men disappeared. And here I was arriving at the back door of Lyubianka.

A man waiting anxiously at the curb opened the side door. He motioned to my seatmate that my shirt-tail was untucked. With his ham-hock hands, he tried to straighten me up, pulling up my collar, buttoning the top button, and trying to tuck my shirt into my pants. It was a half-hearted, embarrassed effort, which left me still looking disheveled.

As I passed the well-polished brass plate to the left of the large door, I realized it said that this was the entrance for the Presidium of the KGB. Impressive at another time, perhaps, but not now.

They led me through small entry hall into a large conference room. In the center was a dark wooden conference table. I was directed to sit in the middle of three seats on the far side with three empty chairs across from me. Two microphones in the middle of the long table added voice to the filmed proceedings. A camera on a tripod located in the corner of the room would film this whole show for a future expose.

I scanned the room. All men, some young, some middle aged, some in suits, some in shirtsleeves, stood against the walls of the room. They were to witness the interview of what they hoped was a genuine CIA spy. A man in a suit, obviously in charge, very stern, almost angry, entered the room. He stood across from me, never sitting down. Clearly, he was the chief interrogator. But, this was to be no interrogation, only a drama acted out for the camera.

Four of us were seated at the table. The man I kicked in the shins sat on my left. When he first sat down he had good-naturedly pulled up his pant leg to show me the welt I had raised on his shin. Before the proceedings began, another man came over to him to show him a Polaroid-type picture of all of us at the site. He was amazed and proud to see himself in this picture, pointing out his face to me. In the photo of me, I was protesting the hands inside my blouse. These instant pictures were obviously new to them. He was amazed at seeing the picture taken less than an hour earlier. I randomly remembered the group at the airport months earlier with the same child-like reaction to these pictures.

Across the table to my right was a nice-looking polite man who I eventually determined was an MFA officer. His role was to protect my rights as an American. He also attempted translate as well. At the end of the table they brought in another chair for a middle-aged stout Soviet woman, who was to write down on sheets of lineless paper everything the chief interrogator said as well as my responses.

The chief interrogator began the proceedings by ordering that they remove my watch and a necklace. The charm on the necklace was called a *figa*, a Brazilian good luck charm, presented to me years earlier by Wayne, a close family friend. So much for that charm. My purse was on the table along with my driver's license. The concrete concealment device was there as well, unopened.

The interrogator began speaking in Russian. "On July 15, 1977, at 10:35 in the evening, Martha Peterson was observed placing a spy cache in a niche on the bridge. Observant citizens called instruments of national security, who came and detained her." This formal statement went on and on, recounting contents of my purse, my remarks, and the fact that the concrete rock was found just where these offended citizens had claimed to have seen me put it. The female stenographer diligently filled page after page.

At last, he had exhausted detailing every factoid about the arrest. He told me to sign the bottom of the pages, pushing them toward me. I told him I didn't know what he was talking about, that he had to call the American Embassy. I repeated the number. This time I added that I knew Cliff, an Embassy official. I was getting tired of the KGB drama.

Miraculously, I had said the right thing. The MFA officer looked surprised and said, "I know Cliff." The interrogator directed him to call Cliff. The MFA officer went to the phone on a small table in the corner by the door and called Cliff at his home. Cliff answered immediately and the MFA officer told him they had detained a woman, giving my last name as Patterson. Cliff replied he would drive down. This was progress, I thought. The only glitch was that my office would be out of the loop and not informed I was here in Lyubianka. It was now past midnight and the 1:00 a.m. deadline approached.

Cliff did not think of calling the Embassy to report that an American had been detained as he was the Consular Chief, in charge of the welfare and whereabouts of all Americans in the Soviet Union. He just thought I was another dumb American tourist who happened to get arrested, which was not uncommon. But the look of shock on his face was priceless when he saw it was me, Peterson. He could hardly believe his eyes, my sitting at the big table surrounded by all these men, lights, and cameras. Cliff had likely assumed I did clerical work in the CIA office. He had no clue I went out on the street at night conducting operations. As he approached the table, he was speechless, an unusual state for him.

He sat down beside me. I quietly but forcefully told him that I knew nothing about what they were claiming. He nodded and that dear, courageous man never faltered in supporting my fiction. He responded every time the MFA officer tried to ask me a question that I didn't know what they were talking about.

Another man had joined us at the conference table, seated to the right of the chief interrogator. I realized with some concern, that we were beginning part two of the interrogation. The concrete package was now positioned in the center of the table on an opened double page of the newspaper *Pravda*, which means "truth" in Russian. This moment devastated me, knowing the package was soon to be opened.

The interrogator nodded to the new man, the technical expert, who stood up and began to dig out the rubble and putty Neal had used to fill the screw holes in the face of the package. He confidently unscrewed all four screws, knowing they were threaded backwards. The purpose in reverse threading was to discourage an innocent who tried to unscrew them, thinking the screws were cemented closed. The technician pried open the lid.

All my senses screamed silently. *They can't open this*, I shrieked to myself. *This is classified. It has been secured in a Top Secret pouch. They aren't authorized to open this, to see the contents, to know any of this.* Undeniably the most excruciating and sickening moment I experienced, I could only sit there watching the KGB open TRIGON's package. It pains me even today to recall that.

The technician placed the lid over to the side of the newspaper. Then he began carefully lifting out each item one at a time. First came a note printed in Russian on a white card. It said, "Friend, if you have found this by chance and are opening it, be warned that this could get you into a lot of trouble. Do not go farther but dispose of this rock by throwing it into the river."

On the top was the same warning note we put in all of TRIGON's. The technician put the note aside. The stenographer was poised with a new sheet of blank paper and began recording a description of this note and each subsequent item. Next he pulled out a roll of 35 mm film with miniature writing on it, tightly wound, and secured with a rubber band. The technician removed the band and handed the film to the interrogator. He began to read aloud the message in Russian on the film.

"Dear Friend. We hope you are well, and we are happy to be in touch with you again. In your last package, you asked for an accounting of the money you have earned during your cooperation with us. It is...."

He stopped abruptly. The amount was outrageous. In a flash, he realized that, if he read the amount out loud to the assembled KGB officers, he would witness a stampede of those in the room to volunteer to CIA. I laughed to myself, wanting to look at the interrogator, but keeping my eyes cast down. I also wanted to watch the faces in the room to see their reaction. But, I needed to act disinterested and unknowledgeable. Cliff sat still, too. I assume the stenographer simply wrote that it was a roll of film with writing on it.

The next item was a plastic bottle. The technician handed it to the interrogator. He looked at the label in English and then began reading the numbers since he could easily translate them into Russian. I was amused when I realized he was reading the Patent Pending numbers for the contents, contact lens wetting solution. The scribe dutifully copied the numbers, likely without explanation as to the nature of the contents of the bottle.

The next item was the lens case with TRIGON's replacement contact lenses. As contacts were not available to the general public in 1977, he had requested in a previous message to us that we refill his Bogota prescription. The interrogator opened the right and left compartments, leaving the lenses in place. He described them as lenses, not knowing their use, possibly concluding they were magnifying lenses to read messages on microdots, a type of miniaturized spy communications. She wrote everything down.

Tucked in around the edges of this top layer of items were rolls of rubles, wound as tightly as possible, and secured with rubber bands. Neal tried to put as much money in as he could, filling each crevice, which made the contents compact and rattle proof. Neal also cleverly packed in several small packages containing emerald jewelry, which CIA had purchased with TRIGON's funds.

The scribe kept on writing as the technician pulled each item out and displayed it on the newspaper. At some point, the cameraman suggested to the interrogator that the newspaper did not provide a clean background to allow clear focus on the various items. They exchanged the newspaper for a large sheet of white paper. This satisfied the cameraman. To me, it seemed so unprofessional, so haphazard. But who was I to comment, sitting in Lyubianka Prison surrounded by a roomful of KGB officers.

When the technician lifted out the large pen, the interrogator quickly and harshly told him to lay it down and not touch it again. The pen severely agitated the interrogator. Only two people in the room, the interrogator and I, knew why this pen caused him such hostility and anger.

But what he didn't realize was that this pen contained the miniature camera. I knew at that moment that the interrogator reacted vehemently to the pen because he thought it contained a vial of poison. This brought me to the most unacceptable and distressing conclusion, yet still a question: Had TRIGON used the poison?

It became the single most important piece of information I gleaned during my arrest and detention. The interrogator knew about the poison pen, and he was angry with me. Later, we could find no other explanation for the interrogator's behavior, only that TRIGON had used the poison and died.

The interrogator regained his composure, and the scribe simply recorded "a pen." Then the technician took out the small capsules, which I knew were the camera cassettes. The interrogator also told him to carefully position them next to the pen. I suppose he thought these might be additional poison reservoirs.

The remaining items, small one-time pads, which TRIGON used to decode radio messages, were itemized and displayed with little description or drama.

The scribe completed the list of items from the concealment device. Picking up her inventory, the interrogator pushed these papers over to me, again demanding I sign them. Cliff told him I wouldn't.

Then, abruptly, the interrogator said, "You may leave." The show was over.

Cliff and I exchanged glances, then, stood up. I had been there since 11:30 p.m. It was now 2:00 a.m.

I reached for my watch and necklace. The man with the bruised shin handed them to me. I said, "*Spacebo.*" I heard a murmur of recognition around the room that, in fact, I did speak Russian. Surely, they realized that the first two phrases you learn in any language are "thank you" and "Where's the toilet?"

But they knew little about me, and even more spectacularly, nothing of the damage I had done to the Soviet Government during my tour in the USSR. I wished I could have been in KGB Center Monday morning when they went to find the surveillance logs of my activities. I wonder how many KGB officers lost their jobs when they found no continuous record of what I had done since arriving in Moscow on November 5, 1975.

Cliff and I exited together through the anteroom. Seated there was the young militiaman. As I passed him, I looked directly at him and winked ever so slightly. I am sure he will tell his grandkids of that night so long ago, when they picked up that young innocent American woman. Or, then again, maybe he didn't really care.

It was a relief to step out onto the sidewalk free of smelly men and intense scrutiny. Cliff's wife sat in his blue Mercedes, waiting patiently for Cliff and his errant American tourist. She, too, was surprised when she saw me.

I climbed in the back seat. Cliff made an amusing excuse, saying I was out kissing militiamen again. We all laughed. I had told Cliff about my first New Year's Eve in Moscow. Upon returning from our celebrations at Red Square, several of us had gone up to every militiaman stationed in front of the Embassy and planted a kiss on their cheeks. How we laughed later when we recalled that most of them were well over six feet tall and had to lean down to accept the kisses. I bet the KGB officers manning the observation post across the street from the Embassy later asked those militiamen some serious questions.

Cliff and I entered the Embassy and went directly to the ninth floor. As we entered the lobby, I saw Neal talking to the Marine Guard. Neal took one look at me, and I read relief all over his face. Without a word, Neal, Cliff, and I headed downstairs to the CIA office. I was amazed to see most of the case officers with Gene, the new Chief, assembled there. Apparently at 2:00 a.m. they had just begun the rescue process. At the time, I was surprised they had waited well over an hour after our pre-agreed upon 1:00 a.m. deadline. But I was relieved to be back to the safety and the company of my fellow CIA officers.

Though not altogether appropriate, Gene hugged me. I was feeling very proud that I had withstood the evening's difficult activities. And now he was going to play macho man with me. In fact, he insisted that I read what he had written on the blackboard in his office. "Welcome back, our little girl!!!"

His total lack of understanding about what I had gone through that night irritated me. I knew more than almost anyone else about being on the streets of Moscow and operating in this most difficult environment.

At that moment, I was glad I was to leave Moscow shortly, as I knew it would be difficult to work for him. I learned he made a comment to a close friend in the office soon after my departure that, if I had seen surveillance that night, I would not have been caught. He just didn't get it. I was ambushed because the KGB had wrapped up TRIGON, and they were waiting for the officer who appeared at SETUN. My being arrested was the final chapter and didn't change TRIGON's fate.

Neal pulled out a small tape recorder. I sat in the middle of the office, re-living the events of the evening, down to the minor details, some punctuated with profanity. Gleaning facts from my lively monologue, another officer composed a cable to HQS informing them of what had transpired. This was sent out at 3:30 a.m. Moscow time, 9:30 p.m. Washington, D.C. time. When our cable arrived at CIA HQS, Jack and the senior division managers were sickened as they read all the gruesome facts. It was an incredibly sad night for everyone to know that TRIGON had been apprehended. He was not only the most highly productive agent we had, but also a longtime friend, someone we all cared about deeply.

CHAPTER **13**

Homecoming - July 1977

After I gave my account of that night, I provided instructions for disposing of my personal effects. From past arrests of CIA officers, we knew the Soviet government would require me to leave within two to three days, in effect be PNGd. It was just a matter of time to prepare the necessary bureaucratic paperwork. In my absence, I requested the CIA office sell my car, my stereo (which we assume the KGB bugged), my heavy winter coat, and leftover canned goods, including, a few remaining jars of Smuckers I hadn't managed to consume.

The trip home was difficult because the office secretary Gene selected as my escort was anxious about the trip. As we changed planes, I knew there were KGB officers watching us in Vienna and Frankfurt airports, but I did not dare tell her because she had already expressed concern about spending the night in the Frankfurt airport hotel without her husband. She worried about waking up in time for our 9:00 a.m. flight to Washington, D.C. She likely sat up all night watching the clock while I slept soundly.

My swift departure from Moscow after a very short night with little sleep reminded me much too graphically of a similar night and flight five years earlier when I left Laos. Maybe this was my karma, change forced upon me by cataclysmic events. Later, I reflected on the fact that my tours overseas were following a predictable pattern, something to remember, if I ever was sent out again on assignment.

Our plane landed at Dulles Airport on Sunday mid-afternoon, a beautiful hot summer day. Trying to act casually as we stepped off the airport bus at the terminal, I was startled to hear my name over the loudspeaker even before we reached passport control. My reaction reflected my Moscow paranoia. I had lived out of the spotlight and in anonymity for the past two years. I didn't want anyone to know who I was. Now, everyone in Dulles Airport knew who I was and that I was there.

I quickly approached the immigration officer directing people into passport lines and told him I had been paged. He escorted us to a side exit where another official cursorily checked our passports, pointing the way to baggage carousels. There had not been time enough for me to return to my apartment before my departure from Moscow. Nor did I want the ordeal of being followed by the KGB as I had been when I went to retrieve my car. In the Dulles baggage area, a friendly customs official pointed to the big black rubberized swinging exit doors that opened out to the waiting public.

As the doors swung out, I spotted Jack and Susie with an unfamiliar officer, identified later as a CIA security officer there in case I had trouble clearing immigration. As we walked to the car, Susie told us she had observed two men in suits hanging out on the fringes of the crowd, ostensibly waiting for arriving passengers. When they saw me, she said, they turned and left. We learned later that local Soviet Embassy KGB officers were directed to confirm to Moscow's KGB Center that I reached the US without any detours. The loudspeaker announcement had assisted them as well.

Home for good, I had been in Moscow long enough. I knew that.

Jack and Susie had arranged for us to stay in their home rather than a local McLean hotel. They had two young children who we temporarily displaced from their rooms. I always believed that Jack wanted to make my return home under these circumstances less traumatic. When he discovered I had not packed any clothes, I could tell he was irritated. The muscles in his jaw under his ear lobe always knotted up when he was displeased. He had instructed Gene to make sure my departure from Moscow appeared orderly to the Soviets, that I was leaving of my own free will. I explained to Jack that the unexpected short lead-time to board our airplane did not allow me to drive to my apartment and then to the airport at the opposite end of the city. So, when Jack told me I had an appointment on Monday afternoon with Stansfield Turner, the Director of Central Intelligence (DCI), I knew the first thing I had to do the next morning was to buy a new wardrobe.

That evening over dinner, Jack told me he was to pick up Tim at Dulles Airport on Monday afternoon. Tim had flown to London the previous Thursday when he departed Moscow. He had just wanted a short vacation before arriving back in HQS. He had no idea that I had preceded him, and Jack was not looking forward to telling him the sad details of the events of that Friday night. Jack and I knew that Tim was going to be very disturbed by this news about TRIGON.

The next morning, Susie was more than happy to take us to Tyson's Corner where a Bloomingdale's store had just opened. The saleswoman was accommodating when I said that I had to purchase a complete outfit. She did raise her eyebrows when I asked whether I could change into the clothes I selected in the dressing room and wear them out of the store. Susie helped me negotiate the store as I selected bra and pants, slip and stockings, shoes and purse to go with the turquoise Diane Von Furstenburg wrap dress, a popular style for the season. Susie laughed as I made my dramatic debut from behind the curtains of the dressing room, appearing totally transformed from my Moscow ensemble of pink pants and top, complete with cork platform sandals. She assured me I looked professional, yet feminine, and totally appropriate to face the DCI as well as SE Division management who anxiously awaited my arrival in HQS to hear the story firsthand. She drove me to CIA and dropped me off at the front door of the HQS building, hugging me and wishing me luck.

I anticipated this was going to be a difficult day, recounting the story over and over, facing SE Division Chief George Kalaris, who might think I was at fault. Interestingly, he was reasonable and practical, wanting to know all the details. In between briefings of key managers, I was ensconced in a large office in the front office suite of SE Division on the fifth floor. I assumed the decision was made to isolate me from my colleagues, who were just beginning to hear rumors of my return. The last thing the Agency wanted was for my arrest to be leaked to the press.

Late that morning, I had a visitor who shared a quiet moment and helped me face the ordeal of having to retell my arrest story, while worrying that they all doubted me. That was Dick, the EUR Division Chief. A very compassionate man with warm caring eyes, he told me he had been in the same situation, although he had been in Moscow only a few weeks. Actually, he said, he held the record for being in country for the shortest period of time before being arrested and PNG'd. We laughed, yet shared the tragedy of loosing our courageous agents who gave their lives for what they believed was right. Dick gave me confidence as I faced difficult moments. He knew firsthand how hard this ordeal was going to be. He cared and wanted me to know he was available, if I needed him.

Of course, the elephant front and center in all my briefings was the question of what happened to TRIGON and how the KGB knew where SETUN was. My surveillance detection route had been long and thorough, leaving me to be certain no one followed me. I knew some officers in HQS still doubted me. But it was also obvious that the KGB didn't have to follow anyone that night, knowing that someone from CIA would show up at SETUN where they could ambush and arrest him. They had pre-staged near SETUN with the van full of men as well as the token militiaman.

I could not explain how the KGB knew where my car was parked. They might have spotted it in a dragnet-type search. Because those at SETUN did not know my name or where I worked before they pulled out my ID, or that I spoke Russian, I believed I was still an unknown at the time of my arrest. The fact that the interrogator referred to me as a courier during the show-and-tell in Lyubianka also confirmed that they knew little about what I had been up to during my tour in Moscow. As we discussed all possibilities, deep down I was more convinced that I had not caused TRIGON's capture by missing surveillance during previous deliveries.

Many theories about TRIGON's fate were posed, but it was too early to draw conclusions. His reporting over the past six months, the anomalies in his deliveries to us, his no-shows as well as the changes in his photography quality were all examined by technical and reports specialists. We discussed the late-June appearance of the man in the military uniform and the unexplained van in the park at LES. We also weighed the probability that TRIGON had already been arrested by then. No one accused me, or even implied, that I might have caused TRIGON's arrest. But I knew that some thought I had become sloppy or had missed surveillance during a critical delivery. It was the mid 1970s, and some thought that they should have sent a man, not a woman.

Ultimately, we learned bits and pieces of information about TRIGON's fate from sources spread around the world. KGB officers and Soviet officials we had recruited eventually heard from KGB Center about TRIGON and how they had uncovered his treachery. The KGB put out many versions but all of them gave full credit to the KGB's counter-espionage skill. The KGB included in these vigilance messages strict warnings against the Main Adversary, KGB speak for CIA. The KGB alerted its officers about possible CIA attempts to use Soviet citizens' vulnerabilities, such as excessive alcohol consumption, inappropriate extramarital affairs, or simple greed, to blackmail and recruit them.

As predicted, Monday afternoon I had a meeting with Admiral Stansfield Turner, the DCI appointed by President Carter in March 1977. He was a CIA outsider and had the reputation of doubting the value and validity of human intelligence. He thought that the only reliable intelligence was collected by technical means, which eliminated human errors in judgment. I did not have a full appreciation of his attitude prior to my meeting, and I found his understanding of the TRIGON case and our operations in Moscow to be limited.

He greeted me warmly in his large seventh-floor HQS office and invited me to sit at his long conference table. He, of course, sat at the head of the table, and I sat to his right. He excused the officer who accompanied me, obviously wanting me to recount the events without any HQS interference or editing. He asked how I was and then requested I provide him with a complete account of the events. I told him the story, of course cleaning up my language. He asked few questions. I learned later that this was my audition, because he wanted to have me accompany him to the White House for his regular Tuesday afternoon meeting with the President. I assume I passed muster, because at the end of our meeting, he invited me to go with him to see the President the next day. He repeated several times that I should plan on only having nine or ten minutes maximum to tell the President my story.

I returned to my office to find Tim waiting for me, fresh off the plane from his vacation. We hugged tearfully. There were no words to speak the emotion we shared, having been so committed to TRIGON and his well-being. I recounted all the details of Friday night's events to Tim. Jack joined us as we began our quest to formulate ideas about what had happened. By the end of that day, our top theory was the belief that TRIGON had been too aggressive in his collection and had been caught photographing documents in his office or carrying them out of the MFA to photograph them in his apartment. Many of us believed all along that we needed to slow TRIGON down; he was too intent on producing for us, perhaps causing him to take unwarranted risks to obtain intelligence. Neither Jack nor Tim implied that I had made mistakes, but I continued to worry that something I had done had caused TRIGON's arrest.

At 1:00 p.m. Tuesday July 19, I was ready, dressed in the same outfit. John, Jack's deputy, picked me up at the front door of the HQS building, and we drove downtown to the DCI's office near the Executive Office Building (EOB). The temperature hung in the 90s with extremely high humidity, a typical Washington D.C. summer afternoon. John's car was an old Ford station wagon without working air conditioning. I had felt nervous, but now I was wilted by the wind from the open windows as we sped down the George Washington Parkway and crossed the bridge into Washington, D.C. John dropped me off at the front door of the DCI's building.

After a brief meeting in his office, the DCI and I walked down the block and entered the lower floor of the EOB where the White House's main security desk was located. I was wide-eyed at just being there, considering I was just minutes from meeting the President of the United States. After being appropriately badged and searched (just wanded, no hands in my blouse this time), the DCI and I entered the tunnel that led to the basement of the White House. I followed him up a small narrow flight of stairs that came out on the main hallway leading to the Oval Office. He showed me the Cabinet Room and pointed out historical pictures as we approached the Oval Office suite.

The President's secretary greeted us and invited us to sit on a floral sofa to await our meeting with the President. The DCI again reminded me I had a maximum of ten minutes to describe what had happened in Moscow. I felt prepared but nervous. At least I was cooling off and drying out. My long hair was thankfully tied up in a knot on the top of my head. Years later, I wished I had a photograph of me with the President to mark that day, but it was just not that kind of meeting.

At 2:00 p.m. the secretary opened the door and we entered the Oval Office. The DCI introduced me to the President's National Security Advisor, Zbigniew Brzezinski, and Vice President Walter Mondale. President Carter entered, saying he had just come from meeting with Israeli Prime Minister Menachem Begin. How amazing, I was part of the President's calendar, being on his schedule right after Begin.

The President greeted me and invited me to sit on the sofa to the right of his wing-back chair. President Carter was short, even diminutive, with a ruddy face broken out in a rash. He looked tired. I placed on a coffee table in front of us the replica of the concealment device and the sketches of the site to help the

President picture what had happened. The DCI sat next to me on the sofa with Brzezinski next to him in a chair facing the President. Mondale sat across from the DCI in a wing-back chair angled slightly away from the President, reflecting his somewhat aloof attitude about the substance of the meeting. In fact, he never said a word.

I began to tell the story of TRIGON, how long he worked for us, how we had communicated with him in Moscow, all very abbreviated to fit it into the DCI's prescribed time limit. But as I began to tell about the night of July 15, Brzezinski began to add details to my story, like the name of the railroad bridge, Krasnoluzhskiy Most, and the agent's true name, and the exceptional value of TRIGON's intelligence information. He had obviously read the cables from Moscow about my arrest. I knew he numbered among the handful of recipients of TRIGON's intelligence reports, being the Assistant to the President for National Security Affairs. He obviously was familiar with the TRIGON case and had greatly valued his reporting.

As I became more immersed in the story of my arrest, it didn't occur to me that the nine or ten minutes had stretched to almost twenty. President Carter was engrossed in my story and the show-and-tell objects. Finally, I concluded with the story of my trip home. The President wondered if I would return to Moscow, but I told him I had been officially expelled from the USSR permanently.

The DCI thanked the President and indicated with a nod to me it was time to leave. I collected my paraphernalia and thanked the President who rose and shook my hand. As I headed for the door, Brzezinski stood to shake my hand and said, "I greatly admire your courage," which the others echoed. I turned toward him, and we locked eyes. I thanked him. He truly understood what I had done, what CIA in Moscow worked so hard to accomplish, and how important CIA's role was to our government's conduct of foreign affairs and the delicate balance of power in the world.

Closing the door behind me, slowly exhaling, I became a bit flustered. I had no clue whether the DCI would expect me to wait for him. I didn't even know how to find my way out down the hall to the stairwell. Deciding that the DCI probably didn't think I would wait for him, I asked the secretary to escort me to the stairs. From there, I retraced our steps out to the street in front of the EOB where John was parked, waiting for me.

Later that day, I received a handwritten note from the DCI who thanked me for a most professional briefing. He said, "You are the only person who has stood face-to-face with the KGB and the President of the United States all within three days. I admire and congratulate you."

I had been instructed by SE Division management not to tell my colleagues I had met the President to personally brief him on what had happened. I assumed they did not want it known that CIA had lost TRIGON, one of our most valuable agents, nor how singularly important TRIGON had been to CIA's intelligence product for the White House and National Security Council. They wanted CIA colleagues to think my arrest was simply a case of mistaken identity, that I was nabbed for no reason. So, for years, I did not tell anyone I had met President Carter although TRIGON's demise was well known within a few weeks in CIA.

I spent the rest of that week attending debriefings with case officers, counter-intelligence officers, and with my peers, telling them the details of my arrest. These colleagues found this information vital to their understanding of what working in Moscow was like, and what I thought might have happened to cause my arrest since they were engaged in supporting current agent operations in Moscow and planning for future operations destined to be run there.

During one difficult debriefing with the SE Division officers, Tim and I were appalled to learn HQS had some serious doubts, more than just anomalies we discussed in the CIA office in Moscow, about TRIGON long before my arrest. These officers hinted they had indicators that TRIGON had come under suspicion and even had been compromised and co-opted by the KGB. Tim and I told them how disturbed we were that this information had not been transmitted to the Moscow office. We might have been able to devise a test to determine whether TRIGON was still free or was being run by the KGB without risking a case officer's arrest. These officers retracted their strong opinion, reducing it to only a question they had discussed, not a fact concluded from any evidence found in TRIGON's reporting.

After that disturbing meeting, Tim and I went out to lunch at a great French restaurant to decompress. As we walked through Georgetown on that beautiful warm July day, we both felt we had been deceived by HQS. HQS officers like to make themselves appear smarter, but many times it is only after the fact. Anyone can make the key plays as a Monday-morning-quarterback. After lunch, we strolled back to the car. I felt something drop on the top of my head. Putting my hand gingerly onto my hair, I discovered a bird had defecated precisely in the center of my head, right on my freshly-highlighted almost-white-blonde hair. Worse than that, the dirty bird had been eating purple berries. I doubted this was good luck as I had been taught as a child. Tim was nauseated by the whole afternoon.

At the end of a week, made sane and comfortable by Jack and Susie and their very smart kids, I traveled to Fort Lauderdale where my parents still lived. They received me home with open arms, too similar to five years earlier. They collected me back into their nest from yet another difficult experience. I'm sure they had their doubts about my continued association with CIA.

I was exhausted, probably from the strenuous nature of working two jobs in Moscow and expending constant adrenaline out on the street. There were no breaks, and no dropping the façade. Most friends in Moscow never knew I led a double life. To explain why I left abruptly that Saturday, July 16, I told friends my mother was seriously ill. They believed I took personal leave to shorten my tour to be with her. Mother was not sick although she and I often laughed about her quick recovery. Mine was slower. I slept long hours, finding that I was utterly exhausted from the challenges of Moscow life and work.

In early August, I purchased a new car, a Pontiac Trans Am, all white once again. I added a blue and red pin stripe down the side. I had every reason to be patriotic. I had rented my townhouse through September, not thinking I would be back in Falls Church, Virginia, before then. So, I had to arrange to evict my tenants earlier than planned. This all worked out, but not without some financial loss. People always think CIA officers make so much money serving overseas, getting special overtime and hardship pay. In Moscow, I only received one paycheck, the one from CIA, and it didn't include any special overtime or hazard pay. The only reason I came home with a full bank account was that I had neither time nor place to spend the money while I was in Moscow. I had been promoted from a GS-9 to a GS-11 by the time I came home, starting and finishing still at the lowest rank of any officer Moscow.

Not only did I have to re-start my life in Virginia by getting my personal effects out of storage and setting up my home again, but I also had to find a position in HQS that was stimulating and made use of my Moscow street knowledge. The Soviets had not publicized my arrest, which allowed me to continue to say little about living and working in Moscow to non-Agency friends and neighbors and rejoin life as if nothing unusual had happened.

When I met with SE Division Chief, George Kalaris, to discuss my future, he said I could go overseas immediately, if that is what I wanted to do. He had several openings and was prepared to nominate me for any one I wanted. But I told him I preferred to stay at HQS for a while. Moscow was a tough assignment, made more difficult by being alone, and I needed to rejuvenate myself.

I decided to take the position as assistant instructor in the Internal Operations Course which trained officers for assignments to difficult operating areas. All officers in Moscow took the course prior to their assignments, learning how to detect the presence of surveillance and how to operate successfully without surveillance observing the operational act. It was a perfect position for me because I loved teaching and had credible on-the-street experience in Moscow. I prefaced lectures with the fact that the KGB did not surveil me while I was there, at least not until the end. Having lived in that fish-bowl environment I could describe realities of life there.

I also lectured on being arrested and how to act. I was proud of this lecture because it filled a void in preparing officers for these difficult assignments. In fact, I gave this lecture for years, not only during this course, but also as a guest lecturer to many varied audiences. Years later, I had officers tell me it was the single most memorable lecture they received in training. Many women said I was the only female operations officer who spoke to their career trainee class throughout their training program, providing them with a glimpse of the particular difficulties that they faced.

One class I was asked to address amused me. I was to tell my story to FBI officers who were taking a counter-intelligence course. They were interested in knowing how I felt to be a KGB target, similar to KGB officers in the US being an FBI target. I told them about life in Moscow and how I was not surveilled by the KGB during my entire tour in Moscow because I was a woman. They doubted this and even told me unequivocally during the question-and-answer period that I just hadn't seen surveillance. I asked them how many female KGB officers they surveilled in Washington, D.C. They chose not to answer my question. They thought women rarely worked on the streets as case officers. Ironically, the FBI and KGB had amazingly parallel viewpoints. Some of the FBI officers became almost argumentative, defending their KGB counterparts' abilities, knowing it was I who was mistaken. They figured I was a woman and could not see that I was actually being followed.

In January 1978, an FBI officer working in CIA HQS asked me whether I wanted to see a video taken of the FBI arresting a KGB officer right before Christmas in Washington, D.C. The FBI officer thought I would find it amusing to see how they treated the KGB officer, knowing I had had a similar experience. I agreed, thinking it could be interesting, but not amusing.

The video camera was hidden among the branches of the Christmas tree in the agent's apartment. The agent was actually an American who worked for the FBI and had strung along the KGB officer, allowing the officer to "recruit" him. The KGB officer knocked at the door, and the agent let him in. There was friendly conversation, cookies were offered, and the KGB officer apparently thought this was going to be another friendly, productive meeting with his agent.

But then the doors in the apartment slammed open, and FBI officers grabbed the KGB officer, violently thrusting him up against the wall, frisking him. The FBI roughly escorted him out of the apartment. I was amazed at my emotion, identifying with the KGB officer's experience. I reacted viscerally to his treatment. It was not amusing although, in reflection, it was great to see the good guys win. I didn't let on to the FBI officer how affected I was, but laughed with him, telling him I knew exactly what the KGB officer was thinking at that moment when the world crashed down around him.

Life became normal after I finally moved back into my Falls Church townhouse, bought groceries, paid bills and enjoyed friends' company. I worked hard to train my colleagues, who often called late at night asking for help in devising counter-surveillance routes and sketching dead-drop sites. I knew this was the right position for me as I contributed to CIA's ongoing successes. Life was predictable although I suspected that the other shoe had yet to drop.

On June 12, 1978, almost exactly eleven months after my arrest in Moscow, an officer from the USSR Branch in HQS called to tell me that Reuter's news agency in London was reporting my arrest. The Soviets had published the story of my arrest in retaliation for the FBI's public exposure on May 21, 1978 of the arrest of three Soviet spies working in the US.

The FBI had selected a US naval officer to volunteer to the KGB, claiming he could provide information on anti-submarine warfare. He set up a meeting with the three KGB officers at a service plaza on the New Jersey Turnpike where the FBI arrested them. The year 1978 was busy in the intelligence war between the Soviet Union and the US. In April 1978, the top Soviet employee in the United Nations Secretariat disappeared right before he was to return to the Soviet Union. He defected to the US. Arkadi Shevchenko had been the Under Secretary General for Political and Security Council Affairs since April

1973. He had previously been a senior advisor to Foreign Minister Andrei A. Gromyko.

The FBI elected to release a press statement about the arrests of the three Soviets. Therefore, as the tit-for-tat game played out, the Soviets published the story of my arrest in their newspaper *Izvestiya*, which meant *news* in Russian, in Moscow. On June 13, 1978, my picture seated with Cliff at the conference table in Lyubianka graced the front page of the *Washington Post*. Jack said he was shocked that morning to open his front door to my unsmiling picture on the front page of his newspaper. From there, the story quickly replayed across the US and then into the international press arena in the overseas versions of the *Time* and *Newsweek* magazines and *International Herald Tribune*.

The story in the *Washington Post* was a carbon-copy of the *Izvestiya* report, claiming I "was a CIA agent who transmitted poison to a Soviet who used it to kill an innocent Soviet citizen." The article in *Izvestia* "alleged that Soviet counter-intelligence agents uncovered the plot when they intercepted Peterson as she was about to transfer espionage gear, including two poison capsules concealed inside a fake rock, to her unidentified contact. Among allegedly captured items were photographic equipment and money."

As this story appeared in US newspapers, friends from my past contacted me to express their support, hoping I had survived this ordeal. Only my parents knew what had really happened. The rest of my family and close friends were aware I had returned home earlier than originally anticipated. Friends in Moscow had believed my "sick mother" cover story, but this news blew the top off that story. Mary, a close friend in Moscow, later told me she thought I became friendly with everyone in the Embassy because my job for CIA was to watch Americans. I told her I just liked people, which is the actual truth. I did not admit to anyone outside of the Agency the truth of the story in *Izvestia*, insisting the Soviets were making up absurd allegations about me.

I hated the implication that I had provided poison for the agent to use to murder a Soviet citizen. The KGB, of course, knew that was incorrect, but it was the acceptable version, given the KGB would obviously not reveal that TRIGON had spied for over two years while he worked in a highly sensitive position in the MFA, irreparably damaging the Soviet Government. Even though I told the TRIGON-as-hero story and arrest account to many people at CIA, I did not include details about the poison.

Eventually we learned how TRIGON was identified and apprehended.

In 1965, a Czech couple, Karl and Hana Koecher, were dispatched by the Czech intelligence service to New York where they were to tell people they had left their country to become free from Communism. His covert reporting to the Czech service was shared with the KGB. The couple integrated themselves into the community, Karl attending Columbia University. In 1973, he obtained a job as a translator for CIA in Virginia. As part of his contract for CIA he was given transcripts from telephone taps to translate. Eventually, some of the calls he transcribed were taped in Bogota. Although the calls Karl translated were not sequential and details were sketchy, over time the KGB pieced together a profile of a suspect, a Soviet diplomat in Bogota. They began investigating various candidates and over time eventually identified TRIGON.

In 1984, Karl and Hana Koecher were arrested, having worked for CIA in Washington, D.C. and in New York, providing the Czech service and the KGB with many years of intelligence. It was during their interrogation that their role in the TRIGON arrest came to light. They were eventually swapped for the Soviet dissident, Anatoli Shcharansky, who chose to live in Israel. The Koechers were sent back to Czechoslovakia.

This is how we pieced the story of TRIGON's arrest together. In early summer 1977, TRIGON was arrested in his apartment and brought to Lyubianka and into an interrogation room. He was stripped to his underwear. Knowing the KGB was eager to learn every minute detail of his work with CIA, and figuring his fate was sealed regardless if he cooperated or not, TRIGON volunteered to provide the full story of his espionage activities on behalf of the CIA. He asked for his pen.

The KGB was eager to obtain enough information to enable them to set up a CIA officer in an ambush, which would, in some small part, be retaliation and retribution for the damage they assumed TRIGON had caused the Soviet Government since his recruitment by CIA.

Opening the pen as if to begin writing, he bit down on the barrel and expired instantly in front of his KGB interrogators. The KGB was so intent on his confession that they never suspected he had poison. Their efforts to revive him were futile.

TRIGON died his own way, a hero.

Epilogue

In 1979, the novel, *TASS is Authorized to Announce,* by Julian Semyonov, a noted Russian spy novelist, was published in Moscow. To CIA's surprise the novel was based on a very loose fictionalized version of the TRIGON case. We subsequently learned that Semyonov had been given access to the TRIGON files by then-KGB Chairman Yuriy Andropov, who instructed Semyonov to write a spy story based on this actual case.

The novel's setting is a fictitious country in Africa instead of Latin America. As the Soviets boycotted the 1984 Olympic Games in Los Angeles, they scheduled to broadcast what became an extremely popular weekly TV series based on this Semyonov novel. The series' popularity was, in fact, compared to the American TV series *Dallas.* The Soviet's intention was to fill the void caused by the boycott with this serialized spy thriller, thereby reducing the displeasure of the Soviet citizenry's not being able to watch the achievements of their world-class athletes.

CIA was interested in what the novel revealed about the KGB's knowledge of TRIGON's cooperation. This was the first time in anyone's memory that the KGB publicly exposed a true case, albeit fictionalized. The most interesting part in the book to me personally confirmed my success in working anonymously during my tour in Moscow and made my mother laugh out loud. The novel's CIA officer, arrested at a railroad bridge at the end of the movie, is a man.

During the first years following my Moscow tour, I tried not to dwell on what might have happened to TRIGON, especially what caused his arrest. I went on with my career, putting energy into training new people, providing them skills and mental readiness for their future challenges. I had confidence I had not cut any corners and had performed to the highest standard in Moscow.

After we discovered Karl Koecher's role in TRIGON's compromise in 1984, I was relieved, but no less sad. The fact that I gave TRIGON poison weighed on my conscience. But if he had been tortured only to die a lingering death in prison, I would have been more distressed. The fall of the Soviet Union in 1991 brought the release of some of CIA's former agents who had been jailed and were serving long years under horrendous conditions in Soviet prisons. TRIGON could have had a similar fate, if they hadn't elected to execute him when they arrested him.

Toward the end of my career, I ran into Bob, a man I had met shortly after my return from Moscow. Now, he owned a company that specialized in training people who traveled to high-risk environments where arrest and torture were not infrequent. He and I recalled our first meeting in the fall of 1977 at a LUMS hot dog restaurant in Arlington, Virginia. At that time, he wanted me to tell him my Moscow story. But he didn't want to know just the facts. He wanted to know how it felt at the moment of my arrest and what I was thinking during the time I spent in Lyubianka. His focus was not to analyze the myriad facts of TRIGON's fate. What interested him were my mental state and thought processes while I was detained.

In telling him my story, I realized I had a type of out-of-body view during my arrest. I also told Bob that I was amused sitting in the conference room in Lyubianka ringed with young men all intently watching me, reveling in the fact that this was a *bona fide* CIA spy caught red-handed by the mighty ten-foot tall KGB. I transposed their faces to those of my fellow CIA colleagues and me, who would have been equally wide-eyed if they had been watching the interrogation of a real live KGB officer caught *in flagrante*.

The man seated beside me showing me his bruised shin from my dead-on aim when I kicked him reminded me of one of my older colleagues in the training program before I left for Moscow. They both shared the same twinkle in their eyes, amused by the attention this young attractive woman was giving them. The chief interrogator supported my impression that he was choreographing a scene in a play. He followed a specific script for the film they were making to be used later in the Izvestiya articles and then the Semenyov novel. He was eager not to reveal much of the secret details to the cast in the room.

My emotional state, seated in the lion's den, was of personal pride and confidence. But I did not feel threatened or fearful. I knew I would be rescued, and with this knowledge, I concentrated on determining what the KGB knew about TRIGON and his work for us over the past years.

And so twenty-five years later, Bob asked me to recount my story to an assembled group of CIA employees who faced situations potentially far more brutal than I experienced. The group was composed of a range of professionals, many retired from previous careers. I'm sure they looked at me and wondered what I could possibly tell them about being arrested or roughed up.

Bob was right. It wasn't the facts of the arrest they needed to know. The essential message was how I felt and reacted mentally. I conveyed these mental pictures, so my audience could reflect on how they might act in a similar situation. Although people like to believe they are invincible, that day each individual came to some realization that he had his own vulnerabilities. They needed to envision how they might respond in an arrest scenario.

They were amazed when I recounted my life story, beginning in Laos, experiencing the death of a young husband, taking on a new career filled with challenges as a female case officer in CIA in the early 1970s, completing almost a year of Russian language training, so I could operate convincingly alone on the streets of Moscow, accomplishing what others had not been able to in this hostile Cold War environment. Before my talk, they may have concluded I was just another professional woman, who had made it to the top by doing staff work. They likely never imagined what I had experienced.

And that is when I realized I had not used my "war story" to an advantage.

People always asked me at the end of my talk what affect my arrest had on my career. I answered that it was just one experience in a long career. But after I gave my talk to this group, I realized I should have used my story differently. War stories are the substance of our oral text books. They reveal the lessons learned through experiences which others might eventually encounter. I didn't tell my story to new officemates, because I didn't want to be known for being arrested by the KGB. There was more to me than that. I recalled others telling their war stories, many times embellishing the story to enhance their achievements and inflate who they were. I wanted to be known as a professional woman, working my way up the career ladder through hard work and creative accomplishments.

In the years following the fall of the Soviet Union, many CIA colleagues were given escorted tours of the KGB Museum when they visited Moscow on official business. The guides pointed out one entire wall devoted to the arrest of Martha Peterson in 1977. One friend, who was in Moscow on a CIA-KGB joint meeting, was driven by the bridge as her KGB escort proudly told the story of my arrest there, asking my friend whether she knew me. She demurred. Actor Robert De Niro and spy gear entrepreneur and benefactor of the International Spy Museum, Keith Melton, were given tours of the bridge and the KGB Museum, all captured in their souvenir photos. The KGB obviously was proud of how they apprehended me and were eager to display to western VIPs the spy gear they confiscated that night.

When I first saw my picture spring to life on a wall in a darkened draped closet in the International Spy Museum in Washington, D.C., I had an instant flashback to the violence at the moment of my arrest, of those men's hands groping inside my blouse, of my loud protests, of my instant grief when I realized that TRIGON was gone. Shortly after the museum opened in the summer of 2002, I asked three friends to accompany me on my first visit to the museum to see *CAUGHT*, the title over the door of the Martha Peterson exhibit. The title depicted the display, but it disparaged what I had accomplished.

As we stood watching the video with my picture larger than life size blazing out on the wall, hearing a deep male voice recounting the facts of the arrest, a small group of people joined us. As we filed out at the end of the story, we heard one of them say, "I wonder what happened to that woman." My friends poked me and laughed. But it was too awkward to acknowledge to these strangers who I was.

On my final work day before I retired after thirty-two years at CIA, one of those men in Bob's audience came to my office, obviously with a mission. He told me I had to tell my story. He believed the story of a young woman left widowed as a result of her husband's belief in CIA's mission, and then her courageous tour in Moscow to avenge his death needed to be told. He said it was time to reveal my past.

Index

W

WAE – When Actually Employed 16
Washington Post 69, 240
West Lot 3, 77
Woonsocket, Rhode Island 60

Y

Yasnaya Polyana – Lyev Nickolayevich
   Tolstoy's home in Tula 210
Yellow River 8, 37

Z

Zhiguli 102, 108, 109, 130, 132, 145,
   181, 191, 209